ALL THINGS THROUGH CHRIST

The Life and Ministry of
WALLACE E. THOMAS

BY
WALLACE E. THOMAS
with
KATE R. THOMAS

WESTBOW
P R E S S
A DIVISION OF THOMAS NELSON

Scripture marked KJV taken from the King James Version of the Bible.

Scripture marked NKJV taken from the New King James Version. Copyright 1979, 1980, 1982 by Thomas Nelson, inc. Used by permission. All rights reserved.

Scripture marked NIV taken from the Holy Bible, New International Version®. Copyright © 1973, 1978, 1984 Biblica. Used by permission of Zondervan. All rights reserved.

Scripture marked NASB taken from the New American Standard Bible®, Copyright © 1960, 1962, 1963, 1968, 1971, 1972, 1973, 1975, 1977, 1995 by The Lockman Foundation. Used by permission." (www.Lockman.org)

Scripture marked ESV taken from The Holy Bible, English Standard Version® (ESV®), copyright © 2001 by Crossway, a publishing ministry of Good News Publishers. Used by permission. All rights reserved.

Scripture marked RSV taken from Revised Standard Version of the Bible, copyright 1952 [2nd edition, 1971] by the Division of Christian Education of the National Council of the Churches of Christ in the United States of America. Used by permission. All rights reserved.

Selected scripture quotations in this publications are from The Message. Copyright (c) by Eugene H. Peterson 1993, 1994, 1995, 1996, 2000, 2001, 2002. Used by permission of NavPress Publishing Group.

WestBow Press books may be ordered through booksellers or by contacting:

WestBow Press
A Division of Thomas Nelson
1663 Liberty Drive
Bloomington, IN 47403
www.westbowpress.com
1-(866) 928-1240

Because of the dynamic nature of the Internet, any web addresses or links contained in this book may have changed since publication and may no longer be valid. The views expressed in this work are solely those of the author and do not necessarily reflect the views of the publisher, and the publisher hereby disclaims any responsibility for them.

Any people depicted in stock imagery provided by Thinkstock are models, and such images are being used for illustrative purposes only. Certain stock imagery © Thinkstock.

ISBN: 978-1-4497-4809-8 (e)
ISBN: 978-1-4497-4810-4 (sc)
ISBN: 978-1-4497-4811-1 (hc)

Library of Congress Control Number: 2012906726

Printed in the United States of America

WestBow Press rev. date: 05/01/2012

ENDORSEMENTS

Wally Thomas was a model pastor for the historic period in which he lived and served. His ministry spanned a period of cataclysmic upheavals and change. Wally was able to adapt his style of minister to be relevant to his time and place, remaining faithful to his core commitment to pastor people with love and compassion.

When I first met Wally, his church was in a transitional community. He introduced forms of ministry that were experimental in the church at the time, and were questioned by his colleagues. But for Wally it was an expression of his passion for winning people to Christ and growing them in the Christian faith.

He served churches of every size and socio-economic distinction. I don't know anyone who has been as effective in such varied settings. He was a leading pastor in assisting us in spreading the Emmaus Walk, because Wally knew this experience was an effective dynamic for transformation and disciple-making.

I am so happy he told his story. The marks of his life are reflected here:

- His genuine humility
- His extravagant love for people which made him an effective pastor
- His ability to shepherd change and transformation without being destructive of community
- The ability to serve the larger church with commitment to the local congregation
- The capacity to lead with grace, doing some radical things without intimidation
- His loyalty to friends that enabled him to be a challenge to their growth

I am one of those friends who was loyal, for whom he was a challenge to be far more than I ever thought I could be.

Dr. Maxie Dunnam, Pastor
First United Methodist Church, Memphis
Former President, Asbury Seminary
Former World Editor, The Upper Room
Author of over 40 books

This is a compelling story of the roots which produced this modern Good Shepherd. He was a pastor to us as he married our children and baptized our grandchildren. But he was much more as administrator, consensus builder, and harvester in the fields of our Lord. One is reminded of Moses in Dr. Thomas' leadership skills. I recommend this book for anyone interested in church leadership in these times.

Charles C. Smith, MD

Reading *All Things through Christ* brought great joy to me because it is the record of the life and ministry of a dear friend—one who had a warm heart and keen insight into what is meant to be in ministry. It is an unusual book because it was mostly written by Wally, but completed by "Kay" due to his death in February of 2009.

The book is the story of a man who came from humble beginnings, but because he surrendered his life to God as revealed in Christ Jesus, went on to become one of the great United Methodist ministers of this century. His life had its share of challenges, but the thing that stands out is how faithful Wally was to God, his family, and to the Church. I've known a lot of ministers, but none more genuine than Wally Thomas.

Dr. John Begley, Chancellor,
Lindsey Wilson College

Wallace E. "Wally" Thomas had a profound impact on my life. As I read through his memoirs in *All Things through Christ* I was reminded of why. First, Wally was a man of Christ-like character. He carried himself with as much integrity as any man I have ever known. Secondly, he truly cared about people. His ministry reflected the heart of our Savior as one that would leave the ninety-nine in pursuit of the one that was lost. Wally was a very effective pastor, but the real passion of his life was to see the lost come home to Christ. He lived this out in front of me and left a legacy for me to "do the work of an evangelist, fulfill your ministry" (2 Timothy 4:5b NKJV). Finally, Wally modeled what it looks like when one remains faithful to God's call while loving and caring for his family and friends. The responsibilities and demands of pastoral ministry never consumed him to the point that he neglected those relationships that matter most. I will forever be grateful that God brought Wally into my life, and to now have the story in his own words in my possession is truly a blessing.

Dr. M. David Calhoun
Assistant Professor of Religion,
Lindsey Wilson College
Founding Pastor, Hope Springs
United Methodist Church

The title of this book tells the marvelous story of Christian faith and family love. From humble beginnings of farm life to productive Christian ministry in town and city—in small churches and large—to heavy administrative duties as a district superintendent, Wally Thomas was a man dedicated to his call to preach the Gospel. Noted for his evangelistic zeal, he was persistent but not coercive. His patient, loving witness was used of God to lead many to faith in Christ. In home as in church Wally practiced a life hidden in God through Christ.

This is a moving story of family life and love, and of God's family on earth. It is a warm and good story, and I heartily recommend it to clergy and laity alike.

Paul A. Duffey, Sr., Retired Bishop
United Methodist Church

The title of this book says it all—*All Things through Christ*. Wally Thomas was called to be a minister. No question about it. Preaching and pastoring were no career path. His entire life was about God and the transformational power that came into the world through Jesus Christ. Wally was a well-grounded Biblical preacher with a heart so warmed with the Holy Spirit that it made him a caring pastor. He made a difference in the lives of many including mine. I'm pleased that he and Kate have unleashed his story for all to read. His life and ministry deserve a place in the history of the Church.

Robert H. Spain, Retired Bishop
United Methodist Church

Kate Thomas writes convincingly and with power. She has soared in her tribute to the life of her husband Wally Thomas. I loved Wally. And he was a dear friend that I could count on. Wally and Kate were *one*. You did not speak of Wally or Kate without including the other. Although anyone in the Thomas family was capable of writing Wally's life story, Anna Kate was the only one who could tie it all together. They were so well-grounded in their faith, marriage, family, and ministry, and because of this, the many who crossed their path gained inspiration for deepening their spiritual life and making their witness as Christians more compelling to others.

Robert C. Morgan, Retired Bishop
United Methodist Church

To read *All Things through Christ* is to have an eyewitness account of the life and ministry of Wallace Thomas, affectionately called "Wally." In the book we follow his joyous journey of forty-two years as a minister of Jesus Christ, and it affords us an opportunity to see life as it is in family, church, and community. It is a joy to read!

Dr. Evelyn Laycock,
Founding Director of the Lay Ministry
Center for the Southeastern Jurisdiction
of the United Methodist Church,
Professor of Religion, Hiwassee
College (Semi-retired)

CONTENTS

FOREWORD

The van was loaded and Karen and the kids were already outside for farewell hugs with my parents, preparing for the drive back to Lexington. Before I joined them, I paused in Dad's office, left him a note on a yellow post-it, and stuck it on his computer. The note read: "Keep writing your story, Dad. I want my kids to know it." In retirement, with Mom's nudging, Dad began a simple memoir, reliving and recording the stories of his lifetime spent believing the promise of this book's title taken from Philippians 4:13—Dad's life verse.

The truth is I would have wanted anyone to know my father's story. I always enjoyed asking him about it and drawing wisdom from the experiences of his life. His was a steady, humble, imperfect (like all of us), authentic life of trusting Christ and offering the Gospel. Dad was a man of love, at home and in the pulpit. Such love will come across, I believe, as you continue reading.

Each page of this book literally became a labor of love. Dad finished a little over two-thirds of the book before being unexpectedly promoted to heaven in 2009. Dad left that same yellow post-it note on the computer until he died. Knowing that Dad intended to complete his memoir, Mom took on the sometimes heavy yet noble task of finishing what he had begun. What you hold in your hands right now is vivid evidence of marriage love lived out even beyond "death us do part."

My sister, Debbie, and I were unspeakably blessed to grow up under the shelter of that kind of commitment in our home. We are among a great throng of people whose lives were made better because of this good man. Those stories became Dad's story, one I am so glad to see chronicled for my kids, and one I am so proud to commend to you.

David R. Thomas
November 2011

ACKNOWLEDGEMENTS

First of all, I am grateful to God, for His Son, Jesus, our Savior and Lord, and for the ever-present Holy Spirit. I am thankful for Wally's and my parents, for the love of my life, Wally, and our children, Debbie and David, for their spouses, Steve Caswell and Karen Muselman Thomas. I am grateful to God for our four precious grandchildren: Katherine Elizabeth Caswell, Luke Christian Thomas, John Paul Thomas, and Mary Esther Elaine Thomas. I thank God for Wally's and my extended families. I am indebted to all the friends in our former churches and beyond who have blessed our lives over the years, and for those who have prayed for my family and me during these three years since Wally went to Heaven.

I am thankful for the contribution our daughter Debbie has made through her additions and helpful suggestions for this manuscript and for our son David's help in proofing, editing, and contributing to this effort. I want to thank my niece Judy Branham, Sandra Stone, and Marti Curtsinger for their editorial expertise. I appreciate Jane Dobson for her timely prayer letter that arrived immediately following Wally's death. I am grateful to Beverly Furnival for her poem entitled "This Child of God" and Mike Cheek's letter that Wally saved over the years. I deeply appreciate these friends allowing me to include these items in this book. I am indebted to those who generously endorsed this book as well as a host of others who have contributed to our life stories.

I want to thank the staff at WestBow Press for their patience and careful attention to all the details of this effort. I could go on and on thanking God for the many people who have blessed, guided, nurtured, and loved Wally and me over the years. My prayer is that your lives have been touched by the life and ministry of Wallace Thomas, and that you will be inspired to trust the promise in his life verse: Philippians 4:13 (NKJV) "I can do all things through Christ who strengthens me."

May God bless every person who reads this book.

Kate R. Thomas

Chapter 1

FAMILY BACKGROUND

James 4:14 in the King James Bible asks the question, "What is your life?" That is a question I ponder as I attempt to write this personal memoir. Mine has been a wonderful life, filled with many peaks and valleys, joys and sorrows, but always guided by the steady hand of God. My mom and dad were good "salt-of-the-earth" people. Daddy, Logan Kenneth Thomas, was one of six children. Mama, Pauline Piercy, was one of five. They grew up within a mile of each other but did not attend the same church or school. However, in their early teens a family in the community had a party to which both my parents were invited.

It was love at first sight, and they married when Daddy was 19 and Mama was 16. Daddy was a member of Neal's Chapel Cumberland Presbyterian Church in Barren County, Kentucky, where I was converted as a 9-year-old. Mama was a member of the Bethel Methodist Church a few miles away. When they married, they joined New Salem Methodist Church. Daddy was soon elected a steward of the church at the age of 20, and he remained in a leadership role there as long as they were members. Later my parents moved their membership to Mama's home church and continued to be active as long as their health allowed.

Theirs was a simple life: they wanted to love God and each other and work hard. With a team of mules, a turning plow, and a double shovel to cultivate their crops, they made their living, raised two children, and made payments on a $2,500 loan by which they purchased their farm. They had some cows, hogs, chickens, and a garden, and they managed to keep clothes on our backs and food on our table.

It was in this humble and God-fearing home that my sister and I were born. My sister, Helen Opal, was born on April 11, 1930. Four years later, on a cold, snowy January 13, 1934, I arrived—feet first! I am told that Helen often said throughout the winter before I was born, "I've just been wishing all winter that I had a little baby brother." I was given the name of Wallace Edwin. It was not until I was in college that I was called "Wally" by Kay and many of my friends.

Due to his realization that I was going to be a breach birth and because of the inclement weather, the doctor spent the night at our house the night before I was born. It is hard to imagine today just how difficult life was for our parents and ancestors. We often say, "We were poor back then, but didn't know it."

Our home was a two-story frame house with three bedrooms, a kitchen, and living room. Our "outdoor plumbing" was at the end of a path in back of our home. Our source of heat was a Warm Morning stove in the living room and a wood cook stove in the kitchen. My bedroom was an unfinished room upstairs. It was cold in the winter, and Mama warmed blankets to wrap around me when I went to bed. She also put a warm old-fashioned iron wrapped with cloth in the bed at my feet to keep them warm. It is no wonder Helen and I were often sick with ear and throat infections during the wintertime.

While life must have been a day-to-day struggle for my parents, they never complained. Instead, they were always exploring ways to improve our life on the farm. They built a brooder house and bought 300 baby chickens. Some of these chickens became hens for our eggs, and some were frozen for food when they were large enough. We didn't have a deep freeze then, so Daddy rented a food locker in Glasgow where the fryers were frozen and stored until we needed them. The remaining chickens were sold, and the money from them was used to buy groceries.

Daddy killed around four hogs and a beef cow each year to add to our food supply.

Helen and I had morning and evening chores each day. We helped milk cows and gather in the eggs. With no running water in the house, we filled the reservoir on the cook stove with water to heat while Mama was cooking. This enabled us to have warm dishwater ready after our meals. Other chores included filling the wood box each day for cooking, the coal bucket with coal for the heating stove, and the water bucket for a fresh supply from our well.

My parents always managed to buy Helen and me some new clothes at the beginning of the school year. Going to town to shop for school clothes was an exciting time, but the most exciting time of the year was Christmas! Daddy always took Helen and me to find a Christmas tree on our farm. It had to be the finest, best-shaped cedar tree that could be found. We would decorate it with strands of popcorn, ribbons and artificial icicles, and, thankfully, Santa Claus would always come to see us. I can remember so well the excitement of those Christmas mornings, coming down the stairs to a warm room and finding our gifts. I will never forget the Christmas I got a new tricycle, and Helen got the doll she wanted.

A favorite family time was mealtime. Mama was an excellent cook, and I can still almost taste those big breakfasts of sausage or country ham, gravy, eggs, biscuits, and sorghum

Wally and sister, Helen.

molasses or jelly and jam. Our conversations during breakfast were often about an article Daddy had recently read in the *Progressive Farmer* magazine or something he had heard on their battery-operated radio.

One morning Daddy read an article about the Rural Electric Association (REA), and then announced with determination in his voice and in his facial expression, "We are gettin' electricity in this old house!" He soon began to work toward making this happen, and it did. Our home was one of the first to get electricity in that area. The first night we had electricity in our house, Daddy and Mama turned on electric lights in every room. They were as thrilled (or maybe more so) as their kids.

I remember Daddy saying, "This place looks like a hotel." Getting electrical power in our home was the beginning of a whole new lifestyle for us. Now we had running water, an electric range and refrigerator, and a telephone. Daddy's leadership was later recognized by his being named to the Farmer's Home Administration Board of Directors, and chairman of the Southern States Cooperative. Daddy later designed and built a dairy barn and formed a Grade-A Dairy Cooperative with Sealtest Milk Company in Louisville.

After they no longer had the financial responsibility for Helen and me, Dad and Mom finally found a plan for the home of their dreams. At the age of 45, Dad built a beautiful two-story, four-bedroom home with plastered walls, hardwood floors, central heat and two baths. I can still feel the excitement of that first night in that beautiful home and the delight of seeing my dear parents enjoy the fruits of their labor and daily walk with God. I am so thankful God allowed them to enjoy this comfortable home for many years.

This kind of home life has carried me through some challenging and difficult times in my life. I am so grateful for my godly, hard-working and devoted parents. Someone has said the main point about Abraham Lincoln was not that he was born in a log cabin, but that he got himself out of it. Mom and Dad started out with love for each other, a dream of a better life, and the faith to believe all things are possible with God.

Chapter 2

BOYHOOD AND YOUTH

Someone has said that for people my age, our childhood experience is a vanished period in history. So many changes have taken place. Not all for the best. Life was so simple during my childhood. Morals and values are lower now. Politics have changed. Methods of war have changed. Experiences of youth are different today. Homes are better and more comfortable, but home life today is a rushed and tension-filled experience. Our clothes, food, medicine, means of travel, entertainment, jobs, customs, and the work force are all different than they were during my growing-up years.

Wally with parents, Kenneth and Pauline Thomas.

We lived about a mile from our one-room school named

Forrest Seminary. Helen and I walked to school most days. It was there that she and I completed our first six grades of education. About 40 students attended and one teacher taught all grades, maintained discipline, and served as janitor. The building had windows on one side, blackboards on the opposite side, and a stage in front for school plays. The big, black pot-bellied stove sat in the middle of the room. In the back corner was a big water cooler, and students had to provide their own drinking cup.

Beside the cooler were shelves for our lunch boxes. The aroma from those lunch boxes and bags whetted our appetites all morning. Some of the things we took to school for lunch were ham or sausage on biscuits, egg sandwiches, fruit, peanut butter and crackers, and sometimes a bologna sandwich for a special treat. If we were lucky, Mama put in a fried apple pie or cookies.

Each grade had its own section of the room. We began the day by filing in the front door where the teacher checked our fingernails to see if they were clean and asked the students if they had brushed their teeth. The morning started with the Pledge of Allegiance to the flag and the Lord's Prayer. Between the stage and the stove was a table with small benches where each class came for instruction. Our mid-morning recess was a time for play. The girls played Drop the Handkerchief, Ring Around the Roses, or Tag. During the lunch hour the boys would often have a quick softball game. On rainy days we might have what we called Railroad Spelling. All the upper grades lined up across the front of the room. The teacher gave out a word to the first student in line. The next person was supposed to spell a word that began with the ending letter of the previous speller's word. On and on it went until everyone had sat down because they could not think of how to start "their word."

The biggest social event for the year was the annual Box Supper. Every girl decorated her cardboard box, filled it with good food, and shared the meal with the boy who was the highest bidder for it. Sometimes there was homemade ice cream for sale as well. The proceeds were used to make improvements on the building and buy teaching supplies. The other big event was our annual Christmas program. The older boys cut a big cedar tree, and each class took turns in decorating. On the last day of school before the Christmas break, parents came for the program of singing carols, reading the Christmas story, and exchanging gifts.

Some of the best teachers of that era were dedicated to teaching in the one-room rural elementary schools. They gave each student personal attention and made learning exciting with the challenge to strive for excellence. Miss Ruby Ward put a blue ribbon on our report card if we made A's and B's. Mrs. Tressie Hatcher wrote a comment on each test with the challenge to improve, even regarding the way we signed our name. This inspired me to try to have the best penmanship possible. Later in college, at what is now Western Kentucky University, I took G.G. Craig's penmanship course. I was allowed to pen my own graduation certificate in Old English.

I guess I literally owe my life to Mrs. Hatcher. She was a great teacher, and taught in a way that made one want to learn. I will always remember her lesson from our health book on ear problems. I was having plenty of ear problems along about that time. The more she talked, the more I was convinced she was describing my ear problem. I went home and told my parents it sounded like I had an infection in the mastoid area behind my ear. The next day they took me to the doctor and Mrs. Hatcher's description was right on target. I had mastoiditis. Before the availability of antibiotics, mastoiditis was a leading cause of death in children. Surgery was performed on the mastoid area, and we were told by the surgeon that another day or two might have been too late for me. God in His mercy spared me.

My parents had no idea of the severity of my ear problem. Mama tried every remedy she ever heard of to no avail. The warm cloths on my ear felt good, but they only helped for a time. She used enough Vicks Salve during those years to just about fill a gallon jug. As I was growing up, our country was trying to recover from the Great Depression. It was a difficult time, and families depended on home remedies during those days.

Many recollections come to mind as I think of those early and formative years. One tradition we had at our elementary school was attending the annual revival at the nearby Cumberland Presbyterian Church. The daytime services were held in the afternoon to allow the school to attend. We marched double file down the dusty road to the church and sat together as a group. The church was filled to capacity, and the singing always included children's choruses. It was during one of those services that, as a 9-year-old, I accepted the Lord Jesus Christ into my heart.

One night during that week, I told Mama and Daddy I was going to the altar at the next day's afternoon service. I wanted them to be present for the service. (I don't know why I was concerned that they be present, because they rarely ever missed a revival service.) I don't recall anything the preacher said, but I'll never forget the great joy of that moment when I knew God heard my prayer and Christ had come into my heart. Later that afternoon, I told my dad I felt like I had a bath inside. This was the beginning of my walk with the Lord, and I will cherish this day as long as I live.

I would like to add here that Kay had a similar experience growing up. She, too, went to a one-room elementary school. She and her classmates played similar games, both in pretty weather and on rainy days. There were eight grades in her school. She also walked with her fellow classmates to a daytime revival meeting, and it was there she asked Jesus into her heart.

I worked hard on the farm. By the time I was 9-years-old, Dad had me driving the

Wally around age 11.

tractor, and I remember having to stand up to see where I was going. I guess it was during those long days of hard work on the farm that a work ethic developed in me that has stayed with me all my life.

Along about this time, I began to want my parents to say grace at our table. Every day I stood by my dad and said, "Daddy, please pray." He put me off for a time but later began to say the blessing at every meal. My dad became a prayer warrior! Later in life he told me to go with him to the dairy barn because he wanted to show me something. I couldn't imagine what was there to see. The herd of Jersey cattle had long since been sold, and dust had collected over the years as all activity ceased around the dairy barn.

"Let's go up in the hayloft," Dad said as we approached the barn. I walked beside him as he slowly made his way up the creaky stairs. I followed him to the far corner of the hayloft. There he stopped and looked down at an old and worn bale of hay. "This is where I have come every day to pray for you and Helen and your families." That bale of hay was Daddy's altar in the hayloft.

Both of our children often recall my dad's prayers at Christmastime. The last and best thing that happened every Christmas was when all 10 of the family gathered in a circle in the living room for prayer. One Christmas, our son David made a tape, without anyone knowing it, of his grandpa praying. What a treasure that tape is today!

Another good memory I have of my growing-up years is when Dad and I would go into town on Saturdays. My hometown of Glasgow was a bustling place around the town square. The streets were full of Saturday shoppers. I remember walking up from the parking lot with Dad. He often took me to a little hamburger joint en route, and those were the best hamburgers I ever ate.

After our lunch, we would walk on toward the town square. Dad would often stop and talk to people. Each time he stopped, I slipped my hand in Dad's hip pocket. Ever so often, he felt his hip pocket to see that I was still with him. I always thought this is how our Heavenly Father wants us to stay close to Him—hip pocket close.

My high school days were full of opportunities and challenges. While at Forrest Seminary Elementary School, I had one teacher and my classmates were children in our neighborhood I had known all my life. In contrast, Hiseville High School was located on the opposite side of the county which meant a three-hour bus ride every day. I got on the bus at 6:00 a.m. and got home at 5:30 p.m.

The bus capacity was 48 passengers, and we usually had a least 60 on the bus by the time we arrived at the high school. Those early high school experiences are still painful to remember. Some of the roughest and most immoral boys in our school rode our bus. It was not unusual to have fights on the bus and for the girls to be sexually harassed. On two occasions, the bus driver put some of the boys off the bus and made them walk home. Every day at the end of school, I would be one of the first ones in line to get on the bus which assured me a seat close to the driver.

Being late in physical development, as well as timid and afraid, I was slow in making new friends and in having anyone reach out to me. I tried out for basketball, but the coach called me a runt and said I was too little for the team. I later became manager.

Life began to get much better when I joined the Future Farmers of America. Frank Newberry, the agriculture teacher and FFA advisor, saw potential in me and gave me opportunities for leadership that would begin to shape my life for ministry. Under Mr. Newberry's leadership, the Hiseville FFA became

Wally wearing his FFA jacket

one of the outstanding chapters in our district. We competed at the county, district, and state level in cattle judging, public speaking, and parliamentary procedure.

One of my FFA projects was the purchase of a purebred Jersey heifer from Mr. Harman Barlow, one of the leading dairy farmers in Kentucky. (Forty years later, our son David served as pastor of the Cave City United Methodist Church. He met Mr. Barlow, and over time they became great friends.) Mr. Barlow was a godly man and was instrumental in helping David start a ministry to the poor in that area.

Dad and I started building our large herd of Jersey cows. I began to dream and see myself with a college education, married, and with a family. I began to set my goal to become a prominent farmer in Kentucky, and I hoped in later years to be the county agent or own and operate a Southern States Farm Store. This was a big dream, but I was growing up in an "all things are possible" environment.

I was elected as an FFA State Farmer and became president of our chapter in my junior year of high school. Our FFA officers competed in the state parliamentary contest and won third place. The chapter honored me by nominating me for a state FFA office. As a nominee, I had to debate issues and make some impromptu speeches on the floor of the State FFA Convention, which was held at the Seelbach Hotel in Louisville, Kentucky.

Now you need to know that this was my first trip to downtown Louisville and my first experience of staying in a big hotel. We ate at the Blue Boar Cafeteria which had an escalator. I hadn't seen many of those down on the farm! It was such an exciting time to be in the city with young men from all over the state and to be representing my FFA chapter wearing my blue FFA jacket and tie.

Soon after this time, I saved up enough money by working with my dad in the Grade-A dairy business to buy my first car. I was looking for a car that would be pretty sharp but would still be within my means. I fell in love with a 1950 black Ford I found at a Glasgow car dealership.

It was a little beyond my budget, but I couldn't get it out of my mind. Before I left town that day, I made a deal with the car salesman. I barely got out of town before I became sick at my stomach that I had spent that much money and still would have to make some payments. I poured out my feelings to Dad. His response was both quick and firm. "Son, you have bought yourself a car. You will stick to your word." I did, and I learned a great lesson from this experience.

While I was being taught to be a good leader and farmer, God had something else in mind for me. The thought of being a minister began to emerge in my mind and heart. One of my close high school friends and a fellow FFA officer said he thought I would become a minister. My pastor, Rev. Glen Lyle, and my minister friend, Rev. Marshall Owen, suggested God might be calling me to ministry. I rejected that idea and continued to pursue my dream of being a dairy farmer and a leader in agriculture.

In order to pursue my dream, I would need to go to college, but no one in my family had ever set foot on a college campus. This would be the greatest challenge of my life so far. I will always be indebted to Frank Newberry, my FFA advisor, who was also my counselor beyond high school. We had numerous conversations about my future and the need to get a good education. None of my friends were going to college, and Mom and Dad could not give me any guidance for this unknown path.

Mr. Newberry came to our home and talked to us about college. He offered to go with me to Western Kentucky State Teacher's College (as it was called then) to explore the possibility of enrolling there. It so happened that Mr. Newberry had a sister that lived across the street from the college and had a room she could rent to me. This was a perfect arrangement for a frightened young man with a vision for life that would take him into many unknown paths.

I was never as scared as I was on the day of registration! Entering mid-year after the crops were in, I found no orientation for beginning freshmen. This meant I had to select courses and fill out forms by myself. Sitting on the floor at the entrance of Cherry Hall, I suddenly felt the presence of someone standing near me. After a greeting, he sat down beside me and offered to help me with registration. Dr. Willard Cockrill, a professor of geography and meteorology, helped me select courses and fill out all the forms.

Dr. Cockrill then went with me to the admissions office to pay my tuition and walked with me to each classroom where I would be attending classes. He also took me by his office and said his door was always open. He invited me to come to his office anytime I needed help. I left his office hoping all my professors would be like Dr. Cockrill. Throughout my journey, God has always been there for me and has provided friends at those critical moments in my life. His promise is true, "I am with you always, even to the end of the age" (Matthew 28:20b NKJV).

Chapter 3

COLLEGE DAYS, MARRIAGE, AND FIRST APPOINTMENT

On January 20, 1954, I became a college student and went to my first class. In walked the professor, Dr. W.K. Wilgus, ready to begin English 101a. I can see him now—about 130 pounds, black wavy hair, a neatly trimmed mustache, and wearing a double-breasted blue suit. After laying his folder down, he stepped out to the front of the desk and greeted us. Dr. Wilgus made a remark about being a freshman in college. Then he said, "Look to your left and to the right. One of you will fail this course." I didn't hear anything else said that hour. I was scared and a bit angry as well.

I lingered after class to meet this Dr. Wilgus. I made an appointment to see him the next day. As I entered his office, he noted I was on time and asked what he could do for me. I said his opening statement frightened me, and I had no intention of being a student who failed English 101a. He listened to me as I shared my background and goals for my life. Then he leaned forward and said, "Mr. Thomas, you will not fail English 101a. I love students with goals and guts. My door will always be open for you when you need help." I passed English 101a, and Dr. Wilgus became one of my best friends among the faculty at Western.

During the spring semester, I met Kenneth Barger and Malcolm Grinstead who became my best friends in college. That fall the three of us rented an apartment and lived off campus, but in close walking distance. This was one of the most exciting times of my life. Barger and Grinstead (as I called them) were very congenial and willing to share in the cooking and cleaning. Each week we put $15 in the grocery jar and developed a rotation system for the housework. For instance, when Grinstead cooked, I cleaned the kitchen, and Barger straightened the remainder of the apartment. Each time we went home, we would return with good home-cooked food that would last several days.

One of the big events of orientation week was the freshman reception for all incoming freshmen. We three upperclassmen, as we thought of ourselves, couldn't wait to go to the Student Union Building to see all the pretty girls. There must have been four to five hundred students getting acquainted and enjoying the refreshments provided by the college. I noticed four beautiful girls sitting on a bench talking to each other and sipping soft drinks. One of those girls was especially attractive to me. I walked by two or three times, and when we made eye contact, she flashed a smile at me that I will never forget as long as I live.

It's hard to put into words, but something happened to me. I thought *I've got to meet her, but I need to be dressed more appropriately.* I rushed back to the apartment and changed into my light beige sport coat and rust pants with a matching tie, splashed on some Old Spice shaving lotion, and hurried back to the reception. When I returned, she was still there on the bench with her three friends. My heart has never beat as fast, and I had never been so excited about meeting anyone in my life. Grinstead and Barger were encouraging me and promised they would wait for me.

I took a deep breath, buttoned my coat, and casually walked over to meet this beautiful young girl. I introduced myself, and she told me her name was Kate Radford. I thought she said Kay Radford, which is the name that stuck with me always. She invited me to sit down beside her. There just happened to be room for one more person on the bench.

She introduced me to her friends, who were her high school classmates from Cumberland County. Becky Parrish was her roommate, and Margaret Radford and Elise Norris were her suite mates. We had a good conversation about our majors, our hometowns, and the excitement of being college students.

Wow, what a wonderful evening! Barger and Grinstead couldn't wait to hear about the conversation. After reliving the night, I realized I didn't find out where Kay lived and wondered when I would see her again. The next week I attended a vesper service in the auditorium of the library. When I arrived, the first person I saw was Kay. There was a vacant seat next to her and she gestured for me to sit by her. Needless to say, I got her address that night.

I took Kay to the dorm after the vesper service, and asked her for a date. It was hard for my feet to touch the ground as I went to the car. There was something very special about this girl. During my first weekend home I told Mom and Dad about my girlfriend. When I described her church affiliation and politics, Dad immediately said, "Son, did you ask her to marry you?"

College life was now more exciting. Kay and I saw each other briefly every day as we went to and from classes. We began to date regularly. Life was good, and I was doing well in my classes. But in my quiet moments the idea of ministry kept creeping into my mind. I clearly saw the hand of God on my life. He was blessing me with new friends, with guidance in decision-making, and with encouragement and support from professors who believed in me. Now, a special girl was bringing joy and enthusiasm into my heart.

I began to wonder: *Is this the hand of God? Does He really have His hand on my life? Is this call for real?* Every day became a day of pondering and reflection, bringing a deeper awareness of the living presence of God in my life. No one knew, or so I thought, about my inner struggle and the call of God on my life. I wanted to tell Kay, but feared she would stop seeing me.

Christmas break meant we wouldn't see each other for three weeks. Neither of our parents had phones at that time, so we could not communicate that way. I asked Kay for directions to her home, which she gave me in detail.

On a sunny but cold Sunday afternoon after Christmas, I decided I had to see my girlfriend. I finally found her at a neighbor's house playing croquet with her friends. After a few awkward moments of introductions, we left the croquet game and went to her home where I met her parents. That was another heart-racing, hand-perspiring moment. After a brief visit with her parents, Kay and I took a short drive before I headed back to Glasgow. We agreed we were anxious to get back to Western and where we could see each other every day.

One semester of cooking and house-cleaning was enough for my roommates and me, so we moved into a rooming house closer to the campus. We were now next door to the Western Lunch Room where Kay and her friends ate their meals. You can surely guess I ate my meals there as well.

We were well into the semester when Dad became ill with a bleeding ulcer, which meant I would have to drop out of school and return to the farm to make the crop. The thought of losing my credits that semester was difficult and expensive in lost time and money. Before I left for home, Kay and I shared our love for each other and committed not to date anyone else. The term that described that commitment in the 1950s was "going steady."

En route home from Western, I stopped in Glasgow to give a pint of blood for Dad, went home, and went to work. This was mid-March, and Dad had been unable to do anything about getting the crops started. I could not understand why I had been forced by circumstances to be away from Kay and return to the farm. What was God trying to say to me? Was He changing His plans?

Looking back on those months, God was using this "Arabia" in my life to enable me to see more clearly my "burning bush." I had a lot of time alone on the tractor and traveling back and forth to Bowling Green to see Kay. I had made my decision to accept Christ as my Savior. Now I was faced with a call to ministry and wondering how Kay might feel about being a preacher's wife. Our love for each other grew with every passing day. God's call to ministry was in my heart and on my mind day and night. I would often stop the tractor and sit against a tree and talk out loud to God. I couldn't sleep at night.

Sometimes what seems like detours are actually God's way of putting us back on track. I needed to talk to someone, and I wasn't ready to share my struggle with Kay. Marshall Owen, a Methodist minister and pastor of a church in Bowling Green, had stayed in our home during two revivals he preached in our church. I felt I could talk to him and get some clarity on my struggles and some direction for my life. After a two-hour visit with him, he helped me understand how God calls ministers and how he believed God was calling me. We had a wonderful prayer time together, and I realized God really had put His hand upon me. Now I felt sure He would not change His mind.

I had wrestled with God for five years and was losing in the fight. Finally, one Wednesday night while Mom and Dad were gone to prayer meeting, I went to my room and closed the door. I remember saying audibly to God, "The struggle is over. I'm all yours. I hear your call. I will be your minister. I am afraid and don't know where to start. Please, God, help me. Where do I start? Give me some word, some kind of assurance that I can be a pastoral minister."

Still on my knees with tears flowing down my face, I reached for my Bible and it opened to a verse I had never read before in Philippians 4:13. These were the words that became my life verse, "I can do all things through Christ who strengthens me" (NKJV). Reading those words gave me the assurance I needed to make this bold step. That night my room was filled with God's presence, and I have never had such peace in my heart. I was experiencing my "Wonderful, Counselor, The mighty God, The everlasting Father, The Prince of Peace" (Isaiah 9:6b KJV). This Counselor has been with me in my journey and I believe His promises are true and can be trusted.

That night I trusted God with my life. I was now ready to tell my parents and my dear Kay about my call and decision to obey God. I knew I could cope with whatever was ahead in my life. I knew that my trust was in a God that would provide for all my needs—not my wants, but my needs! I knew I could rely on God in all the days ahead, because my future was now in His hands.

The next morning I shared with Mom and Dad my struggle and the experience during the previous night. They shared their joy with me, had a prayer of thanksgiving, and promised to support me in every way they could. My next step was to share this decision with Kay. I could more clearly see God guiding me and enabling me to make this decision. In my heart I had assurance that Kay would be encouraging and supportive of my commitment to ministry. Yet telling her was another heart-racing, hand-perspiring moment.

On the following Saturday night, Kay and I went to a drive-in restaurant in Bowling Green and ordered sandwiches and Cokes. After we finished our sandwich and talked about our week, I told her that I had something to tell her. She turned toward me and said, "What is it, Wally?" After a quiet pause, I looked back and said, "Kay, God has called me to be a minister and I answered His call last Wednesday night on my knees beside my bed." She looked at me with that sweet, radiant smile and replied, "Oh, Wally, I'm so happy you have made that decision. I'm proud of you. Tell me about it."

I then told her of the long years of struggle with my decision, and of the convincing presence of God in my life when I surrendered to His call. She then shared her call to full-time Christian service and her surrender at age 12. She was wondering how she could fulfill God's call on her life if she married someone whose life centered in agriculture. In His great providence, God had brought us together. Before we left the drive-in restaurant, we both prayed, thanking God for our lives and for bringing us together.

We were married on January 26, 1956, at the Burkesville Methodist Church. Kay was 18 and I had just turned 21. It was such an exciting event in Burkesville that the principal dismissed the high school in time for Kay's friends and teachers to attend the wedding. Kay's roommate and suitemates—Becky Parrish, Margaret Radford, and Elise Norris— were bridesmaids. My sister, Helen Whitlow, was matron-of-honor. Kay's two brothers, Windell and Allen Radford, my two cousins, Jerry Thomas and Joe Billy Jones, and my brother-in-law, Doug Whitlow, were groomsmen and ushers. Rev. Lewis Piercy, my great uncle, officiated. He wouldn't allow us to kiss at the end of the ceremony, but we took care of that at the exit to the sanctuary.

Following our honeymoon to Cumberland Falls in Kentucky and Rock City in Chattanooga, Tennessee, we enrolled at Western again. To minimize expenses, we moved in with Mom and Dad and commuted to college for that spring semester. During the following summer, I continued to work on the farm. In September of 1956, we moved into an apartment near Western's campus and lived there until I graduated in June of 1959. My friend,

Our wedding day on January 26, 1956.

Rev. Marshall Owen, was there to help us find the apartment; his sister and her husband allowed us to rent the apartment in the back of their house. It, too, was across the street from the college and the rent was $45 per month. I got a job as a shoe salesman, and as a part-time employee became the top salesman in the store. That meager income from Butler Shoe Store plus income from the tobacco was what we lived on for the first year of our marriage.

In January, 1957, our first child, Debbie was born and was a great joy in our lives. She was born on Sunday, and final exams began on Monday. My 8:00 a.m. exam was American Literature taught by Dr. Wilgus who had been my teacher for English 101a. Before we started the exam, I gave him an "It's a girl" cigar (which was the custom then). He asked when she was born, and I told him it was last night. He chuckled and said, "I'm sure you are prepared for this exam." When I completed the exam and handed it to Dr. Wilgus, he never opened it. Instead, he recorded a "B" in his grade book and congratulated me on the birth of our child. I was still working at the shoe store, carrying 15 college hours and doing a course of study for a license to preach.

With the dramatic change in my vocation, I changed my major from agriculture to English. One of the required courses for that semester was algebra, which was a four-hour course. This meant I had a homework assignment every day. I got behind the first week and was never able to catch up. For the first time, I felt overwhelmed and discouraged. Then I remembered the "big meeting" with God in my bedroom and Philippians 4:13 (NKJV) came rushing back to my heart: "I can do all things through Christ who strengthens me." With new determination, I resolved that I would conquer algebra and press on toward the goal I felt God had given me.

Wally leaving for his first pastoral visit.

After completing my license-to-preach course of study, I was ready, so I thought, for my first appointment. My district superintendent, Dr. Oscar Nichols, told the cabinet he had a student that was begging for an appointment. Bishop Watkins created an appointment by taking a church from three different charges, and they became the Mammoth Cave Circuit. The churches were Hall's Chapel in Warren County and Highland and Old Zion in Barren County. (Highland United Methodist Church was one of the churches our son David later served in his first appointment out of seminary).

I preached at Hall's Chapel on second and fourth Sundays and Old Zion and Highland on first and third Sundays. It was a 90-mile round trip to the three churches. Hall's Chapel was unhappy their pastor moved. On the first Sunday as their pastor, the song leader greeted me with, "We don't know if you can preach a lick or not, but we'll soon find out." During our first Sunday at Old Zion an announcement was made that the annual revival would begin in two weeks. Either I would be preaching the revival or I could ask someone to be the evangelist. I contacted an evangelist before sundown. I only had three sermons and I used two of them the first Sunday I was there!

Marshall Owen, who became my father in the ministry, helped me in this revival. Our plans were to live in the community and visit every day. After one night in a home with no bathroom facilities, we decided to commute. This was a 10-day revival with services at 10:00 a.m. and 7:00 p.m. We had a big meal for lunch, and another big meal for supper in a different home. Jokingly, I told the church how Marshall and I loved country ham and fried chicken. Every day we had country ham and fried chicken for both meals, and the country ham was some of the best I have ever eaten.

The ladies at Old Zion were great cooks. By the end of the second day I was sick. One night we went to the church early and stretched out on the floor. I had never been as stuffed as I was that night. Marshall laughingly said, "Wallace, you have to learn to appear to be eating a lot and gracefully refuse seconds." I'll never forget the lessons of my first revival.

About midway through the revival, the father of a prominent member died. While I was eating supper, his daughter came to see me and asked me to preach the funeral. I was speechless, and after a long pause, Marshall said, "Of course Wallace will preach the funeral, and I will assist him." This was my first funeral.

We had a good revival and several professions of faith, and the service of baptism was set for the first Sunday in August in Leroy Landrum's pond. I had never baptized anyone, and Marshall could not be with me for the baptism. Leroy Landrum and Maurice Furlong (at my insistence) volunteered to assist me. The day was cloudy and windy, and the water splashed all over me during the baptizing. It felt ice cold, which caused my voice to sound emotional. After that service, Maurice and Leroy agreed that the place for baptism was at the altar of the church. The United Methodist Church offers three modes of baptism: sprinkling, pouring, and immersion. I believe that after this experience Leroy and Maurice felt satisfied with the mode of sprinkling or pouring.

My former pastor, Glenn Lyle, helped me in my first revival at Hall's Chapel. We had professions of faith at this revival, too. The service of baptism was at the altar of the church on the closing night of the revival. I rehearsed the service of baptism several times, and was so excited about being the pastor of these little churches. Five young adults came forward to be baptized and join the church. They chose sprinkling for their mode of baptism. As I reached for the baptismal font, I realized I didn't have any water. After a long pause, I turned back to the congregation and admitted I didn't have any water for the baptism. The congregation didn't know whether to laugh or cry. I think they did some of both.

With there being no water in the church, the song leader said, "Continue to sing while I go to our Baptist friends down the road and get a jar of water." As Mr. Bratton returned and entered the church, Kay held up a bottle of water which was in the diaper bag for our 6-month-old daughter. This could have been used for the baptism by sprinkling, but Kay didn't think of having the water until it was too late. I'm sure these young adults never forgot the pastor who forgot to have water for their baptism.

The transition from farming to preaching and pastoral care was exciting, and at times, frightening and overwhelming. Every day was a new experience. Kay and I always enjoyed visiting our members. Relating to people has always been one of my strengths. One of our first pastoral calls was with Mr. and Mrs. Chuck Furlong. Upon our arrival, they insisted we stay for supper. I can still feel the warm and contagious spirit of that home. And they were so excited we had taken the time to visit them. Our meal consisted of country ham, corn bread, and cooked cabbage. The ham and corn bread were great, but I had never tasted cooked cabbage. I couldn't even stand the smell of it. But wanting to be a good pastor, I knew I must graciously eat some cabbage. That night I learned to like cabbage and remembered again that "All things are possible through Christ" (Philippians 4:13 NKJV).

We will never forget our first Christmas program at Hall's Chapel. Mr. and Mrs. Simmons invited us to their home for supper before the program. They lived in a little three-room frame house. Mrs. Simmons greeted us by saying that she had worked all day preparing the meal. She had made biscuits and opened a jar of sausage, a jar of kraut, tomatoes, black-eyed peas, and blackberry jelly. The kitchen table was home made with a bench on each side. In preparation for our coming, they had painted the table and benches a bright red. I was wearing my black tweed "going away" suit from our wedding. The bench felt dry when I sat down, but when I started to get up after supper, I was stuck to the bench. I carefully kept my back away from the people and no one noticed what had happened that night after sitting on the freshly painted red bench. Luckily the dry cleaner was able to salvage my suit.

There were times when we needed to come home on Sunday after church and have some time to rest and get ready for our college classes. The fourth Sunday in January during my first year of ministry was one of those days. College finals started on Monday, our baby daughter had a cold, and I needed to study. Kay and I agreed that we would refuse the invitation to have lunch with anyone. Upon our arrival at the church, Mrs. Eadens greeted us with tears in her eyes, saying, "Please come home with us today for lunch and talk to our son. Layton no longer attends church, he's running with the wrong crowd, and he is drinking. We need help." Needless to say, we went home with Mr. and Mrs. Eadens for lunch. I was nervous and did not know how to initiate the conversation with Layton.

Before lunch was over, Layton left and did not return before we went home. I missed the opportunity to talk to him. Being consumed with final exams, I thought no more about this concerned mother and the reckless life of her son, Layton, until the following Saturday morning. The telephone rang before I got out of bed. I quickly answered the phone and heard the broken voice of Mr. Bratton, the song leader from the church, say, "Brother Thomas, we've had a terrible tragedy in our church. Layton Eadens was drag racing down Center Street in Bowling Green last night and ran head-on into a tractor trailer truck. He was killed." He paused and then continued, "He had two friends with him who were also killed." After another pause Mr. Bratton added in a broken voice, "And Layton was drinking."

After a long pause I told Mr. Bratton I would go immediately to be with Mr. and Mrs. Eadens. Those nine miles were some of the longest of my entire life. The words of Mrs. Eadens were ringing in my mind, "Come home with us for lunch and talk to Layton."

Family and friends had gathered in to be with these grieving and heart-broken parents. I parked a distance from the house and prayed, *"Lord, help me. What do I say? What do I do? God, I have failed You and these grieving parents. God, I have failed You and this family. Please, please be with me."* I knew Kay was on her knees back at the apartment praying for me.

When I opened my eyes, Mr. and Mrs. Bratton were standing beside the car. They hugged me and walked with me to the house. When I walked through the door, everyone got quiet. After a moment of embrace, I offered a prayer asking for comfort and strength. I sat on the couch with Mr. and Mrs. Eadens, holding their hands. Mrs. Eadens broke the silence and said, "I'm so sorry Layton left last Sunday before you were able to talk to him." Squeezing my hand, she continued, "We want you to do the funeral."

I had never felt so inadequate and such a failure in my life. I later learned that I would not only have Layton's funeral but would have the funeral of the other two youth also. Again, I claimed the verse that God had given me the night I accepted His call to ministry: "I can do all things through Christ who strengthens me (Philippians 4:13 NKJV).

As soon as I got back to the apartment, I called Dr. Nichols, my district superintendent, and he invited Kay and me to come to the parsonage. He and Mrs. Nichols were very comforting and encouraging to us. He loaned me some books and gave me some ideas that would be good for these tragic funerals. We had a good prayer time together. During the next three days I had two worship services and three funerals. I discovered the truth of Paul's words in II Corinthians 12:9a (KJV): "My grace is sufficient for thee, for my strength is made perfect in weakness."

In January 1959, we had another death in our church. I had just baptized this person, and the following Sunday she committed suicide. This sent a shock wave throughout the community and people were wondering why one as good as this dear lady would take her life. I could not answer their questions. I knew God to be a wise and merciful God, and we could trust this dear lady was in His loving and everlasting arms.

I had certainly "hit the ground running" in the ministry. One thing was for sure: God was with me in my journey and I was being taught to "Trust in the Lord with all thine heart; and lean not unto thine own understanding. In all thy ways acknowledge him, and he shall direct your paths" (Proverbs 3:5-6 KJV). The ministry to which God had called me was much bigger than I am, but I chose to look at the size of God rather than the size of the seminary education ahead of me.

Chapter 4

SEMINARY AND THE ZEBULON-FINCHER CHARGE

I graduated from Western in June 1959, and three weeks later we moved to Atlanta, Georgia. Kay didn't finish her degree until later. I was now ready to enroll in seminary at Emory University's Candler School of Theology. We visited Emory earlier and rented a duplex apartment in Decatur, Georgia. The apartment was only four miles from the seminary.

On July 4 we loaded our car with food and clothing and began our journey of 400 miles to Atlanta. I was ready to begin my studies to become an ordained minister in the Methodist Church. Before we left Kentucky, we traded our old car for a newer car, but it was still a used one with retread tires! We were as prepared as possible for a daylong journey to Atlanta. This was before the days of interstate roads and air-conditioning. The temperature that day was in the 90s. It was also before car seats for children were a requirement, and Debbie rode between us in all our travels. Her arms were often outstretched around each of us.

About 100 miles into our trip, one of our retread tires went flat. This necessitated my unloading the trunk to get to the spare tire. By the time I changed the tire, we were hot, scared, and with no money for emergencies. We were alone and wanted to go home, but we wanted more to obey God.

The truck bringing all our other belongings was also delayed and would not arrive until Sunday. Classes were to begin on Tuesday, so I had only two days to get moved in and buy some tires. On Monday morning I remembered that night in my bedroom when I committed my life to ministry. But in that moment, I wondered how I would ever become an ordained minister.

My first stop for tire shopping was a Standard Oil Station near our apartment. Early in our conversation, the station owner asked why I was in Atlanta. When I told him that I would begin classes the next day at Candler, he put his arm around my shoulder. I will never forget his words of encouragement that followed. "Please know you have one friend in this town. I'm a Methodist also. God has called me to help seminary students, and right now I believe you need some new tires."

God had come to me again through one of His faithful servants. Even in a large, strange city, God was with me and was supplying my needs. I recalled these words of promise in Philippians 4:19 (KJV): "But my God shall supply all your need according to his riches in glory by Christ Jesus."

Like a father, this good filling station owner took me to a bank and helped me open an account, gave me the name of a doctor, and introduced me to his pastor. I couldn't wait to get home to tell Kay about our new friend. That day we knew we were in God's will, we were not alone, and we would not be defeated.

My first day in seminary was a memorable one. I enrolled in two classes—"World Religions" and "The Prophets." I knew nothing about world religions and very little about the prophets. I felt so alone and so far from home. It was a great comfort to know Kay was praying for me. I prayed before I got out of the car. As I walked toward the classroom, I asked God to be with me and calm my heart.

I entered the classroom in Bishop's Hall at Candler, and soon two men joined me. Their names were Dean Chastean and John Ripley.

Both were beginning their seminary education just as I was, and both were taking the same two classes I had chosen. We quickly became friends and soon discovered we all had many things in common: a lot of faith, very little money, and supportive, loving spouses. In two days, God gave me friendships that would be a great source of strength not only during seminary, but also throughout my life.

That short summer session felt like an eternity, and as soon as I finished my final exams, we headed for Kentucky. I got stopped for speeding in Tennessee. When the policeman started writing the ticket, Debbie leaned over to the window beside me and said, "Mr. Policeman, we're just going to see Grandma and Grandpa." The officer looked at her, smiled and said, "OK, but tell your Daddy to slow down." With that, he tore up his ticket and we were on our way home again—in time for supper.

Our time at home before returning for the fall semester gave Kay and me some time to reflect and plan. We decided that by continuing to take summer classes, I could graduate in two years. In the meantime, I could get a job as a shoe salesman to help with our finances. Decatur, Georgia, had the feel of a small town, and on the square was a large shoe store. It reminded me of where I had worked in Bowling Green, except the quality of the shoes was much better. When I asked for a job and told of my experience, they hired me immediately.

Even though Kay did not get to complete her education before we left for seminary, she was offered a job teaching. We spent several hours praying about this decision. We only had one car, and the daycare centers were inferior to what they are today. After visiting some of the daycare centers around us, we made the decision for Kay to be a full-time mother. At Western, she majored in home economics and made her own wedding gown, which was beautiful. We came up with the idea that she could make or alter anything the girls from Agnes Scott College needed.

Agnes Scott was in walking distance of our apartment. We posted a note on the bulletin boards at the college, and in a month she was earning as much as I. She also babysat Bill and Mary Lou Strickland's daughter, Linda. Bill Strickland was also from Kentucky and a student at Candler. Debbie now had a playmate, which was a blessing. Kay also kept a neighbor boy after school for around three hours each day.

One Saturday, while I was working at the shoe store, I got a call from Eugene Dunn, a pastor from the North Georgia Conference. He invited me to preach the next day at one of his churches, Zebulon Methodist Church, to be interviewed to be their youth director. I agreed to think about it and call him back. After talking to Kay, we agreed to go and consider the offer.

The next morning we drove 60 miles to Zebulon and met the Dunns. When we arrived, I was told I would preach that morning at Fincher Methodist Church, the other church on the charge, and also preach at a joint service in Zebulon that night. I only had one sermon and had to put something together for the evening service. I prepared a message on Philippians 4:13 (NKJV), "I can do all things through Christ who strengthens me." I then told about God's call on my life and how God had guided me thus far.

The churches hired me that night to be their youth director and also to alternate with the pastor in preaching during the Sunday morning services. They would pay us $125 per month, and provide us a room on weekends with Mrs. Odessa Slade, one of the Fincher members. So our combined income would be approximately $250 to $275 per month depending on how much sewing Kay was asked to do. We paid our own rent, had no health insurance, and were driving a used car. But we did have new tires!

Working with Eugene Dunn and serving these two strong churches as youth director plus preaching every Sunday were positive experiences in the development of my leadership and preaching skills. Eugene was a good administrator. He taught me the importance of sermon preparation, visioning, goal-setting, and accountability with a calendar for all the church goals. Eugene was also a good preacher. I recently ran upon some notes I took while listening to one of his messages. His three points were: (1) We can walk away from yesterday because Christ is in us, (2) We can walk through today because Christ knows about our heavy loads, and (3) We can walk through tomorrow because Christ is our hope of glory. All of us can claim these promises.

Both Zebulon and Fincher had meaningful and well-prepared worship services. This was my first exposure to an order of worship and bulletin. These were congregations committed to meeting the needs of their people and reaching out into the community. Each year the pastor had a planning retreat for the administrative boards to talk about needs, to set goals, and to develop a budget. Participating in that process was equal to any academic course in seminary and gave me the experience I needed in beginning my ministry as a full-time pastor.

By beginning seminary in mid-summer and attending every summer school, I was within six hours of graduation at the end of my second year. After talking to my district superintendent, Dr. Oscar Nichols, we decided to ask for an appointment in Kentucky and then commute to my church on weekends. When we arrived at Annual Conference, we were told there were no openings except student appointments with an $1,800 salary.

I have been told I was a topic of discussion every time the cabinet met during that Conference. My appointment was changed four times while we were attending the Conference. When I arrived at Conference on the last day, I learned Bishop Gum told Marshall Owen I was going to a good station church that paid more than the minimum salary. I received this message only three hours before adjournment, but I could not find out where this church was located.

I was fit to be tied. Kay had a hard chill the night before; we were not sleeping and were totally exhausted. Finally, 30 minutes before the reading of the appointments, I was told that we were going to Park City Methodist church; only nine miles from my hometown.

After the adjournment of the Conference, Bishop Gum said, "Wallace, I believe in you. Don't let me down. Park City has had a difficult year and the people are threatening to reduce the amount they pay to the apportionments." My district superintendent came to me and said, "Park City does not know you have to go to summer school. You will need to meet with them as soon as possible." He did not offer to go with me, nor did he offer any suggestions on how to tell them that I would be away most of the summer. Kay and I left Conference feeling scared and alone with no one to give us guidance. We agreed that having each other and our Heavenly Father was all we needed, and again we claimed the promise, "We can do all things through Christ who strengthens us" (Philippians 4:13 NKJV).

We drove to Glasgow where Debbie was staying with my mom and dad and told them about our new appointment and expressed joy at being close to home again. I then called Fred Perdue, chairman of the board at Park City, and requested a time to meet with the board. The next day, we traveled to Park City to see our church and parsonage and tell them about our summer school schedule. After brief introductions, Mr. Perdue asked me to make a statement and share our needs for the summer.

Park City received us with open arms and assured us of their support and prayers during the concluding months of seminary. During the first half of the summer, my family stayed in Decatur, and I traveled to Park City every other weekend. At mid-summer, we moved to Park City and I commuted by train on weekends. I arrived in Bowling Green at midnight on Fridays, and left for Atlanta at midnight on Mondays.

The young adult Sunday school class at Park City worked out a schedule to pick me up on Friday nights and take me to the train station on Monday nights. They also helped me with visitation on weekends and were supportive of Kay and Debbie while I was away. My 8:00 a.m. professor learned of my schedule and excused me from the Tuesday morning class, giving me a private session on Tuesday afternoon. Summer passed, and I graduated from seminary on August 19, 1961. What an exciting day that was! Kay's parents, my parents, my sister and her husband, and Kay and Debbie were all present for my graduation.

Seminary graduation,
Candler School of Theology, Emory University.

In reflecting on my days in seminary, I would have to say this was one of the most difficult times of my life. But, through it all God supplied our needs. So often when we had no money for groceries, we would get a letter from a former member, friend, or relative. Enclosed in the letter would usually be a check for the amount of money we needed, a wonderful reminder that God was taking care of us.

When I left for seminary, I had a herd of Jersey cows that was a part of our dairy herd. At the beginning of each quarter, I sold a couple of cows to pay my tuition. I sold my last cow at the beginning of my last quarter in seminary. God had enabled us to obey Him. Now we looked forward to serving Him in our new appointment at Park City. (At the time we were at Park City, the church was called Park City Methodist Church. The word "United" was added during our next appointment which was in Munfordville. However, I am calling this church what it was soon to be named.)

Chapter 5

PARK CITY UNITED METHODIST CHURCH

It had been six years since I answered the call to preach and started on my journey. After these strenuous years of hard work, sacrifice, and empowered by a lot of faith, we were finally living in our first parsonage and ready to begin our new work together.

That word "together" needs emphasizing, for in no vocation is a man's spouse more vitally important to his work than in the ministry. It was over 50 years ago that Kay and I started out as a team. Her talents and dedication have been used greatly to build and bless the lives of our children and me. Beyond our family, she has always faithfully served her church and community. Kay delayed her education while I completed seminary, and she graduated *Cum Laude* from Spalding University in 1977.

Kay has always kept a journal and has shared many of our experiences in her book of daily devotionals which is in its second printing. This book, *New Every Morning: A Touch of God's Faithfulness,* was published in 2001. Kay's second book is entitled *Grandparenting A Child with Autism: A Search for Help and Hope.* She has also published a children's book entitled *Mother Duck Knows the Way* as well as numerous brochures and articles.

While she was never ordained, her ministry has been far-reaching as a Sunday school teacher and author. She has enjoyed her own ministry of encouragement by writing thousands of notes to friends, relatives, and sometimes people whom she has never met who are struggling with life.

For many years Kay held a deep desire in her heart to start a Kentucky Christian Writers Conference. While attending a writers' conference in Nashville, Tennessee, Kay spoke with one of the workshop leaders, Donna Goodrich, about her dream for a Christian Writers' Conference in Kentucky. Donna immediately responded by saying, "Well, why don't you start one?" Kay's reply was that she didn't know how to begin such an undertaking. It was then that Donna said she would help Kay. About a year later on June 27-28, 1997, the first Kentucky Christian Writers Conference was held at Memorial United Methodist Church in Elizabethtown, Kentucky, and has continued to meet annually ever since.

I can't even try to express what home life has meant to me since we started our life together, but I cannot imagine my life without Kay. The author of the book of Proverbs wrote with deep feeling about a good wife, but when it comes to Kay, even these glowing words are an understatement:

"A good wife who can find? She is far more precious than jewels,
The heart of her husband trusts in her" (Proverbs 31:10,11a RSV).

Before moving on with my life story, I want to talk a little more about those early years. I was tossed into my first full-time parish nearly a half-century ago, like a boy thrown into deep water and told to swim when he didn't know how. The seminary courses in homiletics had been of slight use to me. One professor spent a lot of his time on the golf course, and another professor lectured from a book he had written entitled *You Can Preach*. It was already outdated by the time I took his class.

Sermon preparation has never been an easy task for me, and at the beginning it was often exceedingly challenging. Park City Church had two services on Sunday plus a Wednesday night prayer service. This meant I had three messages to prepare every week. One Sunday night I was having a difficult time getting into my sermon and after about five minutes, I paused and said, "I'm sorry, but I cannot preach tonight. Will you stand for the benediction?" I went out the side door to the parsonage without shaking hands or greeting anyone.

The next morning as I was on my way to the post office, Mrs. Sam Crump, my organist, neighbor, and one of the most devoted Christians I have ever known, was sitting on the front porch. When I came in sight, she called to me, "Wallace, come by for a cup of coffee after you get the mail." I was scared to death. Thoughts began to whirl in my mind. *What will she say to me? I have blown it during my first few months here!*

I will never forget that conversation. With love and compassion she said, "Wallace, it took a lot of courage to do what you did last night. You're

Park City Methodist United Church.
First appointment out of seminary.

doing a good job and we're proud of you. Three sermons every week require a lot of study and preparation. You are visiting every day. We're so glad you, Kay, and little Debbie are living in our parsonage." Then she gave me a 20-dollar bill, and said, "You and Kay go to Mammoth Cave for a good meal today, and know that your congregation loves you."

I am eternally grateful for the many faithful and loving people like Ethel Crump in my journey. Only God knows just how much a few encouraging words can lift a person's spirit in those days of discouragement and feeling like a failure.

I have seen many young ministers mistreated in their first parish, so hurt by criticism and so disheartened by meanness and coldness that irreparable damage was done to them. I was fortunate to begin my ministry in a vital congregation with committed, resourceful leadership and a healthy understanding of the mission of the church. Park City proved to be an incredible opportunity for me to develop my skills and work habits for pastoral ministry.

At the time of my ordination, pastors were ordained deacons for a two-year period during which more steps in the ordination process were completed. After a second review, we were then ordained elders, which is "full connection" in the United Methodist Church. I studied the questions the bishop would be asking me on the day of my ordination:

- Will you visit from house to house?
- Are you determined to employ all your time in the work of God?
- Will you observe the following directions: be diligent; never be unemployed; be punctual; do everything exactly on time?

I felt ready and eager to get to work. The Park City Church bought a new desk and chair and created some office space at the end of a hallway. Now I had a place to study, a few shelves for my three boxes of books, and I could have regular office hours.

My office hours were from 7:30 to noon Monday through Thursday with Friday being my day off when possible. The afternoons were given to visitation. Most of the congregation lived within walking distance of the church, and I visited most of the members every quarter and would see the men at the post office every morning at 7:00. At the conclusion of a board meeting one night, the chairman asked if anyone had anything to say. Mr. Sam Crump (Mrs. Ethel's husband) raised his hand and said, "I like our preacher; he goes to work when we go."

Feeling accepted and comfortable with my people gave me confidence about my work. Occasionally in a sermon something would get hold of an idea I was expressing, and it would catch fire. I would feel the congregation's warm response. I'm sure the congregation was as surprised as I was when that happened! I would go home feeling that preaching could be that kind of moving and powerful communication of the truth every Sunday.

Another life lesson was emerging. It was that sermon preparation is not just research and organizing thoughts. It is a prayerful waiting; it is the presence of God that reaches the heart of the congregation. It is heart and mind sharing a word that is convicting, comforting, encouraging, healing, guiding, and redeeming—all inspired by God. It is the greatest hour in the preacher's life! I began to feel a rhythm, a daily routine in my work: prayerful sermon preparation, administration, and pastoral care. Most every day was given to these three areas. Every day is a challenge for pastors and requires our very best.

During my first winter at Park City we had a flu epidemic, and many of our members were hospitalized. I visited as many as I could. One day, wearing dress pants and sweater, I visited my great uncle, J.L. Piercy, who was in the hospital in Glasgow. Uncle Lewis was the minister who married my parents, my sister and her husband, and Kay and me. As I entered the room, he greeted me by saying, "Wallace, you are a servant of God, and you don't go to the hospital dressed like you're going to a ball game. You wear a coat and tie. Now, have a prayer with me and go visit your people." Uncle Lewis was very blunt but honest, and a bit too rigid in his style of dress. He always wore a coat and tie, even at home, and always wore a black suit when he was meeting the public.

I soon realized the truth of my uncle's wisdom concerning the importance of appropriate dress for ministry. A pastor's day is often filled with surprises such as emergency calls, quick trips to the hospital, calls for counseling, and lunch meetings with parishioners. While I do not agree with Uncle Lewis's idea of the black suit and tie every day, I do think the present generation of clergy has gone to the extreme in casual and, at times, sloppy dress. Since receiving Uncle Lewis's unsolicited advice, I have always tried to dress appropriately, keep regular office hours, and discipline myself to regular visitation.

The members of our church at Park City, especially the women, insisted that I adjust my schedule to help Kay and have more time as a family. I tried to do that. Those were such happy times in our lives—our first appointment after seminary and serving a church that loved us.

Prior to our coming to Park City, the congregation completely refurbished the sanctuary with new carpet, light fixtures, pews, and paint. Bishop Walter Gum was scheduled to preach the dedication sermon. It was scheduled for 2:00 on a Sunday afternoon in order that former pastors and members of other churches could attend. This was our first time to have a bishop in our church and my first time to introduce my bishop. I worked on that introduction like I was preparing a sermon, and I rehearsed it with Kay.

Mom and Dad came for the service and were planning to babysit for Debbie while Kay and I took Bishop and Mrs. Gum and Dr. and Mrs. Nichols, our district superintendent and wife, to lunch at Mammoth Cave. However, Debbie decided she wanted to go with us. During the meal, Debbie turned over her milk, and it spilled all over Mrs. Gum's dress. Debbie looked at us and in tears, said, "I want to go to be with Grandma." We started apologizing, and Mrs. Gum graciously informed us of the many times drinks were spilled on her by her own children and grandchildren. She brushed off her dress with a napkin and then held Debbie, assuring her of her love. That experience made us feel comfortable to always include our children in special occasions when we had guests in our church.

Living in a town of 500 people, I soon became known as "preacher" and my ministry expanded to caring for people of the entire community. The Toms family was a large family in the church. Robert "Wimpy"

Toms and his dad Barney Toms each owned and operated service stations which were always open on Sunday. These stations were a hangout for men, especially the un-churched.

My goal was to get Wimpy and his dad to close their stations and attend church on Sunday morning. Finally, one Sunday during Sunday school, I went to Wimpy's station and told him I wanted him to come to the worship service. I then proceeded to close the doors. Wimpy knew I meant business, so he washed his hands and walked with me to church, which was only a block away. That was the last Sunday he had the station open. The church joined me in praying for the salvation of these men.

When we started our fall revival with Marshall Owen, Barney closed his station and attended the revival every night. That week, Wimpy made a profession of faith and Barney rededicated his life. I'll never forget the night Wimpy came to the altar. He was a deer hunter, and he had spent that entire day in his "tree house" he used for deer hunting. All day he had wrestled with God, and God won.

On that eventful night, Wimpy and his family were sitting together on the third pew from the front. About midway through the sermon his son went to sleep in his lap and I thought to myself *this will be his excuse for not coming to the altar.* As we were singing the closing hymn, "Almost Persuaded," Wimpy gently laid his son down on the pew and started toward the altar. Marshall looked at me and said, "Wallace, here he comes!" I almost jumped over the altar rail as I met him at the altar. The whole church had been praying for Wimpy, and now our prayer was answered.

After a time of prayer at the altar, Wimpy stood to his feet and told us about his day in the woods wrestling with God and thanked us for our love and prayers. That was a great night in my life and in our congregation and one of the great revivals in the life of that church.

The next day Wimpy bought a Bible to be used at his service station and started witnessing to his friends who played checkers at the station. He told all of them of his experience and started taking them to revivals in the community. In the next two months Wimpy must have led a half-dozen of his friends to the Lord by taking them to a revival service. Often, I would hear the horn blow in my driveway, and when I went to the door, it would be Wimpy with a beaming smile saying, "Bro. Thomas, George accepted the Lord tonight. Come and have prayer with him."

Wimpy's unchurched friends were added to my prayer list. It became a pattern for me to carry a 3x5 card in my shirt pocket with a list of people for whom I was praying they would become Christians. Some names stayed on my list for five to six years before I wrote "Prayer answered" by their names. As people became aware of my prayer list, they began to ask me to visit their relatives and friends, which I did. Remembering my failure to talk to Layton from Halls Chapel, I always promptly followed up on these requests with a sense of urgency.

Paul's words in II Timothy 4:5 (RSV) became an admonition to me: "As for you, always be steady, endure suffering, do the work of an evangelist, fulfill your ministry." For me visitation was much more than an ordination requirement or congregational expectation; it was building relationships that enabled me to share my faith personally with people in the community. This would become one of the greatest strengths of my ministry.

The youth ministry at Park City United Methodist Church was considered to be one of the best in the district. Kay and I worked with the youth and developed a good relationship with them. Often we would have them come to the parsonage for homemade ice cream or a cookout. One of the highlights of our youth ministry was our summer youth week. Each morning the youth were in classes led by student ministers who were attending Western Kentucky University in Bowling Green. In the afternoon we had activities and swimming. Each evening parents took turns preparing cookouts in their yards. Following the meal, the evening was given to program planning and to a worship time to which the parents were invited. On Friday night, the parents were invited to a parent/youth banquet where we shared our blessings of the week and our goals for the year. Many of the members of the church said our youth week was equal to a revival for them, too.

Growth was taking place in every area of the church. Sunday school and worship attendance were strong. The young adult class led by Jane Arterburn filled their room every Sunday. Park City had an outstanding United Methodist Women's group (called Woman's Society of Christian Service at that time). Mrs. Ethel Crump was the Louisville Annual Conference president while we were there, and later, her daughter, Jane Arterburn, was the Conference president. Jane and Hack's daughter, Janie, served as district president of Methodist Youth Fellowship.

Growth was taking place in our family, too. We were thrilled when our son, David, was born on July 27, 1962. He didn't wait around long to be born once his time arrived. As soon as I parked the car that morning in the Bowling Green Hospital lot and walked back in, the nurse met me with a bundle in her arm! She asked if I was "Mr. Thomas."

I told her I was, and she said, "I am holding your new son!" My immediate response was, "No, that can't be my baby. My wife was in labor 24 hours when our daughter was born." She replied, "Your name *is* Thomas, isn't it?" With that she pulled the blanket back from David's head, and said, "This is your son. Your wife is the only one back there, and the doctor almost didn't get here in time!"

David joins our family.

I noticed the red hair, and wondered again if there had been a mix-up. I couldn't think of anyone in our families right then with red hair. By this time the nurse was getting a bit weary with me, and placed the baby in my arms. I knew for sure then that this was the little boy for whom we were hoping and praying. Debbie was 5½ at that time and was so proud of her new brother.

The congregation immediately adopted David as one of their own. Two weeks after he was born, Hack Arterburn, our devoted superintendent of the Sunday school, said to Kay, "You all are going to let that baby grow up ignorant if you don't get him in Sunday school!" It would be good if we had more Sunday school superintendents who are that conscientious.

When David was 6 months old, our church sent us to the Christmas Conference in Denver, Colorado. I don't know how the church learned about this upcoming Christmas Conference, but they decided Kay and I should attend the event. Gene and Gladys Dunn, our youth counselors, offered to keep Debbie and David for us.

Kay likes to tell of our first airplane flight. The church flew us first class on Continental Airlines. Continental was thought of as the Cadillac of airlines at that time. Soon after our flight took off from Louisville, the stewardess came by and politely asked, "Would you care for an hors d'oeuvre?" I looked over at Kay to see what she was going to say, but since I was near the aisle, I thought she was expecting me to speak first. So, I said, "Well, what all do you have?" The stewardess smiled and started naming stuff I had never heard of, let alone learned to like. She said, "We have goose liver, artichokes," and on she went. So to make it easy for her I just said, "Well, just give me a little bit of all of it!" She did, and I don't reckon I will ever need any more goose liver or artichokes as long as I live.

The Christmas Conference was a special experience for both Kay and me. It was a reenactment of the very first Annual Conference of the Methodist Church in America. We will always treasure the memory of this event and the gracious people at Park City who made it possible. We returned home with a deeper appreciation of our heritage as Methodists and more committed to ministry than ever.

Debbie started first grade in the fall of 1963. (There was no kindergarten in the elementary school at Park City then.) Kay and I were eager to hear about her first day at school. Debbie said she had a good day, but she seemed concerned about her teacher. We questioned her a bit to try to understand what was worrying her. Finally, she said, "Well, my teacher is named Miss Armstrong. Some of the children said she might spank hard." That made sense to children starting their first day of school. For beginners, a teacher named Miss Armstrong might just happen to have strong arms. However, she was a kind and wonderful teacher.

Before Christmas that year, Kay began to prepare for an open house at the parsonage. (She had open house for every church parsonage in which we lived.) David was a toddler at Christmas time, eager to explore everything in his world. The night before the open house, he was delighting in all the sparkling ornaments and lights on our Christmas tree. At first he touched the ornaments hesitantly, then in a split second, decided to pull one from the tree. Before we could get to him, you can imagine the rest of the story. The tree hit the floor and the ornaments scattered everywhere. Thankfully, David wasn't hurt. After the broken pieces were swept up, the tree went into David's playpen, and the open house went on as planned.

Soon we found ourselves needing more space at our church, and at the official board meeting, action was taken to build an addition to our educational building. A part of this plan would include a new fellowship hall. The following spring we began construction of this expansion.

George Wood was my district superintendent at that time. After our having such a good year in the church, he felt that some kind of an increase in my salary would be in order. The official board refused on the grounds they could not raise the pastor's salary while they were in the building program. On the way to the parsonage after the charge conference, Dr. Wood said, "Wally, get your boxes. You're moving."

That year my salary was $4,440 and Dr. Wood was asking them to pay $4,500 for the next year. A $60 raise for the coming year, or $5 per month, seemed too much to them right then. I've always felt there was some conflict between the Official Board and Dr. Wood that brought about that decision.

So we got the boxes, packed our things, and after the 1964 Annual Conference, moved our seven-year-old Debbie and two-year-old David a few miles up the road to Munfordville. We will always treasure those happy years at Park City.

Chapter 6

MUNFORDVILLE FIRST UNITED METHODIST CHURCH— MT. BEULAH UNITED METHODIST CHURCH

In May 1964, I was appointed to the Munfordville/Mt. Beulah Charge in Munfordville, Kentucky, which was only 12 miles north of Park City. One goal for my ministry was that I would serve a county-seat church, and my appointment to Munfordville fulfilled that goal for me. I

Munfordville First United Methodist Church.

borrowed Dad's pickup truck and Doug, my brother-in-law, brought his pickup which together would carry all of our earthly belongings up the road to Munfordville.

The parsonage was in poor condition when we arrived. Some of the windows had no curtains. The basement was not fit for storage. We couldn't lock the outside basement door. Some of the appliances didn't work. While we were unloading the furniture, the storm door slammed on David's finger, and he started screaming to the top of his voice. With my bleeding child, I started down the road, asking the first person I saw where I could find a doctor.

Pointing to the end of the street, a stranger said, "Straight ahead at the stop sign is Dr. Speevack's office." Fortunately, we were able to see him immediately and Dr. Speevack took care of David's finger. He then held David in his lap and gave him a sucker. David liked our new doctor immediately, but didn't like what had brought them together that day.

That was the beginning of a friendship with this good Jewish doctor who cared for our family without any charge for the next five years. Dr. Speevak was a kind, elderly bachelor, and he enjoyed many meals in our home. He would teasingly ask Kay, "Say, you have cooked me a kosher meal?" She looked all over Louisville for kosher food, but we both knew that our meals were not very kosher. Our guest didn't seem to mind, though.

We will never forget the time I asked Dr. Speevak to say our blessing at the meal. He looked at me like he couldn't believe what he was hearing, but he bowed his head and said, "Thanks!" Both Debbie and David giggled, and we gave them one of those looks they recognized. Dr. Speevak said, "Well, isn't that enough? 'Thanks' is sufficient I believe."

When David and I got back to the parsonage after the doctor visit, Mr. Guy Thornberry, a trustee, was there to greet me. He apologized for the condition of the parsonage and indicated the church wanted to build a new parsonage. I agreed with him that they needed a new parsonage and said I would do everything I could to help them get it done. In 30 days we had contracted to build a new parsonage. We never completely unpacked before we moved across town to a small frame house which belonged to Jimmie and Mary Buford Kabler. The church sold the old parsonage to Pete Lawler who moved it across the river three miles from Munfordville.

My new appointment gave me a $500 increase in salary, but Munfordville First United Methodist Church was a struggling church lacking in programming and outreach. They were averaging only 45 in worship and 30 in Sunday school. Often the offering was not enough to pay my salary. I remembered the wisdom of my seminary professor who said, "In the first summer of your new appointment, let dust collect on your desk and the soles wear out on your shoes."

That summer I visited every home in the Munfordville Church and Mt. Beulah congregations. So on the last Sunday of that quarter before taking the offering, I read the financial statement from the treasurer to the congregation. I took the offering and instructed the treasurer and chairman of the administrative board to go to my office and count the offering. They were to bring me a report at the conclusion of the service.

After my sermon on God's Love, I announced the amount of the offering and told the congregation that we would need to receive another offering before the benediction. We received another offering and I asked the church officials to meet me in the Men's Sunday School Class room following the service. The chairman of the administrative board, William Wallace, opened the meeting by saying, "I think you all know why you are here." Nothing more was said and one by one they started giving more money to the treasurer. When some of the men started writing checks, I knew I was making progress.

The only remark made after the opening statement by the chairman was made by Mr. Howard Roop, the treasurer, who simply said, "I move we adjourn." This indicated we had enough money to pay the bills. I was sitting just inside the door which meant no one could leave unless I moved. Our wives were waiting for us outside the church. Kay was wondering if she should go home and start packing. After some silence, one of the men chuckled and said, "I guess that's the first time we have had to pay to get out of the church."

As we arrived for the evening services, I noticed the men were gathering around me. Then one of them began to speak, "Brother Thomas, we'd like to make a deal with you. You just preach the gospel and we'll pay the bills. Please don't lock us in the church again. That was too painful." Then they laughed and said, "We are with you and will support your ministry." Looking back on that day, I know that was a bold and scary thing to do, but it worked. In my five years as pastor, I didn't have any more financial problems in the church.

We were grateful to Jimmie and Mary Buford Kabler for providing housing for us while the new parsonage was being built, but we were ready for the new parsonage. By December 1, the parsonage was completed and we were told we could move in and celebrate Christmas there. On the day we were to move, Kay was sick in bed with flu and strep throat. We moved her bed, wrapped her in blankets and moved her to the parsonage. Dr. Speevak came by to see Kay and started her on antibiotics. Debbie and David stayed with Kay and cared for her while I finished moving.

The next days were spent unpacking boxes and nurturing Kay back to good health. I am sure she never unpacked such a mess as my packing was. She said that all the ingredients in the canister set—sugar, flour, corn meal, and coffee—were spilled all over everything!

The parsonage was beautiful with wall-to-wall carpet, new furniture, central

Kate's parents, Murson and Vina Radford, with Debbie and David in front of new parsonage.

heating, and a full, dry basement for storage. It felt like a mansion to us. It was exciting to decorate our new home for Christmas. Kay has always made every parsonage special at Christmas. We still use a part of the front door decoration we won that first Christmas for having the prettiest home decoration in Munfordville that year.

With lights in the windows, the smell of cedar from our tree, and Christmas music from our new portable stereo, we were experiencing the happiest, most joy-filled Christmas of our lives. Every time someone came to see us, David would immediately ask, "Would you like to see my room?" It was the first time for David to have his own room.

Most pastors would probably prefer having only one church. I always enjoyed pastoring Mt. Beulah. This small church, located a few miles from Munfordville, had preaching services each Sunday at 9:00 a.m. I always looked forward to driving those few miles out to Mt. Beulah. The people were friendly and appreciative of me. Kay didn't get to go to Mt. Beulah as much as she would have liked because she wanted our children to get to their Sunday school classes on time at 10:00 in Munfordville.

Mt. Beulah United Methodist Church.

Kay and I worked hard at getting to know our two congregations. I visited in every home and listened to their concerns and dreams for their church. Despite all our efforts, progress seemed slow. I began to feel tired and, at times, discouraged.

It was about this time that Dr. William James, our district superintendent, and Mrs. James came to see the parsonage. They were very complimentary of our work and the construction of the new parsonage. Sensing our exhaustion and weary hearts, Dr. James invited me to go with him to the Congress on Evangelism in Chicago during the coming January. Little did we know that God was providing an experience for me that would begin to shape my ministry at Munfordville and provide spiritual renewal for my life.

It was there in that big Hilton Hotel in downtown Chicago that G. Campbell Morgan, one of the great preachers of that generation, called us to get on our knees beside our chairs and ask God for a fresh experience of His grace in our lives. This was not about a "second blessing," but a simple time of rededication of our lives to God and the ministry to which we had been called.

With renewed determination and enthusiasm, I started gathering free material and attending workshops. On the last day of the Congress on Evangelism, I attended a workshop on the Lay Witness Mission. This is a laity-led weekend of 15 people from different states who would come by invitation to local churches at their own expense and stay in homes of church members. The plan is for the weekend to begin on Friday night with a potluck supper and be followed by a worship service. During this service led by the coordinator, he or she and members of the team give their testimonies. Saturday is a day for in-home meetings and evening worship. The mission is concluded with the Sunday morning worship service. Before I left that workshop, I got a directory that had names and addresses of coordinators available to lead this special weekend. I knew this was an answer to my prayers.

We had our Lay Witness Mission at the Munfordville Church in October 1965. It concluded with my congregation at the altar on their knees in rededication. My prayer was answered, and the door was opened to a fruitful ministry at Munfordville. Small groups and Bible studies were formed, and people began to pray for their unsaved friends and loved ones. Soon we started having visitors and professions of faith at the morning worship service. My prayer list continued to grow. As I visited and became a friend to those on my list, they became regular attendees. Several were baptized and joined the church. During my five years as their pastor, we averaged 25 new members per year.

One of those new members was the man who married Jimmie and Mary Buford Kabler's only daughter, Jean. Doug Custer grew up in a Baptist church in Florida, and naturally, Jean hoped for him to join her church since they would be living in Munfordville. At the close of one Sunday morning worship service, Jean nudged Doug a little and said, "Aren't you ready to join this morning?" Doug quickly replied, "No." But during the closing hymn, he suddenly closed the hymnal and said, "Let's go!" As they walked to the altar, I couldn't hide my joy and said, "Well, behold, the bridegroom cometh!" Another man who had been considering becoming a member of the church followed close behind. All of this moved Jean's dad to the point that he followed the group to the altar with tears streaming down his face.

The new growth at Munfordville became the talk of the town and district. I began to get several requests for revivals. During the next two years I conducted revivals in Burkesville, Parrish Chapel (Kay's home church), Stovall, and Sonora, just to name a few. The Stovall revival started on Sunday night after a Lay Witness Mission, and we had professions of faith every night. It was a busy but fulfilling time in my life.

Our family was happy. Debbie was in fourth grade and making the honor roll, and David was in a kindergarten that Kay and another parent, Rosemary Custer, organized at the First Baptist Church. Dave enjoyed antiques and loved to trade. Occasionally, he would invite Johnny Hulsey, his much older friend, to come to the house and look over his "loot." Sometimes Kay's first knowledge that Johnny was coming over was when David set two glasses of water on the kitchen table. Johnny and David would sit at the kitchen table and bargain with each other, one as determined as the other. I have often wished I had tape-recorded one of those "tradin' times."

I often sat at the kitchen table for conversations with family and friends. I remember one particular time he was having a deep "theological discussion" with a pastor friend. We were worlds apart in our beliefs, and seemingly were at a stalemate. It was a perfect time for five-year-old David to casually walk by the table and say, "Ah, you all, it's just this 'Christian livin.'"

We had a collie dog named Pal that everybody loved. He was beautiful, resembling the movie star dog, Lassie. Pal would often go down the street to the Houchen's grocery store and lie down close to the door where people would pat him on the head as they passed by. One Sunday night he decided to come to church. Just as I started preaching, in walked Pal. He knew he shouldn't be there, but he proceeded to come down the aisle toward me, wagging his tail every step of the way. Just as he got to the altar he decided to lie down and tucked his head between his two front legs. Pal looked up at me as if to say "I'm sorry . . . I know I shouldn't be here." I stopped my sermon and told Pal to go back home. Pal obeyed and left with his head drooped low.

Debbie and David enjoyed Pal. He was always with them when they were playing outside—swinging, snow sledding, or whatever. He was their friend. These were happy years for our family.

One cannot be in ministry long without seeing the devastating results of alcoholism. Munfordville was a small town with an unusually large population of alcoholics. Organizing an Alcoholics Anonymous group became a vital ministry to many families in our community. Marriages were restored, businesses were saved, and there was new hope for the future. I helped in getting people out of jail, dumping liquor in the river, and counseling with families torn apart.

On my way home for supper one afternoon, I found myself crossing the Green River bridge going toward the Rowletts community instead of going to the parsonage. Turning around in a driveway, I recognized one of my alcoholic friends sitting on the front steps of his house. I proceeded to get out of the car and walk toward him. I suddenly realized he had a gun in his hand. When he recognized me, he blurted out, "What in the world are you doing here? I'm on my way to the river to shoot myself."

After some conversation, James gave me the gun and agreed to come that night to AA at the church. The next day I bought him a hammer-and-nail apron and got him a job with a local contractor who was building a house in Munfordville. The ministry is full of God Moments where God directs us to people in a time of crisis. Munfordville First UMC soon became the gathering place for alcoholics, and I became known as the friend of alcoholics.

Having a Jewish doctor in town meant our members were sent to the Jewish Hospital in Louisville when they needed hospitalization. This involved a 140-mile round trip for hospital visitation. When Grace Mansfield, a dear lady and one of our oldest members, was rushed to the hospital, I left immediately to be with the family. I stayed with the family all night and was with them when she died. The next day, without any sleep, I helped the family with funeral arrangements.

After lunch, when I finally got to the office and was trying to collect some thoughts for the funeral message, I fell asleep in my chair. I was quickly awakened with a knock at the office door. When I responded to the knock, I looked into the eyes of a tired and weary transient person and his wife.

On that particular day I didn't have the patience or energy to deal with one more need. This was especially true when I saw what looked like a dozen children standing beside their old bread truck parked in front of the church. The man looked at me and said softly, "I don't know where to turn. My wife and children are tired and hungry. We have driven from New York with little to eat and no place to sleep. When we saw the stained glass window over your front door with the words, 'Come Unto Me,' I thought I might find some help here."

I followed Joe Patera and his wife to the old bread truck where 11 children were anxiously (and hungrily) waiting for my response. I gave them money for groceries and one meal at the only restaurant in town, and then directed them to the Veterans Park where they could camp overnight.

A few days later when I awakened to a big frost and temperatures in the 30's, I remembered the Patera family. On my way to the office I drove by the park and, sure enough, they were there, cold and sick. I could not walk away from this family and send them on down the road. I remembered our Lord's words, "I was hungry and you gave me no food, I was thirsty and you gave me no drink, I was a stranger and you did not welcome me, naked and you did not clothe me, sick and in prison and you did not visit me. Then they also will answer, 'Lord, when did we see thee hungry or thirsty or a stranger or naked or sick or in prison, and did not minister to thee?' Then he will answer them, 'Truly I say to you, as you did it not to one of the least of these, you did it not to me'" (Matthew 25:41-45 RSV). I immediately took them to the doctor and told them we would care for them.

What happened in the next few days and in the next two years was truly one of the most miraculous experiences of my ministry. The entire community became aware of the homeless Patera family and was ready to be a part of their care. Members of Alcoholics Anonymous were the first to bring money and offer their assistance. James Stanton, a mechanic, offered to furnish a car. Pete Lawler, a furniture dealer, volunteered to provide used furniture and appliances. A total stranger offered a house (shack) that had not been lived in for several years. Church members, alcoholics, community leaders, and youth repaired the house. They put in new windows, cleaned the cistern, and put new gutters on the house. The county graded a road to the house, the women sponsored a pantry/food shower, a clothes closet was set up, a committee was organized, and on and on it went.

In one week, this family of 13 moved from the Veterans Park to the little shack in the woods next to Interstate 65. The Pateras were home again. With tears in his eyes, the father said, "We thought God was against us and didn't love us anymore and was punishing us. You see, our house was destroyed by fire. Suzie, our daughter, was badly burned (I could see her scars), and I lost my job."

The more we heard of their tragic story, the more we wanted to help them. The doctor, druggist, and school system all supported me in caring for this family. The children enrolled in school and made good grades. It was not uncommon for the principal to call and say, "Preacher, come get your children and get them to the doctor" or "Preacher, come and get your children. They have head lice again." It became common for me to enter the local drugstore and see the pharmacist go immediately to the section where the head lice treatment was kept.

Christmas 1966 is a Christmas that Munfordville will always remember as one of their most joyful. On Saturday before Christmas Sunday, I loaded all the Patera kids in the car for haircuts and new clothes. I had no money for the project, but a lot of faith in my people. I started with haircuts and then went to the only department store in town for new clothes. I told the store owner, Vernon Moore, who was a member of the church, that together we could do this. The people responded and when we left the store, the clothes were paid for with enough left to buy new clothes for their mom and dad. It took three trips to get the children and their new clothes home. I still remember the joy and excitement of that Christmas Sunday as the Patera family took their seats for worship. They were home for Christmas, and Christ was at home in their hearts.

Soon after that glorious Christmas, we learned Mrs. Patera was expecting number 12 and if it were a boy, he would be named Wallace Thomas Patera. To abbreviate the story, the baby boy was born, and Joe Patera had a mental/emotional breakdown. Thankfully, Joe was found just before he tried to stab little Wallace. Joe was committed to a mental institution for three months.

In the meantime, two of Joe's brothers came to see the family and began to work with us to move them back to New York. In September 1967, with a rented van, money for overnight lodging, and meals furnished by our church, this homeless family returned to their home state to be near their family and friends. Our churches and community had been so supportive of this dysfunctional family for two years. Today, if you were to ask the older people in Munfordville to describe the best Christmas they remember, the Patera story will likely be told.

On the larger scene, the Methodist Church and the Evangelical United Brethren Church, who had aspects of their heritage in common, merged in 1968 to become the United Methodist Church (UMC). I have always felt the United Brethren Church brought a special spirit to the Methodist Church.

In four brief years, First UMC and Mt. Beulah UMC were experiencing renewal and growth and becoming vital congregations. Kay was busy teaching Sunday school, substitute teaching in the local school, active in the local Woman's Club and Woman's Society of Christian Service, and serving on the district and conference Women's Society of Christian Service committees. Our children were enjoying school, their church, and making friends. Munfordville was feeling like home to us.

I became aware of Mt. Beulah's need for a piano player. Louise Hulsey, who was a member at Munfordville, agreed to go to Mt. Beulah with me and share her talent in music. Her husband, Johnny (David's trading buddy), was not a Christian, but he often went with us to that early service. Those trips became friendship moments and, as a result of those early morning conversations, Johnny accepted Christ and was baptized into membership at Mt. Beulah. Johnny could always be found at Baird Drug Store with some friends. I went by there often and had coffee with them. When I went to Louisville to visit in the hospital, which was usually once or twice each week, Johnny would often go with me. He loved White Castle hamburgers, and on the way home we would get a sack of hamburgers for our "snack."

I scheduled one afternoon a month to visit the Mt. Beulah people. One of the dearest persons in that little church was Betty Wilkerson whose husband was not a Christian and never attended church with her. Frequently, Betty would ask me to drop by for a visit and have prayer with them. I dreaded those visits with Mr. Wilkerson. He never welcomed me and often made hurtful remarks about the church and preachers. One time while visiting the Mt. Beulah people, I had a strong nudge to visit in the Wilkerson home. Betty was piecing a quilt, and Mr. Wilkerson was sitting at the kitchen table smoking a cigarette.

When I sat down at the kitchen table and attempted to engage in conversation with Mr. Wilkerson, he looked at me and said, "Before you pray today I want to say something." He looked lovingly at his wife and said, "Betty, I'm sorry for the way I have treated you and for the pain I've brought to your life. I'm not worthy of being your husband. Recently, this has been very troubling to me. I've spent many nights here at this table thinking about my life. Last night, I looked out the window at the stars and a full moon shining in the window and I started talking to God. I said, 'God . . . God, if you're out there, can you hear me? God, could you come to me? I'm a sinner. Would you forgive me?'"

Turning to Betty and then to me, with a tender smile, he continued in a soft voice, "Last night God came out of the heavens right into my heart. Today, I have peace in my heart. Today, I know God loves me and is present in my life." He then went to Betty and hugged her, shook hands with me, and said, "Thank you Betty. Thank you, Brother Thomas, for not giving up on me."

I can't describe the joy of that moment. The words of an old hymn best describe what I experienced: "Heaven came down and glory filled my soul." Mr. Wilkerson would not tell his story to the congregation, but he was baptized and joined the church. He gave me permission to share with the congregation about his experience at the kitchen table.

On the way home, I stopped by the Mt. Beulah church for a prayer of thanksgiving and reflection. It seemed that, suddenly, God was answering so many prayers and was so present with His guidance and power in my life. God had given me a special gift in relating to people in such a way that they could open their heart to God's saving grace. I promised God that day that I would never give up on anyone who does not know Him as Savior and Lord. I continued to pray, "God show me the way to reach Hart County for Christ. You said, 'Ask, and it shall be given you; seek, and ye shall find; knock, and it shall be opened to you'" (Matthew 7:7 KJV).

I shared with Kay the experience at the Wilkersons' and my prayer time at Mt. Beulah church. Soon thereafter, we received a brochure from the First United Methodist Church in Glasgow saying Tony Fontane was coming for a revival. We had never met Tony Fontane, but we had heard a lot about him. He was known as one of the world's most famous singers, having performed in concert halls and churches around the globe, for U.S. troops on military bases, as well as in the presence of Presidents Eisenhower, Kennedy, Johnson, and Nixon and other dignitaries around the world.

I was tied up and could not attend the first service at Glasgow, so Kay went to Glasgow by herself. She came home saying it was one of the best revival services that she had ever attended. She said, "Wally, he is all that people are saying that he is." We were convinced this could be the answer to our prayer to reach Hart County for Christ.

I found out where Tony would be eating breakfast on Monday morning and was there when he arrived. I introduced myself, and he invited me to join him. I shared with him my burden for the youth and families of Hart County. He listened to my dream and promised to write me in a few days. Within two weeks, I got a letter indicating he would come and he gave me the first week of March 1968. We had six months to prepare for what would prove to be one of the greatest religious events in the history of Hart County.

With the First Baptist Church working with us, we formed a coordinating team that met every month. A Hollywood-style movie had been made about Tony's life. "The Tony Fontane Story" was shown at the town theatre and also the two high schools. Newspaper ads were run in the local newspaper and in the surrounding counties. This being a countywide event, the Hart County Board of Education offered the use of the high school gymnasium. Five hundred chairs were rented from Fort Knox that would enable 1,000 people to attend the services.

A spirit of excitement filled the air because a celebrity was coming to town, and we didn't have a motel. He would have to stay at Horse Cave, a neighboring town.

On Friday before the revival began, some of our members loaded the 500 chairs on a cattle truck to be unloaded on Saturday. That night we had a big snow and the chairs were covered with four inches of it. High school youth and many strangers came to help unload, dry, and set up the chairs in the gym. Sunday was a beautiful day. People had been praying all night. The worship service was like Easter Sunday, and the Holy Spirit seemed to be hovering over our town. I picked Tony up at the airport and we had our second visit traveling from Louisville to his motel. Needless to say, I was tense and nervous, but I had rehearsed everything I was going to say to this Hollywood star.

The local radio station set up to broadcast the services. On that first night the people streamed into the gym like they were going to a ball game. That little gym was packed with over 1,000 people present to hear Tony Fontane sing and preach the gospel. At the conclusion of the service, many youth and young adults came to the altar to commit their lives to Christ. Before the week was over, hundreds of youth and adults rededicated their lives to Christ. The churches found strength in uniting in a common purpose. My dream was fulfilled.

The following week Jim Berry, the manager of the local radio station, called the clergy together to discuss the impact the Tony Fontane revival had on Hart County. By popular demand, a clergy radio talk show consisting of a Catholic priest, a Baptist pastor, and two United Methodist pastors began. Everybody had heard about the revival, and most had heard Tony on the radio or attended the services. There were discussions about the revival in the barber shop, beauty shops, and restaurants.

We were now having the largest attendance in the history of our church. On Easter Sunday, even the balcony was full—a first since the sanctuary was built. Adult men and women were accepting Christ and being baptized at our altar. Dr. Loraine Cave, a Western Kentucky

University psychology professor, made a profession of faith and was baptized. Businessmen made professions of faith at our Sunday morning services. Even James Stanton and Vernon Wright started attending our worship services. Members had said, "You can't get these men to darken the door." Vernon was my neighbor, but he would never let me talk to him about the Lord until he got a blood clot in his leg.

On the night before his surgery to amputate his leg, I got up and went to the hospital to be with him at 3:00 a.m. Vernon, a 350-pound man, was lying there wide-awake. "What are you doing here?" he asked. Taking his hand, I said, "Vernon, I'm your neighbor and friend, and I just wanted to be with you. Try to get some rest. I'll be with you until you go to surgery." The light from the hall enabled me to see his big red face with huge tears running down his cheeks. Standing beside his bed I said, "Vernon, are you in pain?" Looking at me with an expression of anxiety and fear, he blurted out, "I'm scared that I might die."

The bed shook as his body released his pent-up emotions. Squeezing my hand, he said, "Brother Thomas, thank you for being with me tonight." After an hour or more of heart-to-heart conversation, sharing Scripture, and prayer, Vernon accepted the Lord and went to sleep with the peace of God in his heart. I continued to sit by his bed in the old hospital chair. I thank God that He prompted me to get up to be with Vernon. The church still remembers the Sunday Vernon Wright came to the altar on crutches to be baptized and join the church.

Some pastor friends who had told me Munfordville church was dead and had no hope were wrong. This county-seat church was renewed! It was listed as one of the churches in our Louisville Annual Conference that had experienced significant growth in membership and attendance. I received encouraging letters of affirmation for my work (with the Lord's help). Dr. L.R. McDonald, a former district superintendent, closed his letter by saying these words of wisdom, "Always prepare your sermons as if you were preaching to a thousand people." Paul Shepherd, who was my district superintendent at one time, said; "Work hard to build good sermons and develop skills for good pastoral care ministry."

I was quickly learning that dynamic ministry required prayer and daily study, visionary planning, love and care for people, and working at the job every day.

Kay was a wonderful helpmate. She taught Sunday school, worked in Vacation Bible School, Methodist Youth Fellowship, United Methodist Women, sang in the choir, and was a great example of a good mother and wife. She helped organize the Hart County Teen Club in 1968. In 1969 the Munfordville Woman's Club nominated her as Outstanding Young Woman of the Year. A biographical sketch and picture were printed in the 1970 volume of *Outstanding Young Women of America*. That same year, the Munfordville Jaycees presented me with a plaque naming me the "Man of the Year" in Munfordville. Kay and I were deeply grateful for the ways God was using us in ministry.

An important event in the life of our family around this time occurred when Tony Fontane came back to our area. This time he held a camp meeting at the Morrison Park Campground in Glasgow. We went almost every night. David was five years old and listened attentively every night to Tony's message. During the invitational hymn one evening, Tony stopped the singing and began to pray. Our eyes were closed, and when we opened them, we couldn't find David.

I looked up toward Tony, and he motioned for me to come up to the altar. When I reached the altar, there was David kneeling by himself, praying. I prayed with him and Tony did as well. When I asked David what he had experienced that night, he replied, "Dad, I know Jesus loves me, and I just wanted Him to know that I love Him, too." His experience was real, and to this day, he recalls that experience as the beginning of his walk with the Lord.

During the last few months of our fifth year in Munfordville, my district superintendent told us we would be moving. He said I would be going to Scottsville, a strong county-seat church. Life was good for our family at Munfordville. Kay and I had worked hard, and the children were happy. We were not eager to leave this community. And for the first time, we were taking a real vacation—a trip to Washington D.C.

Kay promised her parents when she was a senior in high school that she would one day take them to Washington, D.C. It was a wonderful trip . . . one that we will always treasure.

At the request of the church and community, Tony Fontane was invited to return for another revival which was scheduled for Holy Week of 1969. Hart County had a new high school, and the revival would be held in the new gymnasium. The Board of Education resisted our using the gym, fearing the floor would be scuffed before the school had played a game. Superintendent Marshall Dixon overruled, saying the school belonged to the people and not the Board of Education.

This was another great week in our churches and community. The Easter service the following Sunday found every pew filled and chairs in the aisle and in the balcony. In addition to a great revival, a great friendship developed for Kay and me with Tony Fontane that lasted until his death. Tony spent many nights in our home and was like a member of the family. He called me almost every week. Once he called from Korea to tell me about his service with the military and the hundreds who came to the altar. We've always felt that Tony Fontane's friendship was one of God's special gifts to our family.

As our friendship grew, we came to respect Tony more and more. We learned about his background. He grew up in North Dakota where his parents served a mission church. While his mother scrubbed the mission floors, she sang the words to "Peace Like a River" which she had written. Tony said folks today don't give his mother credit for the song, but she was its original composer.

Tony was a gifted servant of God following his conversion. He broke his contract in show business, and a lawsuit resulted. He lost his riches in Hollywood, and he and his wife Kerry lived with Kerry's mother when we visited them in Los Angeles. This house was quite different from his former Hollywood home which he took us by to see. Tony was faithful to his Lord to the end. I had the privilege of assisting in Tony's funeral, which I will share more about in a later chapter.

Kay and I have always looked upon the years at Munfordville as a formative time in our lives and as years of growth for the church. These were happy years for Debbie and David, too. I discovered that if the preacher could be with his people during the week, they would likely be with him on Sunday morning. In the five short years we were in Munfordville, attendance grew from 45 to 112 in Sunday school and from 55 to 125 in worship. Our new parsonage was debt-free when we left. To God be the glory.

The appointment to Scottsville never materialized. I was being sent instead to a church merger situation in Louisville. Moving our family to Louisville during the years of the turmoil over court-ordered busing was a difficult assignment. But God is faithful, and off we moved to the city in June of 1969.

Chapter 7

SHIVELY UNITED METHODIST CHURCH

When we arrived at the Louisville Annual Conference our district superintendent confirmed that we were being assigned to a church in Louisville. Kay and I had not been to Louisville many times much less lived in that city. We were apprehensive about serving a church in a large city and putting our children in the big schools there. Also, the late 60s were a time of unrest in Louisville with school integration and forced busing causing turmoil in the community. Many people were leaving Louisville and relocating in Bullitt, Shelby, and Oldham counties.

My appointment was to help bring two congregations together. St. Peter United Methodist Church in West Louisville merged with St. John United Methodist Church in Shively, a Louisville suburb. The merger took place in January of 1969 with both pastors remaining to work with this merged congregation until Annual Conference. After six months of worshipping together, they were still functioning as two congregations when we arrived. I found two parsonages with furniture, two administrative boards, two treasurers, two Sunday school superintendents, and a 10-by-12 office with two desks and boxes of records, some of which were a half-century old.

My clergy colleagues were talking about the great opportunity of my appointment, but to us it felt like a disappointment. Kay and I spent much time on our knees asking for understanding and guidance as well as safety and security for our children. Little did we know these next eight years would be filled with pain and suffering, cultural shock, and also many great opportunities found only in a large city. As with every new challenge, Kay and I declared, "Together we can do it" and "I can do all things through Christ" (Philippians 4:13a NKJV).

On moving day we left the children in Munfordville with Jimmie and Mary Buford Kabler to attend Vacation Bible School there. The incoming pastor seemed pleased for the children to stay on in Munfordville for a week while we moved and unpacked. As we left on that beautiful June morning, some friends were standing along the streets with tears in their eyes waving good-bye to us. Kay and I cried halfway to Elizabethtown.

Later that afternoon in Louisville, one of the men of the Shively Church came by and asked if we needed anything. I said I needed a city map, which he quickly provided. As soon as he left, Kay and I got down in the floor and started trying to locate our street. About that time a good friend, Rev. Irvin Owen, came by and saw us on the floor bending over the map. He said, "Where are you going?" In desperation we both said, "We just want to know how to get out of this town!" We felt overwhelmed to be in that big city where we had no friends or relatives.

The first thing we have always done when we move into a new parsonage is set up the children's rooms. When the Kablers brought Debbie and David to their new home, their rooms looked almost the same as they did in Munfordville. Kay made a special effort to do this so they would feel more at home. After they looked at their rooms, Kay asked them how they liked them. David crawled up in Kay's lap and said, "They are OK, Mom. But when can we go back home?"

Being uprooted and leaving friends was difficult for them. Debbie would be in the seventh grade at Butler High School, with an enrollment of 3,000. The enrollment in the entire elementary school in Munfordville at that time was 300. We found there would now be 300 in her math class which was taught by way of television. David would be in the second grade at Schaffner Elementary School with an enrollment of 300. Every time we passed Butler, Debbie would say, "I'm scared. I want to go back to Munfordville."

Our first grocery shopping was an adventure. We all went to the big Kroger store, which was across the busy Dixie Highway. The traffic was congested and moving fast, but we made it safely. On our way home, we stopped by the Dairy Queen for a hamburger and ice cream. One day at a time and one trip to the grocery at a time—we began to adjust to our new home at 2310 Mary Catherine Drive in Shively, and we began to find a place to begin our ministry.

I hired Marietta Woodward, Lewis and Mary Woodward's daughter, for the summer to be my secretary and organize the office. I began visiting the congregation. In three months, I visited the entire congregation of over 200 families, met with all the committees, and began a more focused process of merging these two congregations.

To my dismay, I discovered many people in that area did not even know there was a church on Crums Lane in Shively. Here was a little congregation in southwest Jefferson County surrounded by thousands of people in a three-mile radius, but few people knew the church existed except the 35 to 40 people who attended each Sunday.

I knew the best way to get the attention of the community and the entire city was to have a Tony Fontane tent revival. This was a bold step of faith that would require a $5,000 budget to rent a tent, chairs to seat 1,000 people, and publicity that would capture the attention of the city of Louisville. Tony was ready to clear his calendar for a September date. Violet Holladay, a member of the church, gave a $2,000 donation to rent the tent. We had a publicity campaign with newspaper ads, distribution of flyers door-to-door, and the showing of the Tony Fontane story. I also scheduled Tony to appear on the WAVE-TV Morning Show.

That five-day revival was one of the greatest events of my ministry. The tent was filled to capacity every night. On Sunday night, we had as many people outside the tent as there were inside, and our five-acre lot was filled with cars. This tent revival reached people from all parts of the county and some people attended from surrounding counties. At the end of each service, people who had made a decision for Christ were asked to walk over to the little sanctuary for prayer. The sanctuary was filled with people who had come to the altar to accept Christ or to rededicate their lives.

At the conclusion of the last service, some of the men in my church came to me and said, "This revival has united these congregations and we are ready to go forward as one. The following day many people came back to the site of the revival. They were remembering those services and observing the path of beaten-down grass leading to the altar area and on to the sanctuary where people made their commitment to God. That site would soon be the location of our new sanctuary.

Needless to say, the church responsibilities consumed me. Day and night I was preparing sermons, attending meetings, and trying to move forward with building plans. As my dad would say, "Every day I was plowing new ground." In the midst of this schedule, our children were adjusting to their new schools. Kay was trying to be a good pastor's wife and help the children in their struggles as well. We discovered Debbie's math class could also be seen at home, so Kay watched the math class on television which enabled us to help Debbie with her homework each night.

David, in his smaller school, had much more one-on-one instruction than Debbie. Mr. Sloan, a violin instructor at Schaffner Elementary School, came to the school once each week. David developed an interest in playing the violin immediately. Kay was quick to get him enrolled for violin lessons at the Louisville Academy of Music with Mrs. Ruth French, and we purchased a small violin. Learning to play it became one of the joys of David's life.

Our family was soon enjoying the church and beginning to make friends. During the six weeks following the revival, we received 35 new members into the church and had overflowing attendance every Sunday. Cars waited on the street to get into the parking lot. I realized I needed to start planning for expansion with a new sanctuary. Suddenly my plate was full with work and decisions that had to be made quickly. New leadership had to be put in place immediately. We established new leadership with one-third St. John's members, one-third St. Peter's members and one-third new members.

At the October board meeting, I offered a prepared statement about the revival, the huge increase in attendance, and the purpose of merger to have a large and vital congregation in southwest Louisville. I tried to help the people catch a vision of the emerging reality of a great church. Then I said, "A year from this upcoming Christmas, we need to be in a new sanctuary, and the process must begin tonight!" The response was unanimous in favor of moving ahead. That night we elected a building committee and set a date for church conference.

In 10 days, we had our church conference and named E.J. Schickle to be our architect. We didn't need a capital funds campaign because we had $110,000 from the sale of the St. Peter's facility. In December, we had our initial meeting with our building committee and architect and presented a written description of the facility that would meet our needs. In January we had an architectural sketch of the new sanctuary, an estimated cost, and a suggested contractor. On April 1, we broke ground.

Building a new sanctuary as a merged congregation in a time of great racial tension was overwhelming and filled with almost constant conflict. The church was named Crums Lane United Methodist Church. In my visitation, I asked every family about the name of the church. No one liked it, but they didn't have any suggestions for a different name. I knew we had to change the name when some of my correspondence was addressed to Rev. Crum. In consultation with Bishop Short, we agreed to name the merged congregation the Shively United Methodist

Church. When we had our ground-breaking ceremony, our bulletin had the name Shively United Methodist Church on the front.

On Monday, April 2, 1970, construction began on a 425-seating-capacity sanctuary plus a kitchen, choir room, baptistry, offices, and a large lobby and fellowship area. Shively was primarily a blue-collar congregation that worked hard and wanted a good church.

It was difficult for them to ever have a consensus in decision-making, and when a decision was made, the critics were always anxious to let us know of their unhappiness. I had no choice but to be a hands-on leader. Many times I had to be the decision-maker for this congregation, and there were so many decisions to be made: decisions regarding carpet, color of paint, pews, the design for the altar, altar furniture, kitchen cabinets, and more. That decision always came back to me. We hired the architect to supervise the construction, and he kept things moving pretty well.

The total cost of the building was $460,000. With $110,000 from the sale of St. Peter UMC, we needed to borrow $350,000. We consulted with the downtown banks and bonding companies. St. Helen's Bank was the local bank in Shively, and Aubrey Conway was the president and a member of the Parkview United Methodist Church. It was also where I did my local banking. One morning, I stopped by to see Mr. Conway about a loan and told him we needed a loan for $350,000 at 7% interest. This was 1% less than other banks offered, which would make a lot of difference in the amount of our monthly payment. The bank granted us the loan at 7% interest.

Many of our people wanted to be baptized by immersion, so we included a baptistry in our new facility. We ran a drain pipe from the baptistry to a drainage ditch between our church and a subdivision. Residents from the subdivision thought we were emptying raw sewage in the ditch. I responded by saying they must never get close to the ditch, because what was coming out of the pipe was worse than sewage. I told them we would be draining our sins into the ditch. They chuckled and were OK with that idea.

Before we moved into the new sanctuary, I felt that we, as a church, needed a spiritual renewal weekend. Frank Roughton, a classmate of mine in seminary, in recent years had developed a unique drama ministry. With beard and robe, Frank looked like pictures that portray Christ. Just weeks before our opening service, Frank led us in some incredible worship services with his presentation of the Sermon on the Mount and the last week of our Lord's life. We were exhausted physically, mentally, and spiritually from the stress of the building program, and these days of inspiration were timely. We realized we needed to apply Philippians 3:13a, 14 (KJV), "Forgetting those things which are behind, and reaching forth unto those things which are before, I press toward the mark for the prize of the high calling of God in Christ Jesus."

During the next few weeks carpet was laid, pulpit furniture put in place, and pews and office furniture were delivered. Mr. Carl A. Heil, a member of the congregation, donated an Allen organ and grand piano. Enthusiasm, excitement, and anticipation were mounting. The local newspaper featured an article about a new beginning for a merging congregation. A Louisville magazine had an article about our "church in the round" in reference to the architectural design. It was so

Shively United Methodist Church.

appropriate to have our first service in the new sanctuary on the first Sunday in Advent. It was truly a new beginning for this new congregation.

On Saturday morning, we had a trial run for the worship service with a choir rehearsal, a meeting with ushers, and adjusting the new sound system and furnace thermostats. My office was completely set up with lamps, chairs, and books stacked neatly in the shelves. I had a beautiful new walnut desk and custom-made desk chair. I felt like a little boy with a new toy.

After everyone left that Saturday morning, I went into the sanctuary for some quiet time and reflection. In humble adoration I knelt at the altar. I prayed for the Holy Spirit to fill my heart and the hearts of the people as they entered to worship the next day. I read again the plaque that Kay had placed on the back of the pulpit which read, "Sir, we would see Jesus" (John 12:21 KJV). That summed up my call and my desire for this congregation.

On my way home a policeman stopped me. As he approached my car with a puzzled expression on his face, he said, "Sir, are you all right?" I said, "Yes, why do you ask?" He smiled and said, "You have driven through three stops signs without stopping!" After telling him I was a minister and we were having our first service in the new church down the street, he said, "I will escort you home, and please don't do any more driving today."

It is hard to put into words the joy of that first Sunday in the new sanctuary. In new robes, we began our processional into the new sanctuary singing "Joy to the World." The sanctuary was filled to capacity. The organ and piano music were beautiful, and the congregation was singing with great gusto. I have never preached with more freedom and power than on that day. I preached on the text from Nehemiah 6:3 (RSV), "I am doing a great work, and I cannot come down."

The sanctuary was decorated for Christmas; we were ready to celebrate the birth of Christ in our hearts and in our church. The month was packed with the Christmas cantata, children's programs, fellowship dinners, and Sunday school class parties. We continued to have large attendance with members joining every Sunday. In 17 months, with God's help, we had united two congregations and built a new sanctuary.

So much had happened in such a short time, but there was one thing that remained the same: our home. I often think of the closing prayer I have prayed so many times in the marriage ceremony asking God to look graciously upon the couple, that their home may be a haven of blessing and a place of peace.

Kay has always worked hard at making our home a haven of blessing and a place of peace. We all looked forward to suppertime for Kay always had a hot meal prepared for us. During that time, we talked about our day and gave plenty of time for the children to talk about the good and not-so-good happenings in their day. That was, and has always been, an important part of our day. It was during one of those suppertimes and evenings at home that we talked about a vacation to California and a possible youth trip to Florida. That discussion lasted until bedtime and the children could hardly go to sleep for thinking about our summer ahead. That became our topic of discussion every evening for awhile.

With the completion of the sanctuary, I could now give attention to youth and children's ministry. Our junior and senior high classrooms were filled on Sunday morning, but very little else was offered for them. We started meeting on Sunday night for youth fellowship and immediately had between 30 and 40 in attendance. When I presented the idea of a Florida trip to the youth, they were excited about going, and the church said they would help raise the money. The Florida youth trip redirected our focus away from merger and construction to shaping lives and nurturing our youth.

With work projects, fundraisers, bake sales and special offerings, we collected over $5,000 which would totally underwrite our youth trip. This was the biggest trip some of our youth had ever taken. We chartered a big, air-conditioned commercial bus with restroom facilities.

After riding all night, we arrived at Camp Bethlehem just in time for breakfast. Everyone was ready to get to our rooms for some rest. It was hot, humid, and dusty, plus the air was full of gnats.

Everyone got their room assignments except David and me, and we were allowed to stay in a room with a private bath and an electric fan. David was excited to get our room set up and to get some sleep. He was only nine years old at this time, and there was a class for his age group. We enjoyed hanging out together. Kay and I met with the youth each morning for devotions and prayer time, and after breakfast everyone went to class. The afternoon was free for group activities and recreation. I made arrangements with the bus driver for some short trips in the afternoon just to be in our air-conditioned bus. We discovered a nice swimming pool, so we included swimming every afternoon.

Rev. Ed Robb was the camp meeting preacher and had a powerful evangelistic message every evening. All of our youth made commitments during the week, many being first-time decisions. One night after the service began, I realized that one of our youth, Phil Hill, was not with us. I immediately left the service to look for him and found him in tears behind one of the dormitories. I sat down to talk to him, and he began to share with me that he was struggling with the call to the ministry. After a time of talking and praying, Phil committed his life to the ministry.

Following the service that evening, I called our youth together and Phil shared with the group the decision he had made. That was a special time and resulted in many more decisions of rededication and some professions of faith. One young man decided to read his Bible more. Lying stretched out on the floor and thumbing through his Bible, he asked, "Where in the world is that book of Palms anyway?"

During that week we planned the Youth Sunday worship service that would follow at home. The sanctuary was packed that Sunday. Our youth shared their experiences of the past week, and the service lasted an hour and a half. Parents met their sons and daughters at the altar at the close of the service for prayer and rededication.

With only two weeks until our family would head west to California to visit Tony and Kerry Fontane, we had much to do. This would be the greatest adventure of our lives. I was nervous about borrowing money for a vacation, but my banker, who was also a personal friend, made it easy for me. When I told him what I wanted to do, he complimented me for the decision and gladly loaned me the money. Mr. Patterson had lost his wife and was still grieving. With tears, he said, "Wally, all I have is memories of my wife. I'm so thankful for the trips we took and the things we did as a family. I will always hold those memories in my heart."

With a $2,000 loan, an AAA triptych to guide us, and a new set of tires, we were ready to go. We were scheduled to leave on the first Sunday of August after the church service. A happy congregation stood in the parking lot waving good-bye to us as we left for our trip to the West Coast.

We took the southern route going to California and the northern route coming home. We will never forget the magnificent scenery of that trip. Many times along the way we stopped just to look at God's gorgeous creation and to thank Him for the blessing of living in the USA. One of the highlights en route was seeing the breathtaking beauty of the Grand Canyon. Kay often recalls overhearing a conversation between two little boys as we were leaving. They were discussing how the Grand Canyon was formed. One little boy said, "Well, God made it!" The other replied. "No, that's not true. God is in heaven." The first little boy quickly retorted, "Don't you know God is on earth, too?"

We drove about 500 miles each day and tried to check into a motel by 4:00 or 5:00 p.m., and then made our way straight to the swimming pool. Kay couldn't swim and our project each afternoon was for her to get her head under water. By the end of the week we were all swimming with our heads under water.

Debbie and David have often talked about our arrival in Los Angeles. I was nervous about driving on the freeways in that big city with cars whizzing by like bullets. With both hands nervously locked on top of the steering wheel, I gave orders for silence in the car. Our destination was a hotel in the heart of Los Angeles. A friend's uncle owned an apartment there that we could use until Tony Fontane got into town. For a couple who had grown up in Howard's Bottom in Cumberland County and Walnut Corner in Barren County, we were pretty far removed from our roots.

Disneyland, Knott's Berry Farms, and Universal Studios were fun-filled experiences we will always treasure. We also found the CBS television studio and spent an evening there watching celebrities come and go. As we were leaving CBS, we saw Carol Burnett coming to the parking lot. Our car was parked very near her car, and we had noticed her name on her car. Carol saw us standing near her car and came to us with a warm greeting. Her husband encouraged her to keep moving, but Carol said, "No, these people have waited a long time for me." Running her hand through David's hair, Carol said, "I like that red hair. You're an all-American boy. I wish my red hair was real like yours."

When Tony got to town, he immediately moved us to a nice motel in Hollywood. We had two rooms that looked out upon the big "HOLLYWOOD" sign on the side of the mountain that is often seen on television. One of the highlights of our time with Tony was to eat with him at the Brown Derby. Can you imagine our family arriving at the Brown Derby, met by men in tuxedos to valet park our car and usher us to a reserved table to eat with a star like Tony Fontane? We couldn't imagine it either.

The waiter asked Debbie and David if they saw anything on the menu they liked and offered to prepare them a hamburger. They then brought a grill to our table for the children to watch the waiter cook the hamburgers to their liking. Their eyes were as big as saucers. After the meal we walked the sidewalk outside the Brown Derby where celebrities' names were engraved in stars. That afternoon Tony took us to see many of the homes of famous personalities, including the home he had previously owned. This beautiful home was once owned by Bette Davis. It looked like the White House to us!

After a week in LA, we looked forward to our trip home by another route that would take us through Las Vegas, Yellowstone National Park, the Black Hills, the Badlands, Mount Rushmore, and the Petrified Forest. On the way home we spent a lot of time recalling the wonderful experiences of our trip. Our spirits were renewed and we looked forward to getting home.

Debbie and David were excited about getting back to school. Debbie was doing well in school and was active in Girl Scouts. David was tested for the advanced program in school, and was transferred to Kerrick Elementary School where the advanced program was in place.

God's call has always had a burning sense of urgency about it, compelling me to walk closely with the Lord, work hard, and give the best I have to every aspect of the ministry. So much had happened in such a short time, and my first priority had to be better time management with adequate time for sermon preparation. Our pews were filled on Sunday mornings with persons dealing with their sins and shames, their anxieties and doubts, their griefs and disillusionments. I was feeling the awesome responsibility for preaching like I had never felt before.

Sunday comes every seven days, and many hours of prayer and study must be done in preparation for those 60 minutes with the congregation. Preaching is not just talking about repentance; it is also, by the power of the Holy Spirit, persuading people to repent. It is not merely discussing the meaning of faith, but leading the congregation to become people of faith. It is not merely talking about the power of God available to bring victory over trouble and temptation; it must be the reality of sending people out from their worship on Sunday with victory in their hearts. Preaching is "prayer in action." My prayer became, "O God, some person here needs what I have to say. Help my word to reach him or her."

In two short years, Shively UMC was already recognized as one of the fastest growing churches in Louisville. Merger had succeeded, the congregation was united, and they looked forward to being together on Sunday for Sunday school and worship. New members were added almost every Sunday by profession of faith and by transfer. We were having many first-time guests every Sunday.

The John Phelps family came to the morning worship one Sunday and continued to attend with regularity. John owned the Dixie Highway Auto Wreckage business and was an alcoholic. He had a glass eye, and his body depicted his lifestyle with scars from fights and hard labor, but his heart was filled with goodness and compassion for the needy. He and his wife, Ruth, had four daughters who loved to attend Sunday school and United Methodist Youth Fellowship. The children later attended my confirmation class, made professions of faith, and were ready to be baptized and join the church. When I visited their home prior to confirmation Sunday, I found John lying on the couch drunk, and Ruth's frustration was obvious.

I told John and Ruth the children were going to be baptized on Sunday, and I wanted them to be there. Then I proceeded to talk to them about their lives, their need for a new beginning, and how their daughters deserved to grow up in a Christian home. The entire family attended church that Sunday and on the last verse of the closing hymn, they joined their daughters at the altar. After prayer and consultation, John and Ruth were baptized and joined the church also.

Following lunch that day, John called me to report that he had collected all his bottles of liquor from the garage, closets, and trunk of his car and emptied them in the kitchen sink. John told me many times that from that Sunday forward, he never had a desire for another drink of whiskey. John Phelps was healed of the addiction to alcohol the day he accepted Christ.

Shively became known for our ministry to alcoholics. Early on, I organized an AA group, and it quickly became one of the largest groups in Louisville with 75 to 125 in attendance. One of the faithful members of AA was Garnett Gaines, a member of our congregation. Garnett was an outstanding heating and air-conditioning technician, and a good husband, but he was addicted to alcohol. Sarah, his beloved wife, became weary of living with an alcoholic husband. One afternoon she called to tell me she was finished with Garnett and for me to do whatever I wanted to do with him.

I called a rehab center for alcoholics, and requested that they come to get Garnett. I found him passed out in the front yard, and I literally dragged him into the house and put him on the couch. I then told Sarah to pack her suitcase and to go to the Holiday Inn where I had reservations for her. "Sarah," I said, "It's time for you to get out of this mess." Garnett became angry and ordered me out of his house. My response was for him to either drink himself to death *or* to respond to help that was on the way.

At that moment the men from the rehab center pulled into the driveway. Garnett broke into tears saying, "Sarah, please don't leave me. I need you and I need help. One month later Garnett came home, accepted Christ into his life, and started attending AA. A few years ago, Kay and I attended Garnett's 30th anniversary of sobriety and these years have been the happiest years of his and Sarah's lives.

Working with alcoholics is heart-wrenching and sometimes frightening, work. It is time-consuming and challenging. But it has also been one of the most fulfilling aspects of my ministry. Many of these persons don't know much about theology, and many of them know very little Scripture. But what they do know is that in their utter helplessness they can be introduced to a Power greater than themselves where they can find a Source of help and hope. We serve a God Who makes all things possible. At the end of the day I want to be sure that I have encouraged my people to be connected to our God Who is our refuge and strength.

Writing about these experiences has reminded me of the importance of being a pastor, and of being a shepherd who is with church members when their hearts are heavy-laden. Paul said in Galatians 6:2 (KJV) "Bear ye one another's burdens, and so fulfill the law of Christ." I believe that once people discover their pastor to be authentic and trustworthy, there will be unity among the people and this will build momentum in the ministry of the church.

Not only were we experiencing numerical growth, but also our members were growing spiritually. Sunday school was growing, prayer and Bible study groups were being formed, people were visiting the sick and shut-ins, and young men were hearing God's call to ministry. Phil Hill, Rick Holladay, Allen Canterbury, and Mike Carter answered that call and were in the process for ordination in our United Methodist Church while I was their pastor.

With our beautiful 450-seating-capacity sanctuary, we invited Tony Fontane to return for a "celebration and thanksgiving" weekend. This time, Tony's wife, Kerry, came also and gave her testimony of being healed of cancer. Needless to say, many people came to see and hear this beautiful blonde actress from Hollywood. It was a great joy to see our sanctuary overflowing and our altar filled with people accepting Christ and rededicating their lives to a closer walk with God. The two Tony Fontane revivals were vital to the merger of these two struggling congregations. Tony was a person who could relate to all walks of life, and was a great influence in shaping my ministry. He taught me to be bold and courageous and to expect great things from God.

We were excited about being appointed to Shively for our fourth year. Life was good, and we were comfortable living in Louisville. However, Debbie and David still looked forward to going to the country and spending a week with their grandparents. On Monday morning, July 10, 1973, we were to meet my mom and dad at the rest area north of Elizabethtown, and our children would go home with them to Glasgow for the week.

It was a stormy morning with dark, low clouds and rumbling thunder. As we backed out of the driveway, Kay said she felt reluctant about leaving. But Mom and Dad had already left home, and we had no way of contacting them about the possible storm in Louisville. As we got on Interstate 65, it began to rain which made the road slippery. This was a peak vacation time so there was a lot of traffic. The tollgate at Shepherdsville had a back-up of traffic both north and south, and it was raining harder now.

After we passed through the tollgate, a tractor truck pulling a 12' x 64' mobile home jackknifed and lost control in the oncoming traffic. It then skidded across the median and hit the driver's side of our car, breaking loose from the mobile home. Then the mobile home hit our back door which threw our car into a tailspin and off the road.

I was unconscious most of the time for the next two days, so I am only reporting what the police and the family shared with me. David had only cuts and bruises. Debbie had a broken arm and a severe impact on the head, which left her temporarily blinded. Kay's head crashed through the windshield causing multiple lacerations to her face and injury to her sternum. My head also went through the windshield, and the impact of the tractor on my side forced the steering wheel into my femur just below my left hip leaving me pinned in the car with both Kay and me bleeding profusely.

When Kay regained consciousness, the motor was still running. Turning off the ignition, she thought to herself that the motor would never run again. The truck driver left the scene of the accident and was not seen again for days. Finally, the police found him holed up in a motel. He didn't want to answer the door, saying he had killed an entire family. The police assured him that he had not killed an entire family, so he let them in.

Kay recalls a simple prayer she prayed as she realized what had happened. When she got the children out of the car, they stood in the rain as she pulled them close and prayed four words, "Lord, please help us." Kay still recalls the peace that came over her in that moment. And God did help. Good Samaritans—all total strangers—began to minister to our needs. A woman shared her clean beach towels for Kay's bleeding face. Kay soaked three towels with blood and stayed by my side saying, "Wally, Wally! Please raise your head up." Each time she said my name, I would briefly raise my head. The doctors said later that Kay probably saved my life by helping the blood to circulate to my head. Otherwise I would have gone into shock.

A policeman took our shivering children out of the drenching rain and put them in his car. They started praying without ceasing, thinking I was dead. A trucker used a log chain to pull the wreckage off of my crushed leg. This was before the day of jaws of life, so they hooked chains to my side of the car in order to pry the door open and lift me out of the car. When they released the chain, the steering wheel pressed halfway into the seat, giving everyone an idea of the pressure that was on my left leg. Someone covered me with a tarpaulin to keep me dry as I lay on the pavement. Another truck driver agreed to search until he located my parents at a nearby rest stop.

With a 10-mile traffic back-up, the ambulance was delayed in arriving at the scene of the accident. After approximately two hours, we were in an ambulance on our way to the hospital. Debbie and Kay were in the front seat with the driver. David sat by my side saying over and over, "Daddy, we're all alive, and we're with you. We're on the way to the hospital." The ambulance driver radioed to the University Hospital describing the seriousness of our accident. I awakened long enough to scream, "Take me to the Methodist." (This was the Methodist Evangelical Hospital at that time.) That was my first and only verbal response since the crash.

With so much water on the interstate, the ambulance began to hydroplane. Kay pled with the driver, "Please don't let us get killed on the way to the hospital!" We arrived safely, and soon we were sent in three directions. Doctors and nurses swarmed around us determining the severity of our injuries. David was left alone in the waiting room. We will always be amazed at how at 10 years of age, David recalled names and phone numbers of church officials and notified them. The chaplain at Methodist Evangelical Hospital, Rev. Powell Royster, was a wonderful counselor to David. Later the Shively Police Department awarded David a commendation for his bravery.

Mom and Dad came on to Louisville in a downpour of rain. On the way they saw our car being hauled away. Dad had never driven in downtown Louisville, had no idea to which hospital we had been taken, or where the hospitals were located. Yet, with God's help, he and Mom arrived safely at the Methodist Evangelical Hospital.

In a short time church members and ministers lined the emergency room hallway. David went from room to room to check on us and to tell everyone about the accident. Debbie and Kay were taken to surgery and Debbie's arm was put in a cast. She was admitted for a couple of days. Marilyn Hill, wife of the chair of our church's administrative board, Richard Hill, took David to her house. After my facial and body lacerations were attended to, I was admitted and in a room about 5:00 p.m. I am told I insisted the doctor let me go home, since I would need to preach Sunday. I am sure he smiled to himself at such a ridiculous thought.

Linda Bentley, a member of our church, stayed in the room with Debbie throughout the night and then went to work the next day. Kay had approximately 102 stitches in her face, some on her hand, and her left ear lobe was almost severed. However, it was sewn back on and lived. She was dizzy and weak from loss of blood. The doctor wanted to admit Kay, but she insisted she had to go home to be with David. It was so hard for him to face all of this alone. Dad stayed with me and Mom went home with Kay. Marilyn Hill brought David home later that evening. He kept watch over his mother most of that night. Thus ended one of the most difficult days in our family's lives.

Dr. Rudy Ellis, the best orthopedic surgeon in Louisville and also a United Methodist, was my surgeon. The surgery lasted six hours. Dr. Ellis literally put the crushed pieces of my femur back together and inserted a steel pin into my hip joint to support the crushed bone. Later, he said this involved a thousand pieces of bone. When he visited the family after surgery, his shirt was drenched with perspiration and he was exhausted.

My congregation had never responded to a prayer vigil, but on the day of my surgery, they were praying around the clock. Men stopped on the side of the road to pray. People were in the prayer chapel at the hospital, and some members were in prayer at the altar of our church.

Pastor friends joined with our congregation in undergirding our family with prayer.

After visiting with me a few days later and thinking we were past the crisis, Kay and the family went home for some much needed rest. On that afternoon my body rejected the blood transfusion, and I went into a hard chill and had a dangerously high temperature. When I finally became conscious, I discovered my room filled with doctors, nurses, and equipment. This crisis lasted about an hour. One doctor later said I came very close to death in that hour. This all happened without any member of the family being present. Again, my life had been spared.

Lewis Woodward, a dear friend and our Louisville Conference Treasurer, was appointed interim pastor at my church and would be preaching on Sunday. There was large attendance on that first Sunday following the wreck, and Kay, Debbie, and David attended the service. Kay's face was swollen and bruised. Her body was so sore she could hardly move. With an injured sternum, it was difficult for her to even breathe. She went to the pulpit and stood before a congregation who wept with joy that we were alive.

There was a hush over the congregation as Kay looked at those loving faces and just above a whisper, with her hand pointed toward heaven, she said, "I just have a couple of things to say to you. Thank you so much for your loving care and support, and . . . God's grace is sufficient." I often recall the words from Proverbs 31:10 (NIV), "A wife of noble character who can find? She is worth far more than rubies."

That was one of the greatest sermons preached from that pulpit and a moment never to be forgotten. A few years later when we were living in Madisonville, Kay received a call from a Shively UMC member. Bill Embry said, "Kay, do you remember what you said from the pulpit on the Sunday after your family's accident?" Kay told him she remembered. He then said, "Well, I have just come through open heart surgery, and that Bible verse brought me through!"

Kay would be repeating those words of comfort often during the following four months of recovery. The trips to the hospital for her during the next 23 days, in an old borrowed car, were almost beyond her strength. While she was recovering from multiple injuries, caring for the children and my parents, trying to find clothes for Debbie to wear with her arm in a cast, Kay managed to spend as much of her day and evening as possible with me at the hospital.

Recalling these tense and difficult days continues to bring me to my knees in praise and thanksgiving for God's miraculous and providential care and for my wonderful family. Our family, to this day, still contacts each other on July 10, and thanks God for His wonderful mercy. God brought Kay and me together over 50 years ago. He has given us the strength to endure suffering and pain and has provided guidance and strength for our journey all along the way.

Our family also realized how much we were loved during those difficult days. Tony Fontane flew from California and Ed Robb from Texas to see us and spend time in prayer with us. Marshall Owen, my mentor as I began my ministry, wrote me every day while I was in the hospital. Clergy friends visited me every day. We received over 700 cards and many of these contained words of appreciation for our ministry. On our first Sunday together for worship, the congregation gave us a standing ovation and continued to stand as we entered the sanctuary until the family was seated and I was parked in my wheelchair.

After 23 long days in the hospital and much painful therapy, it was so good to be together at home again. I had looked forward to one of Kay's delicious meals and to the opportunity to sleep in my bed again. October 14, 1973, was my first Sunday back in the pulpit, and I preached from a kitchen stool. My subject was "The Wonder of It All." I talked about the wonder of God's creation, the wonder of God's love, and the wonder of God's church.

We will always be grateful to the Shively congregation for their love and care during this difficult time of our lives and to Dr. Rudy Ellis for his amazing surgical skills and compassionate care. On October 24, Debbie was told her arm had completely healed and I was told I could walk and could return to a full schedule as pastor. We were a grateful family as we celebrated by eating a meal at the Galt House in Louisville.

One has a different perspective about life after an experience like a near fatal accident. Life is so unpredictable, brief, and precious. James 4:14b (KJV) says, "For what is your life? It is even a vapour, that appeareth for a little time, and then vanishes away." I know the most important thing in my life is my relationship with God and my loving family.

When we finally saw our wrecked automobile, we knew our Heavenly Father had intervened and spared our lives. Standing by what was left of the car, we embraced each other and had a prayer of thanksgiving. We made a new commitment to discover God's dreams for our lives and to enjoy every day as though it were our last. We walked out of that junkyard with a new passion to love and care for each other and to make a difference in the lives of people we served in our church and community.

During the year following the accident, Kay enrolled at Spalding University and earned a degree in Early Childhood Education. Debbie became a candy striper at Sts. Mary and Elizabeth Hospital during the summer and a student volunteer in the principal's office at her high school that fall. She was active in her Girl Scout troop and in our youth program at the church. David continued violin with Mrs. French and became principal second violinist in the Louisville Youth Orchestra. He played in the Butler High School marching band and played the keyboard for the Butler Pep Band at home basketball games. Both David and Debbie took piano lessons and sang in the church choir along with Kay.

The church was a more gentle and loving congregation and assumed more leadership than ever before. They realized that the pastor did not have to be present for every meeting. I continued to look for new ways to reach out to our community and the un-churched. One of our most innovative ministries was a 9:00 a.m. drive-in worship service in the parking lot. It was not an original idea of mine. One of my colleagues in ministry, Rev. Bill Bowling, started a successful drive-in ministry at his church a few years earlier.

Our men built a stand-alone worship chapel at the edge of the church parking lot. It was large enough for a piano, pulpit, a small choir, and a radio transmitter to make it possible for people to hear the live sermon on their car radio. Even though the little building was large enough to house these items, it was jokingly called Wally's Bird House. Greeters welcomed each family with a bulletin as they entered the parking lot and were invited to sing along with the choir. Our average attendance was 60 with first-time guests every Sunday.

On one Sunday, Mr. and Mrs. Wright came to our drive-in service for the first time. On Monday I visited in their home to discover they had not been in church in more than 30 years. Mr. Wright shared his struggles with alcohol and the suffering it had brought to their home. The drive-in worship service had been a non-threatening way for them to go back to church, and my follow-up in their home gave them an opportunity to open their hearts to God. They did just that and experienced His saving grace in their lives.

A month later they were planning to come to the big church service as they called it. They were planning to be baptized on that Sunday. On Friday before the big day, Mr. Wright went to the barber shop and Mrs. Wright to the beauty parlor. While Mrs. Wright's hair was being washed, she had a heart attack and died. On that Sunday, instead of baptizing Mrs. Wright, I preached her funeral knowing she had the hope of eternal life.

On another day a single lady visited our drive-in service and later told her story. She was in deep depression and came home one day with plans to commit suicide. On her doorknob was a flyer about our drive-in worship service and an invitation to attend. Realizing that our church was only two blocks from her home, she found herself planning to attend our service instead of taking her life. When the invitation was given, she turned on her head lights, which was an indication that she wanted to talk to me.

After further counseling, this lady accepted Christ, was baptized, and became a very active member of our church. Those two experiences were worth all of our work in providing a worship service that enabled people to receive Christ into their heart in a non-threatening setting. The drive-in worship service became one of the most vital ministries of our church.

During this time my hip was in constant pain and I ended each day with a low-grade temperature. Dr. Ellis x-rayed my hip and discovered infection around the steel pin attached to my bone to hold it together. He put me on an antibiotic which reduced the infection, but not the pain. My leg was swelling and fevered. Upon examination, the doctor said we had an emergency, and he must do surgery immediately. He reminded us that my bone was in a thousand pieces and might not hold together without the pin. But there was that verse again: "I can do all things through Christ who strengthens me" (Philippians 4:13 NKJV).

When Dr. Ellis removed the pin, my femur had healed perfectly and would hold together without the steel pin. The pain was gone, and I could walk again. I began to feel stronger and more energized than I had since the wreck. God spared my life and healed my body. He was with me and was giving me a new future. Opening my Bible, my eyes fell upon these words from Jeremiah 29:11-13 (NASB). "For I know the plans that I have for you, declares the Lord, plans for welfare and not for calamity to give you a future and a hope. Then you will call upon Me and come and pray to Me, and I will listen to you. And you will seek Me and find Me, when you search for Me with all your heart." I recalled that Isaiah 40:29-31 (NASB) says, "He gives strength to the weary, and to him who lacks might He increases power. Though youths grow weary and tired, and vigorous young men stumble badly, yet those who wait for the Lord will gain new strength; they will mount up with wings like eagles, they will run and not get tired, they will walk and not become weary." I was experiencing something like a spiritual transformation of the body and soul.

In looking ahead, this congregation needed to upgrade their parsonage if they wanted to attract good pastors. I had tried to do this once and was voted down. I found a nice tri-level home for sale and in our price range within two blocks of our children's school—Butler High School. After much discussion with key members and the trustees, the church purchased this beautiful home on Fern Heather Drive, but it needed a complete makeover.

The trustees put their heels in the ground again and said we would not make any improvements. We needed $2,500 to install new carpet and draperies and to paint the rooms. In five hours, I collected $3,000 cash with the promise of more if we needed it. With cash in hand, I called a meeting of the trustees together for reconsideration. They said we do not have the money and will not borrow. I then laid the cash money on the table and informed them that painting would begin the next day. Kay picked all the colors for paint, carpet and draperies, and we went through the process of renovating another parsonage.

Just as we had moved twice at Munfordville and built a new parsonage, we were now making our second move at Shively and living in a home comparable to any parsonage in the Louisville Annual Conference. The church had built a sanctuary and grown numerically, spiritually, and financially. Merger was successful and the church was united.

During Advent of that year, we had our first open house for the church to visit us and see their new parsonage. With a cozy fire in the den fireplace and an abundance of goodies to enjoy, many of the congregation visited all afternoon. It was a joy to decorate our new home for Christmas and to celebrate the birth of our Lord around the fireplace with our family.

Spring brought Jack Gray, an evangelist from Texas, who preached our last revival at Shively UMC. The church was packed each night with our congregation, many visitors from neighboring churches, and un-churched people from the community. It was a good time of spiritual renewal for our family and our congregation. On the last night of the revival, we had a time of fellowship before taking Jack, the song leader, and pianist to the airport. Debbie and David came to church that night in Debbie's old Chevrolet she had bought from her Grandpa Thomas. They intended to go home after the service to do homework.

Kay had a strong feeling they should go with us to the airport. Even though she could agree with Debbie and David that it didn't really make sense for them to go to the airport, she still insisted. So seven of us piled into our car and headed out. When we returned home, we immediately noticed that the garage door was open and lights were burning all over the house. Burglars had broken into the parsonage, emptying all drawers in the bedrooms. They evidently carried their loot out in bedspreads, quilts, and sheets. They took all of Kay's jewelry, our TV, and many treasured items.

We were scared, angry, and exhausted. We could hardly walk through the house because it was in such disarray. We felt so violated. Around 4:00 a.m., we heard some music and could hardly believe our ears. Kay, Debbie, and I realized it was David playing on the piano, "What a Friend We Have in Jesus." When we reached the living room with looks of disbelief on our faces, he said, "Well, we *do* have to forgive them. The song says '*All* our *sins* and *griefs* to bear.'"

We joined hands in a prayer of thanksgiving that our children went to the airport instead of going home that night, and that we had again escaped what could have been a terrible tragedy. According to our neighbors, they heard a strange noise about the time our children would have arrived home. This was likely the sound of our basement window being broken. Had Debbie and David gone home instead of to the airport, they likely would have arrived home during the time the burglars were in the house.

Life goes on. The ones who broke into our parsonage were never caught. Satan stays busy with his roadblocks, but we have to remind ourselves that he is a defeated power. God's work must move on, and I was soon to realize He had been busy working in the lives of two men, Ed Carter and Randy Duvall. Ed and Randy had been on my prayer list for six years, and attended Ed Robb's revival. The Lord was nudging me to go see them one more time. When I rang the door bell at Ed Carter's house, his voice came on the intercom, saying "Come on in, Rev." As I entered the unlocked front door, I said, "Ed, how did you know it was me?" He said, "I knew you would visit me tonight because we have something to talk about."

I pulled up a chair, and Ed continued. "Rev, I was traveling down the Western Kentucky Parkway from Owensboro today, and I suddenly realized I was slowing down and pulling off the highway. I heard myself saying, "Rev is right. I do need the Lord." And then I said, "God, I'm ready when You are." Then he looked at me with an expression I had never seen on his face before and said, "Rev, I want Christ in my heart. Will you tell me how I can get him in my heart and will you pray with me?"

I invited Ed to join me in kneeling around the coffee table. He called his wife Sue to join us. Ed asked God to forgive him of his sins and to come into his heart. When he finished, we stood to our feet and after what seemed to be a long period of silence, Ed hugged his wife and turned to me and said, "Rev, thank you for not giving up on me. I really have the joy of the Lord in my heart." I learned again that all things are possible with Christ. I had tried to visit Ed many times in the past and was never invited into his home before that night. God's timing is always perfect. Ed was a happy and devoted Christian the remainder of his life.

The next night, I visited Randy Duvall. Randy always had a lot of questions about what he felt were reasons he could not make the leap of faith. God's prevenient grace had been preparing Randy for my visit, and he seemed to be expecting me when I arrived. After a short discussion, Randy said, "Bro. Wally, you've been to my home many times and I count you to be my friend. Tonight, I want you to help me get Christ in my life."

I asked Randy to pray with me this simple prayer. "Lord, I believe You died on the cross for my sins. I know You love me. Tonight, I want

You to know that I love You. Please forgive me of my sins." I then asked Randy to pray the words of the little song most of us learned to sing as children, "Into My Heart." The Lord did come into Randy's heart and there was great rejoicing. I could now write *saved* beside the two names that had been on my list during the entire time I was pastor of the Shively United Methodist Church.

With a new future and a hope, I began to feel it was time to complete my ministry at Shively and to get ready for my next appointment. Debbie would graduate from Lindsey Wilson College (a two-year college at that time) and Kay would earn the BS degree on the same day from Spalding University. Spalding allowed Kay to receive her degree at Lindsey Wilson so the family could be together that day. David was having a good time in school, enjoying band and violin, playing in the Louisville Youth Orchestra, and giving leadership in our youth ministry.

I felt fulfilled with those eight years of ministry at Shively, and I was feeling it was time to move. I felt sure I had done in Shively about all I knew to do, and I definitely desired the stimulus of a new situation. The New Year began with a 10-inch snow and sub-zero temperatures that lasted for a month. Schools were closed, the Ohio River was frozen, and our family enjoyed our new parsonage with the big fireplace.

I had a date on my calendar to meet with Bishop Robertson to develop an itinerary for evangelism workshops in every district. After completing that task, Bishop Robertson pushed back in his chair and said, "Let's talk about the future of Wallace Thomas." He went on to affirm my ministry and inquired about my recovery from the accident and my goals for the future. Then I said, "Bishop, I need a new set of problems." He had prayer with me and assured me I would get a good appointment. When the appointment was made, Bishop Robertson called to tell me he was appointing me to be the pastor of First United Methodist Church in Madisonville, a church of 1,500 members and a multiple staff.

Our family was excited but a bit apprehensive, too. We had never lived in western Kentucky, and I had no experience of working in a large church. Louisville had become home to our family, and our children were reluctant to leave the city. Yet they were excited about going to a large church. The next weeks at Shively were packed with fellowship meals and a lot of tears as we remembered how Tony Fontane, Ed Robb, and Jack Gray had led us in wonderful, fruitful revivals. We recalled the great youth weekends, the Lay Witness Missions, and many other wonderful times as we grew together in the Lord.

We were very proud of our new debt-free sanctuary which was full of worshipers every Sunday. We were also thankful that a worship experience was broadcast to the entire community from the drive-in worship service. We were so glad people in crisis came to these outdoor services and discovered the powerful grace of God. We felt pleased that our weekly mission work at Baird Street in the west end of Louisville was successful. The city of Shively awarded me a Certificate of Service for my leadership in getting an Olympic-size swimming pool at Western High School and a new football exercise facility added to Butler High School. I also persevered until I was able to get a huge Butler High School sign in front of the school. The sign is still there today. I was awarded honorary lifetime membership in the Butler Parent-Teacher Association.

Looking back on my eight years as pastor of this merged congregation, I often wonder how I got through the experience. The opportunities were always greater than my capacities, and the demands heavier then I could carry. Whether my nerves would stand the strain seemed at times questionable, and the automobile accident threatened to settle the matter. As someone has said, "Being a minister can seem a heartbreaking way of making a living," but I always knew I would not give it up for the world.

I left this congregation with new insights and experiences, remembering the words of Psalm 84:5a, 7a (KJV): "Blessed are those whose strength is in thee. [T]hey go from strength to strength." I would go to serve Madisonville in God's strength, with the strong conviction that Philippians 4:13 (NKJV) is true and can be trusted: "I *can* do all things through Christ who strengthens me." (Emphasis mine.)

Chapter 8

MADISONVILLE FIRST UNITED METHODIST CHURCH

Madisonville First United Methodist Church was like a new beginning for me. We had never lived in western Kentucky, nor had I served a large church with a multiple staff. First Church is one of the great historical churches of our Kentucky Annual Conference. It was organized in 1828 in a small log or frame building. The present sanctuary was completed

Madisonville First United Methodist Church and parsonage.

in 1901. In the 1950s a large colonial style parsonage was built, and in 1965, a beautiful two-story educational building was constructed. With a membership of 1,500 members, debt-free in a growing community with a population of 25,000 people, no church was more positioned for growth and vitality than this church.

A large sign arches over a street in Madisonville saying "The Greatest Town on Earth." The warmth and hospitality of our new church were unlike anywhere we had ever lived. The church personified that spirit in their reception of our family upon our arrival on that hot Saturday afternoon in June of 1977.

We will not soon forget the joy and excitement of that moment, nor the spirit of our first worship service. Both levels of the sanctuary were filled to capacity. David Calhoun, our youth director, and all the youth were seated on the front rows. Imagine 50 young people bowing their heads in prayer as I walked to the pulpit to preach. It was one of the most energizing moments of my ministry. The choir, the pipe organ music, and the congregational singing were awesome.

Everyone wanted to meet the new pastor. Lunches were scheduled and committees met to share their concerns and dreams. We had a staff consisting of a secretary, educational director, preschool director, choir director, youth director, organist, and custodian. The congregation was organized according to the *Discipline* of our United Methodist Church, but the officials were not having planning meetings. The Administrative Board met monthly for about 20 minutes to receive the financial report. The Council on Ministries had never met and had no idea what they were supposed to do.

I soon realized this congregation was eager to be good disciples and become a vital congregation, but was waiting for their pastor to show them the way. So my first order of business was to plan my work and then work my plan. I developed a work schedule for study, administration, and visitation. We had 60 shut-ins I wanted to visit, many of whom were in nursing homes. I also needed to visit the lay leadership, the businesses in town, and the homes of this congregation.

Meetings were scheduled with all committees, and plans were made for a Council on Ministries Planning Retreat.

I immediately went to work and visited all the shut-ins. Once I started, I had to work fast because they were calling ahead informing their friends I had been to see them. The shut-ins eagerly shared with me their journey with the Lord and faithfulness to the church. I asked that they be my prayer team and promised to pray for them and visit them regularly. Being a part of a prayer team made them feel useful again.

My first meeting was with the chairs of First Church's Staff-Parish Relations Committee (SPRC), Trustees, and Finance Committee to make a checklist of needed maintenance and renovation. When we finished, we had two pages on a legal notepad of things that needed to be done to the church facility and parsonage. I suggested this comprehensive list be presented to the Administrative Board so all the work could be done at one time. The list was presented at our first Board meeting, and the trustees were authorized to proceed and return with a cost estimate and date to begin. At that first Board meeting, they also raised my salary $3,000 which was a blessing.

Finances were not a concern for this church. However, in all the discussion about church renovation, there was no mention of parsonage maintenance. And it was obvious the parsonage had not been properly maintained. It had one window air-conditioner that wouldn't work half the time. The carpet was worn to threads, and the kitchen cabinets consisted of one section of metal cabinets on each side of the sink that had rusted-out holes in them. The bathroom fixtures were old and needed to be repaired or replaced. The garage next to the kitchen was a junk room and needed to be made into a den. The parsonage had a beautiful outward appearance but needed much repair and renovation on the inside.

When Dr. Richard Dodds, our family doctor and a member of First Church, visited us before our July Board meeting, he experienced the misery of being in a home with no air conditioning. After sharing his uncomfortable parsonage visit with the Administrative Board, they immediately voted to install a new heating/cooling system and to make the garage into a den. Later, a small side porch was renovated to become my private study. This was a great blessing to have a quiet place for sermon preparation, and it also enabled persons needing counseling to meet with me in private.

At the next meeting, the Administrative Board voted to renovate the parsonage and install new kitchen cabinets, carpet and draperies, and to paint the walls. This trusting Board gave a blank check to the trustees and committees to do their work, which included replacing chandeliers and adding new carpet and fresh paint in the sanctuary and parsonage.

These first 90 days as the pastor of this great congregation were indicative of our relationship and ministry for the next six years. They had respect and appreciation for their pastor and family. They had an energetic spirit and a zeal for ministry. It was a congregation with abundant resources, but little vision for missions and evangelism. I remembered the words of Jesus as He saw the multitudes and, with a broken heart, said, "So confused and aimless they were, like sheep with no shepherd. What a huge harvest! How few workers! On your knees and pray for harvest hands" (Matthew 9: 36, 37 *The Message*). And I was driven to my knees for strength, guidance, and harvest hands.

Our first Council on Ministries Planning Retreat was held at Pennyrile State Park. This was a time for developing relationships, visioning, and making first-year plans. It was exciting to listen to the lay leadership talk about their hopes and dreams for their church and how they could make a difference in their community. It was noted that the church was declining in membership and was a graying congregation. We weren't reaching young adults; therefore we needed to find ways to meet the needs of this growing population in our town. We said we wanted to be a friendly and inviting congregation, a nurturing church with a growing Sunday school, and a church with a strong evangelistic outreach. From that planning retreat, we came home with a priority of building a strong Sunday school.

First Church was not lacking for space. We had one of the largest educational facilities in the Louisville Annual Conference at that time. Many of those large classrooms were never used. We began receiving large numbers of young adults into the church, and Kay started organizing new Sunday school classes. During our six years at Madisonville, she organized five new Sunday school classes, some of which are still strong today.

Every class had monthly fellowship suppers. Some had planned programs while others just ate and visited, but each class had a loving and caring relationship. During Advent every class had a Christmas meal either at the church or in a home. We didn't have church business meetings in December, but we were together in fellowship and special Christmas programs. Kay and I were invited to every fellowship meal. Some nights we would attend two or three different dinners, and were expected to eat at each of them. I had a nice red Pendleton vest that I wore under my coat at these Christmas meals, and one night while visiting after the meal, a button popped off my vest and shot like a bullet across the room. I never lived that one down.

Christmas was a very special time of year at First Church. The sanctuary was tastefully decorated with greenery draped around the balcony. A beautiful Chrismon tree and dozens of poinsettias across the altar and in the windows added a special touch. Many of the people brought personal gifts by the parsonage. On Christmas Sunday the chairman of the SPRC presented my family and me with a nice card and a generous gift of money. Our children still talk about the Christmases at First Church, Madisonville.

But life in the church and the home is not always like Christmas. The New Year blasted us with blizzard weather—a deep snow with strong winds, sub-zero temperatures, and drifts that made many roads impassable. Schools, church activities, and many businesses were closed. We were celebrating my 43rd birthday when the telephone rang. One of our youth, Tommy Rodgers, had been accidentally shot and killed while duck hunting.

I immediately left for their home to be with the family. Neighbors and relatives had already arrived and cars were parked on both sides of the road. Walking a block on the icy road with the cold wind hitting my face, I began to hear the cries and screams of the family. Stopping in front of the house, I prayed, "Lord, what can I do? What can I say?" I was scared and felt helpless as I walked into that home. Having lived in the community for only six months, I was still a stranger to many people.

As I entered, a hush came over the crowd and in a whisper I heard people saying, "The minister is here." Without a word, I began to shake hands with people and make my way to the mother who was in the bedroom. With exhausted sobs, she fell across my shoulders saying, "Tell me this didn't happen. I can't believe this." By now there was total silence in the house and one could sense the presence of God in the calming of our hearts. Sitting on the side of the bed with Beverly, Tommy's mother, I read John 14 (KJV), which was the only thing I knew to do. And then I prayed.

The friend who accidentally shot Tommy was sitting in the living room, crying. No one was talking to him for they didn't know what to say. What do you say to a teenager who has shot his best friend? He must have felt like a criminal. Breathing another prayer for help, I walked slowly over to the young man's chair and sat down on the floor in front of him. Holding his hands, I sat there in silent prayer for him. Then, without a word, the brokenhearted boy slipped from his chair to the floor and into my arms. I embraced him and began to whisper Scripture verses, and then I prayed.

After sitting there for a period of time, we rose to our feet and went back to the bedroom. Tommy's friend looked at Beverly, Tommy's mother, and said, "I'm so sorry." There was nothing more he could say. This was truly one of those times when just being present was all I could do besides pray. After a couple of hours, I left that home and faced some of the most difficult days of my entire ministry.

I knew I would be spending hours with this dear family in the days to come. Other family members would need counseling. The high school needed assistance with counseling, too. So, after only six months in Madisonville, I was suddenly being pastor to the community. Yet I knew my most urgent responsibility was to prayerfully begin to try to put together the message for the funeral.

Another tragedy occurred several months later. Nancy, a beautiful, vivacious 14-year-old member of our youth group, went swimming with chewing gum in her mouth, strangled, and aspirated. The guards did everything they could to save her, but when she arrived at the hospital she was put on life support. After days of waiting and praying, the family had to decide to withdraw the life support—a heart-rending decision. This was another very difficult funeral for another young person in our church.

Nancy's funeral was scheduled for Saturday morning at 11:00 in Harrodsburg, but I had promised to perform a wedding scheduled for 1:00 p.m. that same day at our church. The burial was to be at 2:30 p.m. also in Harrodsburg. We worked it out that another minister friend would do the funeral in Harrodsburg, and I would fly in a military helicopter to the gravesite immediately following the wedding. I landed in the cemetery just as the family arrived at 2:30. Once again, I claimed Philippians 4:13 NKJV) "I can do all things through Christ who strengthens me." I was so thankful that my associate, Greg Hatfield, would be preaching on Sunday morning.

I deeply regretted the conflict in my schedule but was thankful to be able to work it out to have a part in both the wedding and funeral. I want to insert a humorous note here. The groom was very nervous prior to the wedding. At the end of the ceremony, just as I pronounced them husband and wife, he passed out. I quickly began the closing prayer and draped the groom across the altar rail. As I finished the prayer, he looked up and said, "What happened?" I replied in a whisper, "Man, you just got married!" Kay was the only one who realized that the groom had probably locked his knees which usually results in fainting.

Reflecting on my journey, I have realized that much of one's ministry is spent with people whose faith has been driven dangerously close to the edge. We find ourselves wanting to ask, "If God is good, then why? Why do bad things happen to good people?" I have compassionately shared in such struggles of the human soul until I cannot imagine any moral chaos and evil doing that would surprise me. I have also seen the best of human nature and amazing unyielding faith and courage in the most devastating moments of life. I believe pastoral care is best accomplished in being present with people who are grieving, struggling, and hurting. It is helping people stay connected with God through prayer and Scripture. It is confirmed by helping them agree with the Psalmist, "Wait on the Lord: be of good courage, and he shall strengthen thine heart: wait, I say, on the Lord" (Psalm 27:14 KJV).

In the meantime, our family was adjusting to life in a new community and making new friends. Debbie enrolled at Western Kentucky University as she transferred from Lindsey Wilson College. She became very discouraged when she learned several of her courses in education would not transfer to Western even though she had been promised otherwise.

In the middle of her second semester at Western, Debbie withdrew and came home for a few months. After sharing her discouragement with Kentucky Wesleyan College, the head of the education department came to our home to talk with Debbie. He assured her that every hour she had earned at Lindsey Wilson would transfer to Kentucky Wesleyan. We will never forget that professor sitting at our kitchen table and compassionately listening to Debbie's dream. He helped Debbie prepare her schedule for the upcoming summer and fall and also promised some scholarship help. In two years, Debbie graduated from Kentucky Wesleyan and made the Dean's List. She continued her education through Murray State University's Fifth Year graduate program which many teachers and prospective teachers were seeking at that time. Debbie loved her two years working as an instructional aid at Hall Street Elementary School in Madisonville while she completed the Fifth Year program

David soon became known among his high school peers as a person of faith, moral conviction, and leadership. One of the girls in his class developed cancer, and David helped many students find ways to cope with Carol Vaughan's illness. He organized prayer groups that met before classes each day. Carol had been David's date for the junior prom before she became ill. She later died and David had a part in the funeral.

David was active in the Hi-Y Club and became the state lieutenant governor of the Kentucky Youth Assembly. He was elected president of his class during his senior year. The youth in our Louisville Annual Conference also recognized David's leadership ability, and he twice was elected Conference president of the United Methodist Youth Fellowship. Rev. Rebecca Curry was a strong influence in David's life during these years. David was elected to serve on the board for our denomination's National Youth Ministry Organization (NYMO). He represented NYMO at the 1980 General Conference and was a delegate that same year from the former Louisville Annual Conference to the Southeastern Jurisdictional Conference.

Our Madisonville church continued to grow in membership and attendance in Sunday school as well as at the Wednesday night fellowship suppers. With the children's choirs, Agape House worship for the youth (which drew 100+ each week), and Bible studies, we often had 150-200 for the Wednesday night meal and activities. There was momentum, enthusiasm, energy and commitment permeating the church. I was finding it increasingly difficult to keep up with pastoral and administrative responsibilities plus sermon preparation, and still have any time for the family and myself.

First Church was no longer just a large membership church: it was also a growing church with many different ministries. The SPRC was eager to make changes and enlarge our staff. Mrs. Alice Gatton, who served as choir director for 50 years, expressed her desire to retire. The

SPRC named a search committee to begin to look for a new choir director and authorized me to discuss retirement with Mrs. Gatton. During a visit with her, I asked if she would prefer to resign after Easter or after the Louisville Annual Conference. Her choice was to resign after Easter which she did.

We also asked that Bishop Frank Robertson appoint an associate pastor to our church. In addition, the committee hired Rev. Stanley Gwinn, a retired minister who attended our church and was a good friend of mine, to be visitation minister. In the office we added a full-time financial secretary along with a church secretary and upgraded office equipment to enable in-house printing for bulletins, newsletters, and promotional materials.

Kay and I purchased a camping trailer along about this time, and parked it on a concrete slab at Barkley Lake. This wonderful little get-away place became known as our R & R trailer. Many of our ideas for new ministries and programs in our church were born at this trailer. Ralph Teague shared with me that the SPRC was aware of my work ethic, and they wanted me to take blocks of time off when needed. He suggested that I take a Sunday off every two or three months. Our congregation was committed to the love and care of our family, and it is such a joy to recall those happy and fulfilling years in our lives.

Dr. Stanley Baldwin, who was chairman of the Administrative Board, gave our family a membership to the country club. Stanley said, "With additional staff, you will be free to play golf with us on Thursday." I had played a little golf in Louisville but really knew very little about the game. Stanley also paid for some golf lessons for me, and I have enjoyed trying to play the game ever since. Later, after my retirement in Brandenburg, my golf buddies and I formed a foursome and looked forward to our golf day every week—weather permitting. They accused me of formulating my own rules, but none of us were too serious about rules of play. We were in the game for the fun of it.

As I mentioned earlier, I was introduced to the Lay Witness Mission movement during my pastorate at Munfordville. Later on, I introduced it to our Kentucky Annual Conference. Many churches became involved in the Lay Witness movement and were blessed and strengthened by it. Now, 13 years later, I was invited to participate in Cursillo #1 in Nashville. The Cursillo movement was introduced to me and to the Madisonville congregation by Rev. George Morris, a United Methodist pastor who helped pioneer the Emmaus Walk program in our denomination and beyond. George contacted me and asked if he could come and speak at a Wednesday night service in our church.

I thought this retreat-like weekend sounded like a good program, but the date that was set for the Cursillo in Nashville was the weekend of our church's Commitment Sunday. This is always an important date in our churches because this is the time that members make their financial pledge for the upcoming year.

Kay listened intently to Rev. Morris' presentation that night and left convinced this was an experience I needed. Later she shared her thoughts with me. I immediately told her there was no way I could be away on Commitment Sunday, especially since I was so new in this church. Kay didn't mention it any more for about a week. However, she did bring it up again, and she assured me that she didn't want to bug me about this. She told me she felt convinced in her heart that this experience would bless me and she hoped I would reconsider.

So my answer was, "OK, Kay. If you are that convinced I would benefit from this, *you* check it out with the Administrative Board." She said later that inside she was thinking she couldn't do that, but her words that came out were, "I will!" Before she could get cold feet, she called the chair of the Board, Ralph Teague. Kay was pretty sure that if Ralph endorsed my going, the Administrative Board would follow.

Kay and Ralph talked, she gave him the one brochure she had on the Cursillo, and asked that he study it and let her know his thoughts. A few days later, Ralph called Kay and said he had looked over the brochure and didn't see anything he would question about the event. He said that as far as Commitment Sunday was concerned, he saw no reason it could not be held on another Sunday.

Early that fall in 1978, the first two Cursillo model weekends were held in Nashville. Four laymen from our church and I were privileged to attend. The Cursillo originated in the Roman Catholic Church and simply means "short course in Christianity." The purpose of this movement is to strengthen disciples within the local congregations. A component of this 72-hour renewal weekend was to hear 15 carefully prepared talks—five by clergy and 10 by lay people—on the 15 distinctive basics of the Christian walk.

Following this first model weekend, The Upper Room in Nashville received permission from the Catholic Church to rewrite the talks using United Methodist terminology and changing the name to the "Emmaus Walk." Soon afterward we five from the Madisonville UMC along with some from the local Presbyterian Church started the Emmaus Walk movement in Madisonville. The Emmaus Walk experience was a turning point in my ministry. I was working hard in my church, but trying to do everything in my own strength. At the Cursillo in Nashville, I realized in a new and profound way that I have a Counselor and Guide by my side: the Holy Spirit. I guess I had known this for a long time, but now I committed my life and ministry totally to God and became assured of my ever-present Helper.

We soon had a waiting list of people from many churches in our area who wanted to go on this Walk. Persons who attend the Cursillo and Walk to Emmaus are urged to get into a small reunion group of no more than 10 people and meet once each week. It was exciting to hear about reunion groups meeting in banks as well as doctors' and attorneys' offices before and after office hours. My reunion group met every Thursday morning at 6:30 in attorney Tom Rhoads' office. Tom was a member of First Baptist Church in Madisonville. Stanley Baldwin, my dentist, was also a member of that group. These were such meaningful times of sharing our faith, and we developed deep friendships. When I moved, my reunion group gave me a golf putter with their names engraved on it. Some men in that group are still meeting today.

It was encouraging when people who attended the Walks to Emmaus came and shared with me their experiences and their new commitment to Bible study, prayer, and other Christian disciplines for the first time. It was exciting to see our people begin to reach out and share their faith with their friends. Some began to visit shut-ins and participate in ministries of the church they had never been a part of before. It blessed me to visit the hospital and have the patient tell me about my members visiting them and praying with them.

Our people loved God and one another in a new way. And God truly had His eyes on our church and was blessing our ministry. I was reminded of the words of the Psalmist when he said, "Behold, the eye of the Lord is upon them that fear Him, and upon those who hope is in his steadfast love" (Psalm 33:18 RSV).

The Madisonville First United Methodist Church began to put more and more emphasis on the Sunday school. Our first step was to host a Sunday school lab for teachers which would be led by personnel from the General Board of Education of our denomination. Twenty-plus churches participated in this lab weekend where we were exposed to a variety of teaching techniques and materials for children, youth, and adults. This was a major undertaking, but immediately our Sunday school began to improve. We followed up with a Sunday school enrollment campaign and testimonies on What Sunday School Means to Me during morning worship.

With an enlarged enrollment, each class sent cards or made calls to members who missed two Sundays. If it were discovered that people were sick, a visit to their home or follow-up contact was made. This new atmosphere of caring created a loving spirit that permeated our church family. Believing that "all things are possible," I have always been bold in inviting special people to church. Cheryl Prewitt, a former Miss America who had just finished her term, was known for her Christian commitment. I contacted her agent and discovered she would come to our church for $2,000. After much discussion, the finance committee agreed to extend the invitation to her.

Cheryl was a beautiful and talented lady. She grew up in a small United Methodist Church and attended Sunday school every Sunday during her childhood and adolescent years. I will never forget Cheryl sitting at the piano in the chancel area that Sunday morning as she blessed us with her music and singing. Her testimony lasted for 45 minutes as 700 spellbound people were moved to tears, joy, and laughter. Over and over Cheryl talked about the spiritual formation in her life that took place during her years of attending Sunday school. People left that service with commitments to make Sunday school a part of their Christian experience.

We also had a Henderson District Rally that afternoon which filled the church again. The impact of that one day with Miss America was like dropping a pebble in a pool that sent ripples across our community and district. We even had visitors attend who later became members of our church.

That night, after this mountain-top experience, Debbie shared with us she did not have a class just for her age group. So plans to start another new class got underway. The last vacant Sunday school room became the space for a new College-and-Career young adult class. Debbie asked Dr. and Mrs. Condit Steil if they would be willing to teach this class. They agreed to do this even though their lives were already full with work and raising a family. The class grew and was a great blessing to the church.

The following year we had a teacher appreciation banquet on our Sunday School Celebration Sunday. We recognized teachers who had taught many years as well as new teachers who started teaching as a result of the lab school. Each teacher now had a substitute when needed. We discovered that our teachers represented a collective 150-plus years of service to the church.

In preparation for the Sunday School Celebration Sunday, every class was asked to make a theme banner. Working on the beautiful banners became an exciting endeavor in and of itself. Attendance was again promoted from the pulpit and in every class. Our goal was for each class to have perfect attendance on Celebration Sunday, and many classes achieved their goal. I can still hear the singing and feel the excitement of that day as the teachers processed down the aisle with a parade of colorful banners. Each banner was then displayed across the front and sides of the sanctuary.

With the introduction of each teacher, the class stood and reported his or her attendance. A brochure listing the classes and the literature used was inserted in the bulletin. The Seekers class, a class Kay organized, was recognized for largest attendance. We had a record attendance of 546 in Sunday school that day and 670 for worship. We achieved our big goal of having classes in every classroom with an attendance of over 500 in Sunday school and over 600 in morning worship.

Kay and our associate pastor at that time, Greg Hatfield, enjoyed working together leading Sunday school class retreats. Articles about our growth in the Sunday school appeared in various church magazines. Kay was asked to write a leaflet on How to Start a Young Adult Sunday School Class, and later she was asked to write a leaflet on How to Plan a Sunday School Class Retreat. The General Board of Discipleship invited a dozen pastors to come together and share stories of success in growing Sunday school. During that quadrennium, I served on a special Sunday School Development Committee.

In 1978 a new 500-bed Regional Medical Center was dedicated in Madisonville. The town was known for its good doctors and good medical services. Many of these doctors were active members of our church. I was asked to offer the prayer of dedication for the new medical facility. Subsequently, I was asked to speak to some of the department nurses. This opened a door for counseling and outreach.

I was frequently asked by a nurse or doctor to visit a patient from out of town or an un-churched person who had no pastor. This led to a volunteer chaplain ministry in the new hospital. To initiate this program, a clergy/physician seminar was held to look at the ways doctors and pastors can better understand the team effort that can take place in the care and treatment of the sick. Today, the Regional Medical Center receives patients not only from all over western Kentucky, but also from Indiana and Tennessee.

Another blessing that came my way was when Kentucky Wesleyan College presented me an honorary Doctor of Divinity degree. I told Bishop Frank Robertson I didn't feel worthy to receive this honor. Bishop Robertson replied, "Wally, honorary degrees are bestowed for various reasons. You have worked very hard as a pastor. In my eyes you have earned it. Now accept this graciously." Through the years I served on the Board of Trustees of Kentucky Wesleyan College in Owensboro, Methodist Community Hospital in Henderson, Lindsey Wilson College in Columbia, and also served as Chairman of the Board of Wesley Manor Retirement Community in Louisville.

Madisonville First UMC was the place to be on Sunday morning. It was also a great church for hosting Annual Conference which we did in June 1979. The Louisville Annual Conference (which we were called at that time) was excited about coming to our town and our church. In my opening words of welcome, I shared with the Conference that we were celebrating our 150th anniversary and I invited them to enjoy our refurbished sanctuary and to celebrate with us the renewed vitality of growth in Sunday school, worship, and outreach. It was no small task to host 600-700 people. In those days all retired clergy and spouses were kept in homes and fed at the church. We also provided meals for the bishop, district superintendents, and other Conference leadership. It was a great opportunity for us to practice hospitality and to "put on love, which binds everything together in perfect harmony" (Colossians 3:14b RSV).

No stone was left unturned in preparing for this big event. It was easy for this congregation to practice hospitality for that was their nature. The mayor of our town owned the corner drug store and he sold ice cream for 25 cents a cone. The word got around about his ice cream, and during one break there was a long line outside the drug store waiting to get a cone of ice cream. Our hospitality committee made the Fireside Room into a large living room with comfortable chairs and an abundance of cookies and drinks. The church's Craft Group made beautiful gifts for the bishop's wife and each of the cabinet wives. Many of our members were available for assistance and conversation as many people were inquiring about our church's growth and outreach.

When David gave his report as Conference youth president, he began by welcoming everyone to his home church and made a reference to my bald head. He said, "This is your opportunity to decide which Thomas' light you prefer: a red glow or a shiny glare." The crowd erupted with laughter! There was a large delegation of youth in attendance at this Conference. After David gave his youth report, he was given a standing ovation. Later during the Conference, he was elected youth delegate to Jurisdictional Conference. These were defining moments in David's life. The following summer David would be moving to Nashville to begin his college education at Vanderbilt University with a good academic scholarship. We will forever remember that moment of departure when we left David standing alone in front of his dorm at Vanderbilt. Within a week he found the Campus Crusade ministry and other Christian groups. David began to make friends and participate in Bible studies. He also started attending student government meetings.

Bishop Robertson named me to be one of the delegates to attend the World Methodist Conference, which would meet in Hawaii in 1981. Our church immediately followed up on that announcement by indicating they wanted Kay to attend along with our children. This wonderful congregation raised enough funds to send the whole family to Hawaii to attend this Conference.

On Monday, July 20, 1981, our family went by American Airlines to Honolulu, Hawaii. We were one excited bunch! We were impressed when we learned of the growth of Waikiki during the past 20 years. There were three hotels in Waikiki back in 1961. Now there were 172. Local people said the island had actually sunk three inches with so many new buildings. Debbie was a senior at Kentucky Wesleyan at this time, and David had just finished his freshman year of college, which made this trip extra special.

We were thankful to have a little time to tour before the World Methodist Conference began. On Tuesday we went on the Circle Island Tour, and saw Diamond Head, Hanauma Bay, the Blow Hole, the Rain Forest, fields of pineapple and sugar cane, shrimp farms, and the Wiamea Falls. During the following two days, we went to Germaine's Luau and later to the Polynesian Cultural Center with our friends Eugene and Louise Dunn and their daughters, Lynn and Kathy. We took a cruise to Pearl Harbor where my uncle was stationed when it was bombed. Thankfully, he was not injured.

We worshipped the following day at First United Methodist Church in Honolulu. What a rich experience this was! I will always remember hearing the choir from Tonga sing "Into My Heart." On July 26, the entire delegation and visitors from all over the world walked together to a rally in the Waikiki Shell, a beautiful outdoor amphitheater. Later that day we celebrated David's 19th birthday before leaving for home the following day.

We experienced one scary event while we were there. One afternoon, our family had a little free time to go to the beach outside our hotel. The weather was perfect. The water was a beautiful sky blue. All four of us were enjoying wading around the shore when all of a sudden, a guard yelled, "That girl has drifted too far!" That girl was Debbie! The undercurrent had caught her, and without any of us realizing it, Debbie was in real danger. The life guard immediately swam to Debbie and brought her safely back to shore. Angels surely were watching over her, and we will forever be indebted to that lifeguard and God's protection.

Kay got her first teaching position in Hopkins County at St. Charles Elementary School (about 10 miles from Madisonville). Those kindergarten children quickly had a spot in her heart! It was exciting to hear her tell stories about the happenings of the day in her classroom. After one year, she was transferred to Anton, which was closer to the parsonage. Life was about as good as it gets. Our children were doing well in college, Kay was enjoying being a teacher, and I looked forward to every day of being pastor of Madisonville First Church.

It was during this time that our parents began to have health problems. My mother, Pauline Thomas, fell and broke her hip while watering flowers in their yard. Kay's mother, Vina Radford, was told she had a spot on her lung and needed further tests. She was given a choice of going to Louisville or Madisonville for the tests. We were so pleased she chose to come to the Regional Medical Center in Madisonville.

After a biopsy and CAT scan, she was told she had lung cancer and would need radiation. I had been with many members of our congregation when they were told this terrible news, but it was different when told to a member of our family. The family met with the doctor to discuss the plan for treatment. She could stay with us and go to Evansville for treatment for six weeks or go to Louisville. Again, we were pleased she chose our area.

The doctors were so sensitive to our hurting hearts and spent time talking about the future. Dr. Jack Hamman shared with us that what we had been given was a human prognosis, but the Great Physician may have a different one. David found a verse of Scripture that was helpful for the family. "The Lord will fulfill his purpose for me; thy steadfast love, O Lord, endures for ever. Do not forsake the work of thy hands" (Psalm 138:8 RSV).

The following Sunday, all of Kay's brothers and sisters, their spouses, and other family members came to Madisonville and worshiped with us. Kay organized a new Sunday school class that Sunday morning with 21 present and also prepared a meal for the family.

The next day, Kay and I took Mrs. Radford to Evansville for her first of 33 treatments. Kay remembers visualizing two streams of power flowing into her mother's body: God's power and the power of radiation. The waiting room was full of patients who had one thing in common: cancer. Everyone had a story to tell and were holding on to hope for healing of this dreadful disease. There were days of cold temperature with snow and rain, but soon the spring days of March came with budding trees and flowers showing signs of new life. On one trip, Mrs. Radford observed the pretty willow trees and blooming daffodils and said, "These trees and flowers have survived the winter, and I'm going to survive this battle with cancer."

The church joined us in storming heaven in prayer for Mrs. Radford. Many visited with her and offered to share in the trips for the treatments. When x-rays were taken at the end of the six weeks, the cancer had reduced. The doctor said she had a fantastic response to the treatment and she would not have to return for a checkup. She went home March 25 enjoying the springtime scenery and the new hope in her life. Mrs. Radford put out her spring flowers and resumed her visitation with patients in the Cumberland County Hospital.

On May 2, 1982, Mrs. Radford developed a kidney stone and had to be hospitalized at the local hospital. The kidney stone passed, and she prepared to go home. Before she left, the doctor said she should take a few iron pills to build her up. In trying to swallow the first pill, she strangled, aspirated, and developed aspiration pneumonia. In a couple of days she went into cardiac arrest and died in another two days.

Mrs. Radford's funeral was on Mother's Day. Brother Stanley Gwinn, my minister of visitation who had been Mrs. Radford's pastor at one time, officiated at the funeral. I assisted him, and David sang "Because He Lives." The many kindnesses shown us from our Madisonville church and other friends were a great source of strength and comfort.

The funeral was a great service of celebration for a person who loved God with all her heart and lived a saintly life. The family recalled precious memories of a wife, mother, grandmother, in-law, and friend. She knew the One who promises that all who live by faith will have a home in Heaven for all eternity.

Kay was exhausted and spent several days in bed with pneumonia following the funeral. She was grateful to her principal at school for his understanding. Murson Radford, Kay's dad, was 84 years old at this time, but he wanted to continue to live at home. All the children lived in the county where Burkesville was located except Kay, and she made frequent trips there to visit with him.

Our family had to adjust to a new normal—a life without Mother and Grandma—and a new understanding of sorrow and grief. Someone has said that in the time of pain and grief, we can turn our struggles into something helpful for others. With renewed strength, Kay went back to her dear children in kindergarten, David and Debbie went back to college, and I moved back into my schedule. It was also a good time to look at a new normal for my ministry life, which was very full.

Along about this time, our church was engaged in a capital funds campaign to raise $100,000 for our Louisville Annual Conference pension fund for pastors. They raised the suggested total which once again expressed the spirit of our church. Kay and I are deeply grateful today to this church, and all the others throughout the annual conference, for their generosity in establishing a good pension program for the pastors.

With a new and enlarged staff, I revised our job descriptions. Greg Hatfield and Stanley Gwinn took more responsibility for the care of the congregation. Greg became more involved with day-to-day activities and the Council on Ministries. Our Emmaus community prayer groups were finding ways to care for people. I no longer attended all of the church functions and meetings, which freed up some of my nights and gave me more family time.

Dr. Wayne Lowe, a pediatrician, volunteered to teach Sunday school. People enjoyed passing by his room on Sunday morning to see Dr. Lowe sitting on the floor with his preschool class and telling them the stories of Jesus. He would often invite his class to his home on Saturdays for hotdogs and then take them to a movie. While he saw more patients than most of the doctors in town, he seldom ever missed being in Sunday school and worship. When we announced that a Volunteer in Missions team was going to Haiti, Dr. Lowe was the first to volunteer. While the team was building a school there, Dr. Lowe was treating children and giving shots. It was inspiring to hear their stories and share their slides. These mission trips helped the church get a larger vision of what the church should be doing. (Kate's note: When

Dr. Lowe's daughter, Dr. Vickie Lowe, visited Wally before his death, she remarked to David about what close friends their dads were.)

Frank Ramsey had been a star basketball player for the University of Kentucky in the 1950s, and was a member of our church. You can imagine what big UK fans my congregation was. Our Administrative Board met on the first Monday night of each month, and when UK was playing, they brought their ear phone radios with them. We would be in discussion about some important issue, and a big cheer would rise up from the group when Kentucky scored. The scream would about be deafening when the team won!

On one occasion, Frank Ramsey invited me to his office for a cup of coffee. After some small talk, he said he wanted to do something in memory of his father and in honor of his mother, and he wanted my suggestion. I always had a list of things in my mind for people like Frank. I told Frank we needed a grand piano, but that would probably be more than he wanted to spend. Frank said, "I don't care what it costs, get a grand piano and get the best that is made." We purchased a baby grand piano which cost $20,000. Uncovering the piano on Sunday morning and hearing our choir director, Jon Baldwin, play his special arrangement of "Blessed Assurance" made for a great worship moment in that congregation.

It seemed I was getting more and more invitations to preach revivals in churches. Many times there would be planning retreats along with the renewal services. These churches were eager to get some practical how-to ideas from our church who was striving to meet the spiritual needs of the people around them and beyond.

Life for David on the campus at Vanderbilt became challenging. He realized that most of the student body there was from upper class homes and few if any ethnic minority persons were a part of the student body. His vision for the student government was to establish an ethnic minority scholarship fund that would open the student body to being a more diverse group. During his junior year, he ran for student government president and won the primary. His opponent appealed the election. The general election was held and again David won. The opponent challenged the outcome again, making accusations of foul play. The controversy continued for six weeks.

The Scripture says "Wherefore take unto you the whole armor of God, that ye may be able to withstand in the evil day, and having done all, to stand" (Ephesians 6:13 KJV). I felt it was time for us to stand. I called the dean of students and told him of the verbal abuse, some of which Kay and I received while walking across the campus. I told him that if the mess was not cleared up by the next day, I would bring a busload of character witnesses and a lawyer to the campus. In due course, David called to say he was cleared and confirmed as student government president. Soon needed steps were taken to confirm David in his new leadership role on campus.

To see his dream of an ethnic minority scholarship fund established, David went to various campus administrators to discuss the possibility. This required several conversations and lots of research to convince the dean that this was a rational and workable idea, but the administration finally got on board. David and a group of student leaders went to the University of Virginia to study their fundraising gala called the Restoration Ball. They hoped to use it as a model for an event at Vanderbilt that would generate seed funds for ethnic minority scholarships. This seemed like something that could be done at Vanderbilt, and off to work they went.

In the fall of 1983, the first Accolade was held at Vanderbilt. Kay and I were on campus that night, and the place was aglow with luminarias lighting the walkways all over the campus. Everyone was in formal attire. Kay thought she didn't have anything appropriate to wear. Her good friend, Jean Custer, came to her rescue. She lent Kay a beautiful pink dress and mink stole for that night.

We felt we were totally out of our element, but it was a wonderful evening. The event was a total success leading to what is now a multi-million dollar endowment for the Chancellor's Scholarship program for minority students. David graduated with honors from Vanderbilt, and I agree with Paul's wise words in I Timothy 4:12 (RSV): "Let no one despise your youth, but set the believers an example in speech and conduct, in love, in faith, in purity."

The life of a minister can never be removed from life's raw, hard experiences of living in the world. We are all living around people who have not found the One who is the way, the truth, and the life. As a pastor, I have shared in the struggles of human souls with every kind of guilt—murder, adultery, alcoholism, sexual perversion, and more—until I can imagine no revelation of evil-doing and suffering that would surprise me. Persons can become consumed with the darkness and wickedness in the world. But I also have seen extraordinary character in ordinary people who exhibit amazing strength and a positive attitude in times of crisis. I remember visiting with a dear friend suffering with cancer who lived across from the 18th green of the golf course. Looking at the beautiful green fairway, she said, "I'm in the rough, but watch me get out."

In Madisonville a couple named Charles and Kathleen Dickerson lived with a burdened heart for many years. Their son left home at an early age, and they had not heard from him for more than 20 years. They kept his room as it was when he left, and every day they went to the post office hoping to hear from him. I visited in their home many times and joined them in praying for their son. (In recent years, that prayer has been answered.)

Charles was not a Christian, but was a good, gentle, and kind person. One morning Charles came to the parsonage office to visit me. After a moment of greeting, he said, "Bro. Thomas, I want to know your Lord. Will you help me to accept Christ?" After sharing some Scripture on how to accept Christ, I prayed for him and then asked him to pray. "I don't know how to pray!" he exclaimed. I said, "Charles, praying is talking to God. You simply tell God what you told me, that you want Jesus to come into your heart." He bowed his head and in tears prayed, "Lord Jesus, I know You love me because You died for me. I am sorry for rejecting You in my life and I want You to know that I love You and want You to come into my heart." We then prayed, and Jesus did come into Charles' heart that day and filled him with great joy and peace which he never lost.

There were times when I went to the golf course just to be alone. On one occasion just as I was about to tee off, a stranger approached me and asked to join me. We introduced with first names and began our game. Between shots we talked and started getting acquainted. On about the sixth hole, I asked him where he went to church and he said he belonged to the First United Methodist Church. On the next fairway, he asked me where I worked. When I told him I was pastor of the First United Methodist Church, he almost croaked. Now he was a good golfer, but for the next three holes he played in the rough. When we finished nine holes he quit and left. Playing golf with me was not the highlight of his day. I later visited him in his home and he started attending church. After more visits and more golf, he accepted the Lord in his life, and before I left Madisonville, I preached his funeral.

In 2004 I received a letter from a member of my congregation who moved to another state soon after we left. I will always treasure this letter and many others I have in my file. I want to share this one letter:

Dear Wally,

Everyone (well, every lucky one) encounters someone in their life who had a significant impact on their spiritual life. Wally, I want you to know that for me that person is you. It was while in Madisonville that my "real" conversion happened. And like so many new Christians, I was willing to drink from the proverbial fire hose. June and I were being fed by our Roman Catholic friends in the community (Life in the Spirit, Marriage Encounter, etc.), by the newly found Cursillo-based renewal, and the charismatic non-denominational church in town. But in the midst of all this, there you were, demonstrating a solid maturity in the faith that has stuck with this wretched soul ever since. You tapped me for some leadership positions and

I learned so much working with you. And every Christmas Eve, bar none, I remember that time you "broke down" while reading the Christmas story from Luke. This past Christmas, since going to a Christmas Eve service just could not fit into our plans, I read the same story to my family that fortunately was altogether in Dallas. The other Christmas Eve memory I have is serving Communion with you to the First Church congregation. I felt honored and humbled. You will always be my pastor.
Brother Wally—thanks!

Mike Cheek

I share this letter and these experiences not for any self-gratification, but to praise my Lord who, through His miraculous grace, could take an ordinary country boy and help bring about hope in others for a better life. My last year in Madisonville was filled with counseling with people in crisis and with hurting souls wanting to know Christ.

Bishop Paul Duffey scheduled a workshop on worship to be held at our church on a Monday in the spring of 1983. He came on Sunday

Bishop and Mrs. Paul A. Duffey.

afternoon and spent the night with us. During a break we went to the parsonage and he gave me a book to read about being a district superintendent. "Wally," he said, "I want you to come into the cabinet next year. You think about it, and we'll talk later."

Needless to say, this came as a surprise, and I don't remember much else that was said that day. It would be difficult to leave this church especially during the greatest year of my entire ministry. Debbie and David were still in college, and to go on the district would mean a $10,000 salary cut for me plus Kay's loss of her teaching salary. With our combined salaries, we had been able to come close to covering the children's college expenses. I felt honored that Bishop Duffey would want me to be a part of his cabinet but sad about the thought of leaving an incredible ministry for an administrative position. Kay and I had to hold this request in our hearts without talking to anyone.

I called Bishop Duffey's office a few days later and got an appointment to see him. It was a good visit, and he was open to the possibility of our not being moved at this time. I shared with Ralph Teague, the chairman of the SPRC, that I might be moving. He then had a meeting with Bishop Duffey, pleading for him not to disturb the greatest years in their church. Ralph met with Bishop Duffey again and offered other incentives for me to stay. I later got a call from Bishop Duffey saying that if I thought I should stay at Madisonville I could do that. But he went on to say again that he needed me in the cabinet. I responded by saying I had promised to go where I was sent, and it was his call. There was a pause, and then Bishop Duffey said, "Wally, I am going to appoint you to the Louisville South District."

The following weeks were jam packed with meetings, fellowship suppers, invitations to homes, golf outings, and some final counseling sessions. The church was grieving not just because we were leaving, but because they were also losing their associate pastor and wife, Greg and Sandy Hatfield. They had been a perfect team and our brother and sister in ministry, and we all loved them. Debbie and David were loved, too, and each had made a significant contribution to the ministry of the church and community.

During a Sunday morning worship service, Kay was presented a silver platter, and on it were the engraved names of the five Sunday school classes she helped start. Following this presentation, a class member read I Corinthians 13 as a description of her life. The congregation gave Kay a standing ovation. Those of you who know me can imagine the emotion that filled my farewell message to this great congregation. At our going away reception, the line extended to the parking lot. It was a memory day that we will hold in our hearts for Eternity.

It is these special experiences of being with my people (in the good times and the not so good times) and the many letters from people whose lives I have touched that mean so much to me today. They continue to put the stars back in my sky and cause me to get up each morning with energy and excitement to do the work my Lord has called me to do.

It is difficult to leave a congregation you have loved, worshiped with every Sunday morning, traveled with through their valleys, and shared with them great moments of joy. Moving to a new appointment is a time for reflection and new beginnings. One can always learn from mistakes, but there has always been one constant in my ministry: I have always loved and cared for my people. I believe that when a congregation knows that about you, they will trust you and follow you. This move was going to be different from any I had previously experienced. I would not be serving a congregation, but would be a district superintendent and have supervision over 30 pastors and 60 congregations. One thing was not different. The success of my serving as a district superintendent would have the same bottom line as serving a congregation: I would need to develop a trusting, caring relationship with my pastors and their churches.

Chapter 9

LOUISVILLE SOUTH DISTRICT

As a young child, I remember the excitement of my small church, New Salem Methodist Church, as they prepared for the Quarterly Conference. The four churches on the charge united for worship to hear the sermon from our presiding elder (later called district superintendent) and receive Holy Communion. After a big potluck meal, we gathered for the Quarterly Conference to elect officers, set the pastor's salary, and collect the "quarterledge" (it was called that because the presiding elder visited

Louisville South District.

our charge once each quarter and collected the money for the apportionments). When there was a change in our pastoral appointment, the Pastor-Parish Relations Committee, of which my dad was a member, made a trip to meet with the presiding elder about getting a new pastor. I have always held this office of elder in our church in very high esteem, but I never dreamed one day I would be a preacher and be appointed a district superintendent.

Now, 49 years later, we were living in the beautiful Louisville South District parsonage. For the first time, Debbie and David would not be moving with us. David had a summer job with the YMCA in Madisonville and one more year at Vanderbilt. Debbie had a teaching position in Hopkins County, so both of them stayed in Madisonville. This was a lonely time for Kay as she searched for where she could find her niche now. She was no longer a pastor's wife, and didn't know what her role as the wife of the district superintendent should be.

Kay had a long-time dream of writing a devotional book. David reminded her of her dream and said, "Mom, this is *your* time to start writing and to get deeper in the Word." That is exactly what she did as much as time would allow. For the first time she could focus on her own personal desires and dreams as well as being my partner in ministry.

Epworth United Methodist Church was down the street from our parsonage, and Rev. Bill Stratton, the pastor, was quick to make a pastoral call and invite us to attend his church. Kay joined Epworth, and for the first time in our marriage, Kay had a pastor who was not her husband. Bill was a wonderful pastor. When we had a death or a need in our family, the first person at our door was Bill. It felt so good to have a pastor for a change. Later, his wonderful wife, Ann, volunteered to be the director for Debbie's wedding.

For me the congregation was now the parsonage families of our district. We were eager to visit them in their homes. It was a great blessing to visit these dear families, hear their stories, and let them know of our love and appreciation for them and their ministry. I have always believed leadership begins with the heart and not the head. I didn't know how to be a district superintendent, but I did know how to love people and have a loving and caring relationship with them. So I set up county schedules to visit the parsonage families, inviting them to share their concerns and dreams and to allow me to pray with them. I shared with them that I was a part of their staff in ministry and also their pastor in their time of struggle.

Like our congregations, our parsonage families have burdens, disappointment, sickness, loss of loved ones, and I feel the district superintendent can and should be a pastor to them. I hoped this initial visit would assure them that I sincerely wanted to be their pastor. Pastors and their families need a lot of encouragement. The writer of Hebrews tells us to keep urging each other on. "And let us consider one another so as to stir up love and good works, not forsaking the assembling of ourselves together, as is the manner of some, but exhorting one another, and so much the more as you see the Day approaching" (Hebrews 10:24-25 NKJV).

Visiting parsonage families in the district was good preparation for charge conferences which were scheduled for September through December each year. One recurring question at our Charge Conferences was about the Emmaus Walk that had been such a vital part of my ministry at Madisonville. It soon became apparent that one expectation of both clergy and laity was that I would bring the Emmaus Walk movement to the Louisville South District. Roy Webster, pastor of Memorial United Methodist church in Elizabethtown at that time, graciously offered his church's family life center as the site for the weekend. Dr. Wayne Lowe, a pediatrician from Madisonville, was named lay director for the men and Kay was named lay director for the women. The first Walk to Emmaus was held in March of 1984.

Team preparation for the Emmaus Walk consisted of six formation meetings where each speaker's talk was critiqued. The plan for the Walk always has the men attend first, and the women follow about two weeks later. We knew we would need to use leaders from Madisonville who had experienced the Walk to Emmaus already. So we worked out the dates when we would drive to Madisonville for the formation meetings. Kay and I attended each of these meetings, driving often on snow-covered roads.

We secured 50 cots from Fort Knox which had to be delivered to Elizabethtown and set up. A trucker from Madisonville came to Fort Knox, loaded the cots on the trailer, and brought them to the church where they had to be set up before each of the Walks. All of this extra activity was in addition to a demanding cabinet schedule and consultations with pastors and Pastor-Parish Committees. We were often stretched beyond our limits, but both clergy and laity responded to this 72-hour weekend. Registration for both men's and women's Walks was quickly filled.

Kay's dad was sick at this time, and she often traveled to Burkesville to help care for him. In early February her dad was hospitalized in the Glasgow hospital. He improved and was scheduled to go home. Kay visited him in the hospital and had a good conversation with him. After she had a prayer time with her dad, she returned to Louisville. Exhausted, she slept until 9:00 a.m. the next day. She was awakened by a telephone call from her sister telling her that Mr. Radford had died during the night. Kay had lost both her parents within 21 months.

Mr. Radford's funeral was held in Burkesville, Kentucky. David sang "When the Roll Is Called Up Yonder," a favorite hymn of Mr. Radford's, and I gave the funeral message. David's roommates from college—Gif Thornton, Jeff Bailey, and Rob Courtney—drove from Nashville to Burkesville to be with us. I shared a conversation Mr. Radford and I had during a revival at Burkesville. One night we talked and prayed until early morning, and I will never forget his telling about his faith and his relationship with God. I also shared in the funeral message about the revival at Parrish Chapel United Methodist Church where he rededicated his life to the Lord. Mr. Radford loved the Lord but had become lax about faithful church attendance.

Our family stayed at the home place the night after the funeral— our last time to do this. It was a good night of remembering our children's grandma and grandpa and Kay's mother and father. The entire Murson and Vina Radford family returned for a Christmas or two to the house after both parents passed away. After the home place was sold, Christmas gatherings were held in a local church, the town library, a home, or at Dale Hollow State Park.

Located within the bounds of what was then the Louisville South District is the Fort Knox military base. There was a large population of Koreans in the Fort Knox area. One group was meeting in the basement of a real estate office for worship and wanted to become a United Methodist congregation. The pastor made an appointment to see me, and when he arrived, he had the entire congregation with him. It was difficult to get 30 people in my small office and a real challenge to communicate with them without an interpreter. However, the pastor spoke enough English to convey he was a United Methodist minister and he wanted his congregation to be a member of our Annual Conference. They were all very kind and soft-spoken, but persistent in their requests.

In consultation with Bishop Duffey and the General Board of Discipleship, we began a year-long process with this small group of people to help them become a United Methodist congregation. The General Board of Discipleship had a Korean section that would provide training regarding the polity as described in the *Discipline of the United Methodist Church.*

At my first Louisville Annual Conference as a district superintendent, this Korean body of believers was recognized and named The First Korean United Methodist Church of Kentucky. Radcliff UMC shared their facility, which made it possible for them to move from the real estate building to a church. This small congregation used the Radcliff UMC for more than a year for worship, fellowship suppers, and prayer meetings. They were a praying people and often prayed several hours at a time for their sick friends, for lost people, and for the future of their church.

I received another call from this Korean pastor for an appointment with me. I set up a time and told the pastor to bring a committee. The purpose of this meeting was to purchase a building they had found for sale. The building could be renovated and would provide them with their own sanctuary and a basement for fellowship suppers.

After Pastor Kim shared his request for help in purchasing this building, I inquired about the asking price of the building. He hesitated and then said with a question in the tone of his voice, "$10,000?" I smiled and said, "I believe the building is worth more than $10,000." He then replied "$100,000?" I agreed to look into the matter and get back with him. After many meetings and phone calls, I was able to get a grant from the Board of Global Ministries which included a low-interest loan for the balance to purchase the building. The grant money was used for renovation which was done by the Koreans and supervised by a construction worker who had married a Korean lady.

There was yet another surprise. This group of Korean Christians later came to see me in a new van they had purchased, but there was no way they could make the payments. I called the Ford dealership and informed them this congregation could not make this kind of purchase without my approval. Pastor Kim then returned the van. I later helped them purchase a new van from a United Methodist dealer at his cost.

The Korean project was time-consuming but also rewarding. After months of hard work, they finally moved into their own facility. A big day was planned with Bishop Paul Duffey preaching through an interpreter, followed by a potluck meal in their new fellowship hall. They gave gifts to Bishop and Mrs. Duffey as well as to Kay and me. (They had gifts for us every time we visited their church.)

Their charge conference was an interesting experience. When I asked for the report from the Pastor-Parish Relations Committee and the pastor's salary for the next year, they immediately went into a discussion in their language. Sometimes they became emotional and the pastor also entered into the discussion. After several minutes, the chairperson turned to me and said in English, "He's getting enough salary!" No chance of a salary raise that year. This little congregation paid for their church and it still exists today.

Kay and I enjoyed traveling the district for the charge conferences. Many of the churches had fellowship hours to welcome us to the district. In each charge conference, I invited the people to share their hopes and dreams for their church/charge and I concluded with a brief message of encouragement and hope. I always tried to complete the charge conferences by Thanksgiving before churches became busy with Christmas activities.

The Louisville South District was a district with diverse congregations. There were suburban churches, county-seat churches, circuits and small station churches, a Korean church, and one African-American church. There were churches in interracial communities that needed to integrate. The fields were ripe for new churches to be planted.

Walker Memorial United Methodist Church was a white congregation in a changing neighborhood and was struggling to survive. In conversation with the pastor and the congregation, it was a consensus that we appoint an African-American minister to this congregation. Our Louisville Annual Conference had a limited number of African-American ministers, making this a difficult task. The Board of Global Ministries offered financial assistance to facilitate interracial appointments. During my six-year term on that district, I appointed four different ministers to that church. After a few years passed, Walker Memorial closed because our Louisville Annual Conference didn't seem to have ministerial leadership with passion and vision to reach people of that community.

While Rev. Carman King served as district superintendent of the Louisville South District, a 12-acre plot of land near Middletown was purchased for a future church site. The terrain was terrible, but it was a good location. An architectural consultant from the Board of Global Ministries walked the land and concluded that a church could be constructed. A sketch was drawn for a church building with landscaping suggestions. The bishop and the cabinet (district superintendents) appointed John Slider to this new church, which was later named Advent United Methodist Church. They met in an elementary school for several years and experienced significant growth. They were able to build the first phase of their new facility, but, sadly, this church no longer exists.

The Middletown UMC was landlocked in a location that would not accommodate much growth. The Holloway family donated 25-plus acres of land, and the church relocated to that site. Today, it is a growing church on the edge of Louisville.

Hodgenville UMC was an older church in downtown Hodgenville with Sunday school rooms in the basement. Roger Newell, the pastor, was visionary and led that congregation to purchase 25 acres with frontage on the by-pass around the town. However, the vote to purchase the land was not a consensus of the congregation. Some of the members of the Charge Conference, who were opposed to the purchase, did not attend the meeting. In time, however, the decision to purchase the land was approved with a strong majority. The congregation relocated and constructed a beautiful facility. The church has experienced growth and has added a new wing to the structure in recent years.

Many years later our son David was assigned to Hodgenville United Methodist Church. He had three good years as pastor of this congregation. Three weeks after David arrived, his youth director introduced David to one of his classmates at Asbury Seminary, Karen Muselman. Karen later became David's wonderful wife and mother of our grandchildren: Luke Christian, John Paul, and Mary Esther Elaine.

Another church with a challenge was Muldraugh UMC. The little town of Muldraugh was a military community adjacent to Fort Knox. The community consisted of elderly residents who lived mostly in houses and young adults who lived in apartment buildings. The Muldraugh UMC was struggling to survive and worshipped in a small Bedford stone building with a basement. It was so sad to visit that church and see classrooms that had not been used for years. In those rooms was old literature covered with dust and trash, and mold was evident on the walls. Kay and I left from that first worship service at Muldraugh remembering those seven people in attendance who were pleading for help.

Rev. Alice Scott, an ordained elder and native of that area, shared our concern and agreed to come to this church as their new pastor. Rev. Scott and her husband, Jack, loved and nurtured these people. They worked with the seven people in cleaning the basement, scrubbing and painting the walls, and in purchasing some used kitchen appliances. Jack played the piano, Rev. Scott preached, and people started coming to the little church to worship God. During the week she visited the apartments and began to relate to those young mothers whose spouses were in the military. Kay assisted her in starting a new Sunday school class. Rev. Scott offered Bible studies during the week, and the ladies of the church babysat so the young mothers could attend.

Alice (as I called her) and I invited Bishop Duffey to preach at Muldraugh, and you can imagine the excitement of that day. The church was impeccably clean, and the sun rays were shining through the beautiful stained-glass windows. They seemed to add a radiance to the joyful faces of those who filled the sanctuary.

It was a special day when the bishop came to preach in little Muldraugh. We three preachers, in our robes and stoles, processed down the aisle as Jack played the call to worship. I've never heard better singing and preaching. It was an emotional day for us all. After the worship service, we all gathered in the fellowship hall for lunch. The church again had hope and faith in their future. We started a building fund, and I helped them raise some money. We put a steeple on the church, renovated the parsonage, landscaped both buildings, and paid for it within a year.

Our denomination has always had dedicated clergy with passion and vision who are willing to make the sacrifice to serve places like Muldraugh, but we've never had enough of them. That's what makes the work of the district superintendent so challenging.

I want to share with you some of my observations that helped me to clarify my role as a district superintendent. I would attend many meetings and make appointments that affected the future of both the churches and the pastors, but the greater challenge was motivating and inspiring the clergy and parishioners to believe in themselves. Jesus started working with people at the level of their commitment, but He never left them there. He said in John 14:12b (KJV), "He that believeth on me, the works that I do shall he do also; and greater works than these shall he do; because I go unto the Father." I felt connected to the ministry of my clergy and each of their churches and I wanted to see them prosper and fulfill the Great Commission.

To assist our pastors in their spiritual life and leadership development, I had annual retreats and invited motivational seminary professors and visionary clergy to be our leaders. Our district secured a church consultant who provided demographics for our churches, and, in some instances, provided consultation to individual churches. Bishop Robert Spain, who followed Bishop Paul Duffey, was a great preacher and led a seminar on sermon planning and structure. We also had a workshop on covenant ministry to encourage our clergy couples to form small groups for prayer and fellowship that would meet once each month. Twenty years, later some of these covenant groups are still meeting in that district.

Several of our church official boards went to Camp Loucon for spiritual and visioning retreats. It is a powerful moment when church leaders get on their knees together in prayer for a closer walk with God and for God's guidance and vision for the future of the churches. It was in these settings that pastors searched the Scriptures for a better understanding of God's purpose for the church. Kay often followed up with overnight retreats with spouses. Bishop Spain and Herschel Sheets helped with planning a year of preaching. I offered workshops on How to Lead a Person to Christ. I am always amazed that there are clergypersons who have never led adult persons to Christ.

I restructured some charge boundaries in order to help pastors serve with less travel and stress. Previously ministers traveled great distances—some all the way across the district—just to preach on Sunday morning. And the worship service was the only thing happening in those churches. To regroup churches to make possible for the pastor to be in the community and it not be a long distance phone call was encouraging to these people and a very simple thing to do.

One pastor lived in Louisville and served City Road Chapel UMC on Dixie Highway and Webster UMC in Webster County. Webster UMC was an hour drive from City Road Chapel and only 10 minutes from Irvington, a struggling county-seat town. Putting Webster and Irvington together gave the Irvington pastor a $5,000 increase in salary. I then put City Road Chapel, who had no parsonage, with West Point UMC, who had a parsonage. This brought together two churches that were only a four-mile drive apart.

Some might say these decisions were good superintending or good leadership, but I want to say these decisions were a ministry of encouragement. These dear people now had hope for survival. These decisions lifted their morale, re-energized their hearts, and raised their expectations. Both charges have had long pastorates since that time and still have hope for the future.

There is an old saying that what goes around comes around. I concluded a church conference one evening for a congregation who had voted to build a new parsonage. One of the members, John Rowe, promised to get all the materials at cost, making it possible to build a nice home at a great financial reduction. As I was leaving, I whispered my thoughts, "If I could get a deal like that, I would build a home at Doe Valley." Mr. Rowe overheard my quiet comment and, taking my arm, he said, "I'll do the same thing for you. I'll get the materials for you to build your home at cost."

I rushed home to tell Kay and we immediately began to dream about building a small home on the lot at Doe Valley that we had purchased in 1973. Two months later in July of 1985, we began construction of *our* get-away home. We appreciated and enjoyed the parsonages each church had provided, but now we would have a place of our own for the first time in our marriage. Many people have enjoyed this little house—missionaries and other Christian workers, family, and friends. Kay had several retreats for pastors' spouses there. It was also located in the center of our district and was convenient to drive from there to several of the charge conferences. This little house later became our retirement home.

It was so exciting to drive to Doe Valley and walk through the rooms as the house was constructed. We dreamed about our first night in our own home but realized the times there would be limited until we retired. We hoped construction would be completed by October before David would be leaving for England for a year of study. But as luck would have it, it was not completed before David left. These 12 months of studying the life and works of John Wesley were supported by a Rotary International Scholarship.

In 1986 we had our first Christmas in our newly-completed home. The furnishings were scarce and our Christmas tree was a home-grown cedar tree we located in Doe Valley. Still everything would have been perfect had David been with us. This was our first Christmas without him since his birth, and Christmas day was difficult. Debbie sang "Infant Holy, Infant Lowly" to David over the telephone as he traveled through Switzerland. Several tears were shed during those moments.

Phil and Ruth Logsdon, our friends from the Shively days, lived in Doe Valley and invited us to their house for a meal that Christmas. After the meal they told us they wanted us to go to England to see David. Then Phil said, "We have two round-trip tickets we are giving you to make the trip." He had been awarded them because of the good business in his waterbed stores. I can still feel the joy of that moment and the deep appreciation for our friends' generosity. Debbie had enough money in her savings account to buy her ticket which made it possible for her to make the trip with us.

Along about this same time, the bishop named me to be a delegate to the World Methodist Conference which would be held in Nairobi, Kenya, that same year. We wondered how in the world we could make two such trips abroad in the same year. At the January Louisville South District Council on Ministries meeting, it was announced the district was raising money to send us to this meeting. We had never been out of the country before; now, we were scheduled to go to two different countries within four months. That would be a lot of travel for country folks like Kay and me!

We left for England on March 26, 1986, and David met us at the airport in London. His British Rotary sponsors, John and Gill Cleverdon, arranged for us to spend the weekend with them. On Monday, we rented a compact car and began touring England. The big adjustment was driving on the left side of the road which seemed the wrong side to us. David served as our navigator with a map in his lap. Intersections were called roundabouts, and we often drove around and around several times before deciding which road to take. We learned that gasoline was called petrol, the hood of the car was called the bonnet, and the trunk was called the boot.

Before we left for England, David often asked us on the phone what places we would like to see while there. Kay always said the main site for her was to see where the Sunday school started. When we discussed the trip with David, he would ask, "Have you all decided where you want to visit? Now, Mom, you don't have to answer. I know where you want to go!" What a thrill for her when we finally located the little building in Gloucester where the first "School on Sunday" was held. Townspeople with whom we spoke were quick to tell us they knew the story of the Sunday school which has been passed on from generation to generation for over two centuries. They expressed appreciation for the difference it made in that community.

In 18th century England, there were no child labor laws and no public education available. Only rich children could hope to get an education. Children worked long hours during the week and were free to roam the streets on Sunday. A man by the name of Robert Raikes had the idea of starting a school on Sunday in a back alley of Gloucester. His intent was to provide some moral and educational training for these children and to get them off the streets and out of trouble. They were a rough and tough bunch of kids, and Robert Raikes is said to have literally tied the children to the log seats, which didn't go over well with the pastors, parents, and church laity.

John Wesley, before the Methodist Church was founded, heard about this situation and met with Robert Raikes. He told Mr. Raikes he thought the idea of a school on Sunday could work. He said it could become a "nursery" for young Christians. And isn't this what the Sunday school should be for us today—a place where we are fed spiritually, nurtured, cared for, encouraged, and loved? I am so thankful Sunday schools still exist after these many years.

We visited Epworth, the birthplace of John Wesley, and Stratford-Upon-Avon, the home of William Shakespeare. We stayed in bed and breakfast homes, often spending our evenings with the family around an open fire. One of the richest experiences of our trip was discussing family traditions and customs with our hosts. The nights were cold and there was usually no heat in the bedrooms. We learned that often the British people sleep at night with an open window. Perhaps this is one reason they are such a hearty people.

After our final weekend in London, we said our good-byes, and David left for Spain to have a few days in John and Gill Cleverdon's condo. Kay, Debbie, and I crossed the English Channel to Amsterdam, Holland. One of the desires of Debbie's heart had been to visit Holland and see the beautiful fields of flowers. I think she stooped and smelled the aroma from every daffodil she saw, because her nose became yellow with pollen! A few years after this trip, she planned her wedding to be in March when daffodils would be in full bloom.

When we arrived in Amsterdam, the bus driver didn't seem to understand where our hotel was, so he took us to the general vicinity. There we stood on a street corner with a bunch of suitcases, looking like three vagabonds. Thankfully, an elderly lady came around the corner and must have sensed our being lost. I could not understand her Dutch, but I gave her the piece of paper with the hotel address on it. She looked down the street in the distance and gave us an idea of the direction to go. Kay had learned a few Dutch words and was able to come close enough to "thank you" for the lady to understand. It surprised and pleased her so that she embraced Kay, and then off we trudged down the street to our hotel.

On our return trip across the English Channel to London we spent the night in a fierce storm. Everyone was sick, and the boat was cracking and popping as though it would come apart. (We later learned this was the boat's final voyage before going to dry dock for repairs.) Every single person on the boat was seasick. Furniture turned over in every direction and so did people's stomachs! The crew ran out of motion sickness medicine. I could then understand the disciples awakening our Lord and begging Him to calm the sea. That was now our prayer. After a day of rest in London, we were eager to get back home to Kentucky.

Four months later, we prepared to leave for Kenya and the World Methodist Conference. Unlike our trip to England where we were greeted by our son, the person greeting us at the airport in Nairobi was a Kenyan assigned to take us to a college dormitory. The dorm on the campus of Nairobi University would be our lodging until we left to attend a Family Life Conference prior to the World Methodist Conference.

We six delegates with all of our luggage boarded an old van at 1:00 a.m. following our 30-hour flight on a crowded airplane. After some discussion with each other, we began to wonder how far it was to the dorm. In broken English, our driver assured us we would soon be there.

We finally came in sight of an American Marriott Hotel. I asked the driver to stop and get directions to the college where we would be staying. It was 3:00 a.m. and the desk clerk wasn't even familiar with the college where we were to stay. The passengers in the van were exhausted, dirty, hungry, and angry. Then the driver announced he was almost out of gas. When we asked him to stop at the next gas station, he replied he had no money. We all pooled our resources for some gas money, and just as the day began to break, the driver shouted, "There's the college, and I've been circling around it all night!"

We finally found our dorm and got to our room as the roosters began to crow. After being in our bed for about 30 minutes, there was a knock at our door announcing it was time for breakfast. With my three-day-old beard and red eyes, our dirty bodies, and in clothes we had worn for three days, we made our way to the cafeteria.

Kay, especially, wanted to attend the Family Life Conference prior to the World Methodist Conference. We went as a group of around 60 Methodists from all over the world out to the Meru Province. The Methodist Church has had a strong influence in this area over the years. Roads out to Meru were paved years earlier by British investors in tea production in that area. Many potholes had developed over the years with little or no repair work done. The bus was old and rickety. Bouncing along on the long journey to Meru, I said to Kay, "Don't ever get me into a situation like this again!" In retrospect, however, I look upon this experience as one of the most meaningful and inspirational in my life.

We were met in Meru by our host for Saturday night and Sunday, Justus Muthee. He and one of his children were waiting to take us from the reception to their home. This was a two-hour drive from Meru, and roads were washed out in many places by the recent rainy season. Once, Kay and I had to get out of the van to walk through the darkness up a hill in order to lighten the load.

We were greeted at the front door of Justus' home by the smiling faces of three other children and Eunice, their mother. The house was built by Justus and his relatives from hand-hewn rocks and was extra nice by African standards. Other family members lived nearby, and Justus' mother was in the kitchen preparing our three-course meal. The older children were quietly helping their grandmother as the night moved along. They were so proud of their "running water" which consisted of a pipe running from a spring, up the hill above the house, and passed by the kitchen cook stove where it heated a bit. When they took us to our bedroom, Justus proudly told us that the bath had hot water. I believe the fire in the kitchen went out before we got to the bathroom.

Following this evening meal, Justus said they always have family devotions before bedtime. He called the family back to the table for singing, Bible reading, and prayer. What a wonderful time of worship! We were familiar with the songs they chose. The Scripture was from Isaiah 40:31 (KJV), "They that wait upon the Lord shall renew their strength; they shall mount up with wings as eagles; they shall run, and not be weary, and they shall walk, and not faint." Not a sound came from these precious children during this entire time. Finally, it was time for the closing prayer. Kay and I were so touched at the way Justus recalled every concern we had expressed and asked for God's help and blessing for our needs.

The next morning we left with Justus for the tour of the 12-point circuit which included his home church. Just as we were leaving, Justus told me I would be preaching that morning. You could have knocked me over with a feather! You can guess where my mind was as we visited those churches en route.

I will never forget the sweet voices of the children, with faces beaming, singing their hearts out in each church along the way. In one of the churches the people proudly showed us their "resource room." The room was nearly bare with only a folding table and a few pieces of curriculum materials on it. The materials were tattered and yellowed from use and age. At another church we noticed tea bushes around the church and questioned Justus about these. He said selling tea leaves was the way they raised their funds to pay their benevolences (mission giving). A local lay person proudly showed us their framed certificate for paying 100% of their church's part for benevolences.

Then came the outdoor worship service. People were streaming into the open field from every direction. Most of them were not wearing shoes even though many had walked all morning just to be there. The presiding pastor of this 12-church circuit introduced both Kay and me and then asked Kay to say a few words. This was another surprise as neither of us knew we would be called on for anything. The crowd was very responsive to both of us. Women gathered the offering in large woven bags many tourists buy for purses. They were laden down with coins as they brought the offering back to the podium.

Following the outdoor service we were invited for lunch. The only thing Kay and I can remember about lunch was that we had roasted ears of corn. We were to pull the fully developed kernels from the ears to eat them. (It reminded us of shelling corn on the farm when we were growing up.) We were deeply concerned that there were so few eating. We, Justus, and the pastor were all we can remember being at the meal except for those who served it. We felt sad that 500 people had walked many miles since daybreak and would walk home with no lunch.

After lunch we were eager to see the Mother church where Justus and family belonged. He had shared so much about the Mother church helping build the other 11 churches on the circuit. So we walked a few yards toward a thicket of trees, and he told us the church was on the other side. We rounded the corner to find only a partially built church made out of cinder blocks. I said to Justus, "Where is the church? I thought you said this is the Mother church." Justus replied, "This *is* the Mother church. We wanted to help establish these other churches before we finished ours. Oh, we will soon have a nice church. You see, we had a harambe (when African people work together in unity and pool their resources for a special project), and we have all the funds we need to finish our church now." Justus explained that the other churches had come to the harambe and thereby generously returned enough funds to help the founding church build their own sanctuary.

I guess Kay and I were standing with our mouths dropped open because Justus said rather firmly to us, "Don't you remember the words of Jesus when He said, 'Seek ye first the kingdom of God, and his righteousness; and all these things shall be added unto you'?" (Matthew

6:33 KJV). We will never forget this lesson. Eunice prayed a beautiful prayer over us, then we got in Justus' van and started back to catch the bus to Nairobi.

All of a sudden Justus whipped the van into another church yard. We were a little disturbed by this because we were very conscious of the time, and we didn't want to miss our bus back to Nairobi. Kay said we needed to move on soon or we would be late for the return journey. Again, in the teaching tone of Justus, he said, "Just remember that the experience is much more important than the time."

We parked in the yard outside this church, and beautiful singing was wafting through the open windows. Kay said to Justus, "Is this church having a worship service this afternoon?" He replied, "No, they have come together for a time of praying and singing to encourage each other." Kay commented later that it would be so wonderful if churches in the western world took the time to come together just for singing, praying, and encouraging one another.

The World Methodist Conference that followed the Family Life Conference was truly an experience we will treasure all of our lives. Delegates of the Methodist tradition from all over the world were in attendance. It gave us a new perspective on the outreach and influence of our denomination through the past centuries. We will treasure these memories always, but we were now ready to get back to Louisville and take up the work of the district again.

One unhappy experience on the trip was Kay getting a light case of malaria. Even though we took all the recommended shots before going, she still got sick. She put up a good front as we went through customs for fear she would be sent to a local hospital. It took several weeks to fully recover, but we will always feel the trip was well worth the discomforts we experienced. I will always be grateful to Bishop Paul Duffey for naming me as a delegate and to our generous Louisville South District for making the trip possible financially.

Back home in the Louisville South District, there seemed to be a real interest in my helping start the Emmaus Walk movement in

Louisville. I got busy with the same process of organizing the Walk that I had experienced at Madisonville and Elizabethtown. Then from the Madisonville, Elizabethtown, and Louisville Walks to Emmaus, Walks were started in Indiana, Bowling Green, Cumberland County, and many other places. Someone has said that unless we attempt more than we can do, we will never do all that we can. I certainly felt I had taken on almost more than I could do with the Emmaus Walks, but I feel my involvement in the Emmaus Walk program made a strong statement about my life, my relationship with God, and my love for others.

These were Wally's last words to write. He became ill on February 24, 2009, following his introducing our revival speaker at Brandenburg United Methodist Church. Within three hours, he was in a coma from which he never recovered. I will share at the end of the book the events during those four days in Hardin Memorial Hospital in Elizabethtown, Kentucky, his Celebration of Life and Ministry service on March 3, 2009, and how God has walked this lonely road with my family and me.

I have delayed completing this book for several months. This task will not be easy. No one could tell Wally's life story as well as he, but he had put too much time and energy into this effort for me to leave his incomplete manuscript in a desk drawer or filing cabinet.

I know many of you reading this now have prayed for me and my family. I am so deeply grateful for your love and support, and I covet your continuous prayers.

Wally's priority in life was truly his relationship with God and love for others. From the time he was a little boy, his heart was to serve God. I believe God placed His hand on Wally at a very early age. He did take on more than he could do at times as he said in his last paragraph, but he was willing to do this because of his love for people and for His Lord.

As I try to go on with his book, I will rely heavily on Wally's journals as well as my own for the chronology of events. I wish so much that Wally could have finished the book because he would have added so much more to my comments.

———————————— Kate (Kay) Thomas ————————————

During these years on the Louisville South District, Wally developed a Five-Star Sunday School program for the district that seemed to energize churches to meet the five goals in this program. Most of the churches were willing to participate in this program, and we saw growth in the Sunday schools in our district.

We had a Louisville South District Sunday School Rally during which a person from each church walked into the sanctuary carrying their Sunday school banner. John Wesley was well portrayed by an actor that afternoon and added a special spirit to the event. Every year he had a "D-Lite Event" for training church leaders.

Wally and I together planned a district-wide "Catch the Family Spirit" conference. This was one of the most successful events during our six years on the district. The goal for this six-hour emphasis was to enhance the quality of the Christian home by exploring concerns and celebrating the family's potential. This event was held at Bethany United Methodist Church and neighboring churches pitched in and helped. United Methodist Women donated snacks and desserts for the catered dinner. Members of Bethany were wonderful in helping decorate the fellowship hall with colorful miniature hot-air balloons tied to baskets holding cut-out figures of families ready to take off! Churches throughout the district created beautiful banners around the theme of the event. These were in the sanctuary for the opening program and we moved to the fellowship hall for the dinner.

Every possible means was used to publicize the event. Letters were sent to every local church family coordinator. Bulletin inserts and posters were given in bulk to each church in the district. Three articles with registration forms were carried in the annual conference newspaper. The event was presented through a skit at a district United Methodist Women's Day Apart. A local radio station carried the announcement, and many personal contacts were made. The Wellspring Christian Bookstore set up an excellent array of books and materials related to family life.

Families sat together, played together, and sang together. Children and youth shared through a musical presentation for the closing service. Nine workshops were offered for adults, and activities were planned for every age group of children and youth. An abundance of free materials for strengthening the family was available. Each adult was given a nine-page handbook containing practical helps for families and churches.

We also had Valentine banquets and retreats for our parsonage families, and the Christmas dinners were always enjoyable. Six couples from our district performed in a Christmas Pantomime one year. It was hilarious—but not sacrilegious. Much of a pastor's life is so serious they need time for laughter. It's healing!

Our children were moving on in life. Debbie became engaged to a young, industrious farmer named Steve Caswell on September 13, 1987. David accepted a job at Bankers Trust Company in Atlanta and settled into his apartment there. During this time, he accepted his call to ministry and served as youth director at Glenn Memorial United Methodist Church on the Emory campus while he later attended Candler School of Theology. On June 21, 1987, he preached his first sermon at my home church, Parrish Chapel United Methodist Church, in Cumberland County. Ironically, Wally preached his first sermon there 31 years earlier in June of 1956.

It seemed life became more full with every passing day. Wally was elected in 1987 to lead the delegation of ministers from our former Louisville Annual Conference to our denomination's General

Conference in 1988. Debbie and Steve set their wedding date for March 26, 1988. Several showers were given for Debbie and Steve. One of our pastors' wives, Eleanor Brinson, generously hosted a shower for Debbie and invited all of the pastors' wives in our district. What a wonderful occasion this was!

I had to have surgery in October of 1987 and wondered if we could get all the preparation done for the wedding in March. While I was recuperating, I made all the gifts for the bridesmaids, maid-of-honor, and flower girl. By March, I was able to prepare most of the food for the wedding reception except the cake. I also invited all of our family on both sides who attended the wedding (about 30) to the district parsonage for a meal after the reception. God supplies our needs!

Debbie's wedding was a beautiful and meaningful occasion. Daffodils were in full bloom. We had around 500 in attendance. David gave her away, because Wally would be giving the vows. Debbie's pastor at St. Paul United Methodist Church in Louisville at that time was Dr. Emil McAdams. Dr. McAdams and Dr. Paul Shepherd, a long-time friend,

Wedding day for Debbie and Steve.

assisted Wally in the ceremony. Many kind and wonderful friends and family members assisted with the wedding, and we were so grateful.

During our last year on the Louisville South District, David chose Candler School of Theology for his seminary years even though he was offered a full scholarship to both the Yale and Harvard Divinity

Schools. Wally's six years on the district were completed in May of 1989. We had no idea where we would be sent next. Bishop Robert Spain, who became our bishop following Bishop Paul Duffey's retirement, spoke to Wally after one of the cabinet meetings. He said, "Wally, I have made four different lines of appointments. With every one of these, you come out at Christ Church United Methodist."

When Wally came home that day, he said he could tell I had a pretty good idea of where we were going to be sent. I said, "Wally, you know where we are going, don't you?" His answer was, "Yes, sit down." There is no experience quite like the anxiety that comes at appointment time.

According to my journal, my reaction to what Bishop Spain said was that I was almost numb. After several seconds passed, I said, "If love really works, that church will respond to us." I entered these words in my journal that day, *"Dear Lord, please help us. All glory is yours."* Bishop Spain met with the Christ Church Staff-Parish Relations

Bishop and Mrs. Robert Spain.

Committee on April 6, 1989. The committee wholeheartedly accepted us, and Bill Eaves was appointed as associate pastor.

Christ Church had the name of being the largest United Methodist Church in our conference at that time. Wally wanted to hear how other pastors went about serving larger churches, so the first thing he did was set up a meeting with Dr. Maxie Dunnam for April 18, 1989. Maxie was very helpful and shared many experiences he had while serving a large church in Memphis, Tennessee. (Ironically, Maxie had visited Wally at

Madisonville when he found out he would be pastor of Christ United Methodist Church, Memphis.) He encouraged Wally, as did many other friends. I will never forget that Bishop and Mrs. Paul Duffey sent us a Precious Moments figurine entitled "Expect a Miracle!"

Debbie and David sent us encouraging notes. Debbie sent these Scripture verses:

> "The joy of the Lord is your strength" (Nehemiah 8:10b KJV).
>
> "They that wait upon the Lord shall renew their strength" (Isaiah 40:31a KJV).
>
> "Lo, I am with you alway, even unto the end of the world" (Matthew 28:20b KJV).
>
> "The Lord is my light, and my salvation; whom shall I fear?" (Psalm 27:1a KJV).

She also suggested that her daddy ponder the words of the hymn "A Mighty Fortress Is Our God."

David sent Wally a letter in which he wrote:

> *"I continue to think more and more about you going to Christ Church. I am so glad for the reception you are having from the members there, and from many preachers. You are in excellent health, full of really amazing energy, and both of your children are relatively settled now into good lives. I don't know . . . it just seems that a whole lifetime of preparation, hard work, experience, and steadfast and consistent Christian living is culminating now as you move to Christ Church. You are equipped; you are ready. I don't think you have a thing to worry about . . . only great joys to anticipate.*
>
> *I just can't think of anything more important than prayer. God gives us opportunities that are beyond our own powers!! He prompts us in this way to depend on Him, thus*

ensuring greater successes than we could imagine. I am praying regularly for you. I am fasting every Wednesday morning's breakfast for your ministry at Christ Church and mine at Glenn Memorial. Just link up with Him, Dad! Marshall the vast resources of this great church to be a dynamo—a channel of God's grace—in Louisville."

With the blessings of our children and the presence of our Lord with us, we moved on to a new challenge at Christ Church United Methodist, trusting in our all-powerful God!

Chapter 10

CHRIST CHURCH UNITED METHODIST

Wally preached his first sermon at Christ Church United Methodist on June 4, 1989. It was wonderful having both of our children with us that day, and we were given a warm welcome. We attended a reception at 8:00 a.m. for those who would attend the 8:30 service, and another reception at 12:15 for the 11:00 attendees. Although we enjoyed our six years on the Louisville South District, we felt thankful to be back serving a church.

Debbie and Steve helped us finish packing the following day, and we moved to the Christ Church

Christ Church United Methodist.

parsonage that afternoon. Wally had a meeting to go to that first night, and he had a hard time finding a tie to wear. It brought back memories of our first night in Madisonville when our whole family was urged to attend a Sunday school class picnic on a sweltering hot evening, and we had no air-conditioning in the parsonage. There is nothing quite like having to go to a meeting on your first night in a parsonage!

We were grateful Debbie could stay with us for a week to help unpack. Church members brought an abundance of food which was a great blessing. On our second Sunday there, Wally and I visited different Sunday school classes. Sherry Jordan, our associate pastor's wife, and I joined the church that day. On June 13, I attended my first United Methodist Women's meeting. I enjoyed my experience with this group and served as Membership Chair during my four years at Christ Church. At the last meeting before we left, we honored 25 new members for that year. Christ Church has, through the years, had a strong United Methodist Women's group. When the former Woman's Society of Christian Service became United Methodist Women in 1968, Christ Church organized around 13 circles and interest groups.

Our first summer at Christ Church was a busy one: unpacking, getting acquainted, visiting Sunday school classes, performing weddings and funerals, and attending New Song at Camp Loucon, two family homecomings, and a conference at Lake Junaluska.

Attendance began to pick up in September from around 700 to 1,000, and we were having around 260 for the Wednesday night fellowship supper. The highlight of that September was the hiring of Dan Stokes from Belmont United Methodist Church in Nashville, Tennessee, as our new choir director. He still serves in this capacity today after these many years.

The parsonage was a large, comfortable brick home located near the church, but it needed much work done on it. Neither the microwave nor the wall oven worked. So the parsonage committee bought both of these items from a "scratch and dent" place in downtown Louisville. Neither appliance fit the space where the old ones were, so they were returned. When the replacements came, they were covered with smoke and had been salvaged from a fire. Eventually, things shaped up and the parsonage was renovated. Book shelves were added in the large den, chairs covered, and new draperies hung. Some partitions were added in the basement, creating an additional bedroom down there as well as a home office for Wally.

On January 1, 1990, Wally entered these words in his journal:

> *My spirit is humble as I begin this New Year. I have never seen more evidence of the power of God in my ministry than I have seen since coming to Christ Church. I know I am where God wants me to be. I also know I will need to read these words many times in the years ahead.*
>
> *I will always remember the day Sam Swope called and told me to come and pick out a new car. He said "Anyone who has the depth of commitment and caliber of leadership that you have, and any one who has done what you have done for Christ Church, deserves to drive a new car."*

Mr. Swope's encouragement and kind words blessed Wally so much that day. For the entire time we were at Christ Church, he provided a vehicle for Wally at the cost to the church of $1 per year. Wally was always so grateful for any kindness shown to him and, in turn, gave God the credit. He went on to say on the following page in his journal:

> *Whatever I am and whatever I have accomplished is because God is present in power and is the guide for my life. I want to begin this last decade of my active ministry with every part of my being committed to the One who made me a minister. God, please go with me into this year and make it a great year for You.*

I have always been touched by Wally's love and appreciation for his family. A few months later, Wally was anticipating our 34th wedding anniversary and entered these words in his journal on January 25, 1990:

> *Tomorrow Kay and I will celebrate our 34th wedding anniversary. We have had a wonderful marriage. We have seen our children grow up to be dedicated Christians and mature adults. I am thankful for the gift of Kay in my life. She has been so faithful and supportive . . . she is so sensitive and caring. I hope and pray we will continue to have good health and will have years together after retirement.*

I noticed Wally didn't pray for any specific number of years. He didn't even say he hoped for many years. He just said he hoped and prayed for years together. God saw fit to allow us to have 10 wonderful years together in our retirement home. On a lighter note, one thing I will always remember about our short 34th anniversary trip, which included a visit to Cincinnati, was a sign in a shoe shop window that read, WE CAN HEEL YOU AND SAVE YOUR SOLES. Wally didn't claim to have any gifts of healing, but his heart's deepest desire was to see souls saved.

Things were happening in the world along about this time. The Berlin Wall came down, and what a day of rejoicing that was! Communism fell in Czechoslovakia, Romania, East Germany, and Russia. On the home front, encouragement *and* discouragement seemed to be our daily fare. Attendance was up at Christ Church and the budget was underwritten. Yet there seemed to be an attitude among some of the members that was not conducive to growth.

The computer system in the church was in total disarray to the point that no computer repair shop was interested in working on the computers. Our friend from Meru, Kenya, Justus Muthee, sent us a note during this time simply saying, "His Son makes the very difference." Good advice! God makes the difference when computers are down or when our spirits are down. The Scripture I entered in my journal during this time was Zechariah 4:6b (KJV), *Not by might, nor by power, but by my Spirit, saith the Lord of hosts.* Following this verse I wrote these words, *Claimed for Wally's ministry at Christ Church. Whatever happens for good at Christ Church has to happen through God's Spirit working among us.*

Wally's parents' health was in decline. Mrs. Thomas fell and broke her hip and fractured her shoulder. Wally was often torn between loyalties. He loved his parents dearly, and he was constantly under the stress of where he was most needed. We tried to go to Glasgow every week, staying two or three days sometimes. When Wally couldn't go, I went alone. He often said he felt guilty most of the time. When he left things undone at Christ Church to see about his parents, he felt guilty all the way to Glasgow. Coming back to Louisville, he felt guilty all the way home because he couldn't help his parents longer. I marveled at how Wally carried this double load. As someone said of him, "Wally was a man of courage and character."

It was difficult to keep Wally's parents in their home. The help would only last for a time, and we would be back looking for assistance. We continued to make trips to Glasgow. I would usually take food, and while I was there, fix Mrs. Thomas' hair, and often cut both parents' hair. Wally's sister, Helen, was retired and lived nearby and she was a great help to her parents. Her husband, Doug, was also retired and was helpful as well. Wally continued to carry a load of guilt about where he was needed most.

Wally and I began plans to start a new young adult Sunday school class at Christ Church. I was told attempts had been made in the past to start a new young adult class, but these had failed. I knew the need was there and continued to talk to young adults who were not in a class. Our new class was a bit slow in getting off the ground, but after a few months it jelled. I treasure the memories with this group of young adults and all the special experiences we shared. We named ourselves "Partners in Christ" and worked hard at painting and fixing up the room. I made swag curtains for two walls of windows, and I believe they are still hanging today.

During this time David went to India as a part of a class assignment at Candler School of Theology. He became very ill while there and could not get antibiotics until he returned to London en route home. I well remember our concern when he called us and the only words we could understand were, "Mom, Dad, I'm in trouble!" No more communication for about three hours when we had another call from David. Even though we were sorry he was sick, we were relieved it was not something worse. At that time there was a good bit of bombing of buses in India.

Debbie stayed busy substitute teaching and working on the first presentation of the "Living Christmas Tree" in their church in Upton, Kentucky. This had been Debbie's dream since she and Steve married. The church got behind the idea, built the frame for the tree, and decorated the frame with beautiful greenery and lights. Other churches joined in and helped, and the program still continues periodically today.

Christ Church seemed to be moving along well. On March 15, 1990, Wally wrote these words in his journal:

> *What a wonderful day! We had 1640 in attendance and a $30,000 offering. The music was great. Everyone was happy. This day was a culmination of many things: healing of past hurts, a new spirit of unity, a ministry that looks both forward toward the future and outward toward people's needs.*

Around this time, a great joy came into our family! Debbie and Steve were expecting our first grandchild. I will never forget seeing the first ultrasound of the baby on March 8, 1991. To this proud grandma, the picture looked as though the baby was cradled in a hand, and to us, it was the hand of God. Little did we know then that approximately three years later, our Katie would be diagnosed as being on the autism spectrum. Her parents were told Katie had PDD or Pervasive Developmental Disorder, an "umbrella" term for covering all degrees of autism on the spectrum. This diagnosis was changed to autism a year later. The God who had her in His hand on the day of the ultrasound was the God who would carry us through all the challenges of autism later.

A few months later, Debbie was in Elizabethtown shopping when she felt the baby move for the first time. She said it thrilled her so much that, before she realized it, she was jumping up and down. Then she immediately looked to see who was watching. Our family joined her in her happy anticipation. Debbie was given several baby showers, and a dear friend from the new Partners in Christ Class, Sally Euson, provided her with 12 useful items for the baby including a baby bed.

Wally's dad was hospitalized with pin strokes in April of 1991 and went from the hospital to the nursing home in Glasgow. Wally's mom was still at home, but finding and keeping help for her was difficult. She later entered the same nursing home and shared a room with Wally's dad.

On September 24, 1991, my sister Jewell's husband, Elver Davis, fell and broke his hip. He died the following day after the surgery, and his funeral was two days later. Although Elver's health was declining, his sudden death came as a shock to everyone. Elver loved the Lord and had made a public acknowledgement of it and joined the church several years earlier.

Our granddaughter, Katie, was born on September 28, the day after Elver's funeral. The last 20 minutes of the delivery were difficult, and Katie was born just as the medical staff was contemplating a C-section. When Steve brought Katie out of the delivery room for us to see, her eyes were wide open. Due to the difficult delivery the last 20 minutes, she was placed for a time in the transitional nursery. Four pediatricians examined Katie, and all four said she was fine.

Debbie and Katie were discharged in two days, and I spent the following 11 days with them in their home. When Katie was 5 days old, her eyes followed a baby rattler and also focused on our faces. She responded to music and has loved music ever since. David flew in from Atlanta to see his new niece. They have a close attachment to this day.

David continued to serve as youth director at Glenn Memorial United Methodist Church during his seminary days. This was a successful yet challenging experience. Many of the youth were sons and daughters of teachers and staff at Emory. One of the parents became mentally ill and threatened David's life. Glenn Memorial paid for David to stay four nights in a hotel for his safety. The man received extensive counseling and later apologized sincerely to David.

For many years David participated in the Big Brothers of America program. He was given a little boy named David who lived in Louisville. We called him "Little David." Little David lived with his mom and two siblings in a car for many months. He seemed to love the times he visited us at the Louisville South District parsonage and he later visited us in the Christ Church parsonage also.

We were so pleased when Little David's mom and the man with whom she was living decided to allow Wally to perform their wedding ceremony. Now, Little David, his stepfather and his two children, and Little David's mother and her two other children could be a family. They moved to Brandenburg, so the wedding was in the United Methodist Church there. Jack Eller was pastor then, and he was very supportive in helping this family. Little David's mom found a wedding gown at a consignment shop. She didn't try it on until she got to the church, and found it to be at least six inches too long. I rushed around and found some masking tape, and taped a six-inch hem in it. It held throughout the wedding and the little reception we provided for them following the wedding ceremony.

Later, the whole family came to Christ Church for an 11:00 a.m. worship service. The parents and Little David's sister sat in the cab of the truck, and the four boys rode to church in the back. Our people welcomed them warmly when they went to the hospitality room for refreshments following the service. Some generous hearts gave them donations of money totaling $2,000. Our David still tries to stay in contact with Little David (who is no longer little!).

Our schedules at Christ Church continued to be full with weddings (Wally had 34 in one year), funerals, meetings on many nights during the week, and continuous trips to Glasgow to see about Wally's parents. Mimi Mulvey, a friend at Christ Church, said to "Just Philippians 4:8 it." I immediately looked up this Scripture in the KJV and found these words, "Finally, brethren, whatsoever things are true, whatsoever things are honest, whatsoever things are just, whatsoever things are pure, whatsoever things are lovely, whatsoever things are of good report, if there be any virtue, and if there be any praise, think on these things." That was good advice. Life can sometimes pull our spirits way down, but God can lift them way up if we will only concentrate on the good things in life!

After serving two years as Christ Church's Associate Pastor, Bill Eaves, announced he would be leaving at the next Louisville Annual Conference. Jean Watkins became the new Associate Pastor, and Paul Schultz was hired as church administrator. Wally took on an extra load by serving as chair of the Wesley Manor Retirement Community Board. It was at a time when things were at a low ebb there, and this responsibility was added to his already heavy load. However, Wally provided needed leadership at a crucial time for Wesley Manor.

In November of 1991, some young adult men from Christ Church began meeting with Wally each week for a prayer time in the parsonage. John "Rocky" Rawlings, Russ Wardlaw, Eric Martz, and Steve Yackey called themselves the "Covenant Group." This was a great blessing for Wally. We also had other church groups in the parsonage often. One year I prepared four different staff dinners and enjoyed all of them.

Wally and I needed to get away for a few hours, but often when we reached our destination, we would receive a call that there was a need at Christ Church or in our family. During one of the times away, we were called back home for the second time within a week due to deaths in the church. In times like these, nothing comforts like God's Word. Psalm 46:10a (KJV) says, "Be still and know that I am God." My friend, Anita Kuvin, reminded me of Psalm 37, which records the words of the psalmist David urging us to have confidence in God in times of struggle.

Anita's husband, Neil Kuvin, and Wally became good friends. He and Wally had breakfast together often. Neil grew up in the Jewish faith, but as time passed, he began to discuss Christianity with Wally. Neil began to realize there was more to God than he had experienced. He felt something was missing in his life. On the day after Thanksgiving, November 29, 1991, in Wally's office at Christ Church, Neil accepted Jesus into his heart. He has been a devoted, radiant Christian and a leader in Christ Church ever since.

Around this time two special people visited our church: Sir Alan and Lady Winifred Walker from Australia. They were giants in the faith and were such a blessing to our church. One thing that has always stood out in my memory of Sir Alan was that before he spoke, he always knelt in prayer behind the pulpit. Both Sir Alan and Lady Winifred spoke on the subject of Family Survival Techniques and were well received by our people.

In January of 1992, a Long-Range Planning Committee was formed. In March they came to a consensus as to priorities for Christ Church at that time. These priorities were:

- Grow spiritually.
- Reach out to the unchurched.
- Minister to the needy in Louisville, Kentucky, and the world.
- Encourage total participation in the Sunday school and worship services.
- Grow the church with new members.
- Study how to better utilize the church facility and expand as needed.
- Strengthen financial resources.

The committee seemed to have a meeting of the minds for moving forward.

Around this time Wally was asked to serve on the General Conference Commission for eight years. When General Conference was held in Louisville in May of 1992, he was a delegate again. Wally also served on the hosting committee for that Conference. Dr. Bill Hinson from Texas, who served what was at that time the largest United Methodist Church in the United States, was in Louisville for General Conference. He preached for both services at Christ Church on May 10.

The following day David was to graduate from Candler School of Theology at Emory University. Wally and I left immediately after the 11:00 service and headed toward Atlanta. We arrived in Atlanta just in time for the Covenant Service and the reception at Cannon Chapel. The following day brought joy to our hearts as David graduated first in his class.

David soon received the news that Bishop Robert Spain was appointing him to the Cave City-Highland Charge. On June 1, I flew to Atlanta to help him pack and also helped unpack in Cave City a few days later. I remember how the youth at Glenn Memorial kept coming by David's apartment to say their good-byes over and over. Lunch meetings took place every day, and at one point this mother said, "Dave, no more appointments until this apartment is packed!"

David was ordained deacon on May 21 at our Kentucky Annual Conference which met that year at Fourth Avenue United Methodist Church in Louisville. He settled in at Cave City in this first appointment out of seminary. He formed some very special relationships with the people of the Cave City and Highland charge. One of these was with an elderly lady in the Cave City United Methodist Church named Gladys Mouser. Gladys had married quite young and worked hard all her life alongside her husband in the motel business, which began to thrive after the opening of Mammoth Cave National Park in the mid-1940s. Gladys was at the motel seven days a week, rarely having time off throughout her life to go to church until her later years.

Gladys never had children and felt a kind of motherly connection with David when he became her pastor. That good chemistry became instrumental as Gladys began to respond to David's preaching with a desire for spiritual growth. He eventually had the privilege of sharing in Gladys' profession of faith and baptism, after which she described her life as more full of joy and purpose than she had ever known before.

The following year, after David moved to Hodgenville United Methodist Church, Gladys died from bladder cancer, crossing over into the heavenly reward she had become sure of. Not long after that, David was surprised to learn that Gladys had included him as residual beneficiary in her will, the full proceeds of which David passed along immediately to the Kentucky United Methodist Foundation. He believed that the blessings of knowing Gladys had come through the Kingdom of God, so this gift from her estate needed to stay in the Kingdom of God. Later on, he and Karen set up the Channel of Grace fund within the Kentucky United Methodist Foundation, which has supported worthy United Methodist projects ever since.

Wally and I attended the Jurisdictional Conference at Lake Junaluska, North Carolina, in the summer of 1992. During this time Wally served on the Episcopal Committee. A part of his responsibility was to interview candidates who, if elected, would serve as bishops in the Southeastern Jurisdiction of the United Methodist Church.

During the following days four new bishops were elected: Robert Fanning, Kenneth Carder, William Morris, and Jack Meadows. The question then was "Who will become the bishop of the Louisville Area?" Bishop Robert Morgan, who had been serving as bishop in Mississippi for eight years, was assigned as our bishop. Bishop Morgan and Martha led the Louisville Area for eight years. During this time the former Kentucky and Louisville Conferences merged and became known as the Kentucky Annual Conference.

Bishop and Mrs. Robert C. Morgan.

In August of 1992, Wally attended a Regional Church Conference in Oklahoma City. It was a helpful experience. When he returned he discovered a conflict within the leadership at Christ Church. A few people were attempting to circumvent the rotation system for church leadership that was firmly in place. Thankfully, this was a once-in-a-lifetime experience for Wally. Someone has said the only way conflict resolution takes place is when people of good will and common sense provide a system by which fair play is extended to all persons. A life of grace does not guarantee the absence of conflict. But a life of faithfulness to God, regardless of our circumstances, is what counts.

We had open house at the parsonage in October of 1992. Over 200 people came and were so proud of all the work that had been done on the parsonage and yard. Soon thereafter, we were notified of a burglary at Wally's parents' home. All of Mrs. Thomas' beautiful quilts were taken. Why would anyone take only quilts when the house was full of other valuable items? This will remain a mystery to us, but we were thankful that no more damage was done. In the midst of this challenge, our little Katie started walking. What a thrill to see one's first grandchild take her first steps! Again, joy was mixed with our struggles, which is typical in life.

In January of 1993, Bishop Morgan contacted Wally and said he needed him in the cabinet as a district superintendent. Bishop Morgan knew plans for a building program were now in place at Christ Church, and Wally would have to make a decision whether to stay the course through this building program or finish his last six years of ministry serving on a district. Bishop Morgan insisted Wally was his number one choice to come back into the cabinet.

Attendance was holding up well at Christ Church and the Staff-Parish Relations Committee voted unanimously for Wally's return. A few days later, Bishop Morgan offered Wally the choice of three open districts. Now that the two former conferences were united and district lines changed, both Wally's and my home churches were in what was then called the Campbellsville District (now the Columbia District). We felt it would be a blessing to serve in the district of our roots, and after much prayer, we decided this is where we should go.

Ten days later, Wally announced his leaving to the Christ Church congregation. The congregation was totally stunned! All afternoon, the phone rang off the hook, and a continuous line of people were at our door. One of the persons who had undermined Wally earlier called that afternoon with compliments on Wally's work. While this felt a bit like a stab, we remembered that no hurt is unknown to our Lord. He knew first-hand about betrayal. These experiences enable us to be a more effective "healed helper" as someone put it. God doesn't let any experience be wasted. He uses these experiences for someone's good and His glory.

On March 10, 1993, Katie had eye surgery to correct a problem of focus called strabismus. She came through this well and was a little trooper as she has been in everything she has faced. A short while after this, there were signs of autism although we didn't recognize them at the time. Her fanning her fingers out and her high-pitched squeals seemed fascinating to this grandma, and I certainly didn't see in them any warning of the struggle ahead. Around that time I entered in my journal, *"Katie is such a joy and delight and such a good child."*

In April of 1993, Wally and I felt we needed some time apart before he began his work on the Columbia District. We went to Fairhaven Retreat Center near Elizabethton, Tennessee. Nestled in beautiful Roan Mountain, this is an ideal place of respite for Christian workers. Over the years Wally encouraged and, at times, helped supply funds for pastors and spouses to go there for some rest, relaxation, and counsel when needed.

While we were at Fairhaven, we spent several hours with a wise counselor on the grounds. Wally shared how a few people at Christ Church wanted to control. The counselor suggested that the problem with persons who are determined to control is likely to stem from the evil one, or else they are dealing with authority issues in their past. The counselor pointed out that Wally's nature had been to absorb hurts. He said, "Wally, God has allowed you a graduate course in conflict management. This will help you relate to pastors and spouses in your new district who are dealing with antagonists in the churches." He went on to say that Wally's serving Christ Church was within the sovereignty of God, and the problems were there before Wally arrived. He added, "Wally, you were of the right nature for the need."

We returned to our parsonage refreshed and ready to move on. Easter was near, and we enjoyed going to David's Tenebrae service at Highland United Methodist Church near Cave City. Easter dawned bright and beautiful on April 9, 1993. A huge crowd of 1,860 attended our last Easter service at Christ Church. Debbie, Steve, and Katie were there for the 11:00 service. David had 144 people in attendance at Cave City, which more than filled the sanctuary.

Wally left for the cabinet meeting the following day. On Tuesday I gave the devotional at our United Methodist Women's meeting. Many kind words were spoken on my behalf. One lady presented me with a birthday cake she had made. She also had a huge, over-sized birthday card that read, "We had to find you a card big enough to hold all of our love!"

A week later, David and Sally Euson hosted a Partners in Christ Sunday School Class going-away dinner for us at their home. It was a memorable event. I still have the picture of this group hanging in my home. Class members showered us with gifts, and the church administrator and his wife presented a "Wally and Kay Rap" song. I continue to keep up with several of these couples, many of whom have scattered throughout the country. I wish I could include every Sunday school class God has allowed me to help start.

Partners in Christ Sunday School Class.

Three days later, Katie came down with pneumonia. This news was followed by the word from a neighbor in Brandenburg that our retirement home had flooded. We were using my deceased parents' old washer and dryer, and the hose to the washer burst. The house had water damage in the upstairs and basement. As I mentioned earlier, times of struggle seem to follow times of joy and vice versa. But through it all God is with us!

Many of our last evenings at Christ Church were filled with dinners in the homes of members and potluck dinners with Sunday school classes. David preached for the first time at Christ Church during our final weeks there. Following annual conference, we attended our going-away reception at Christ Church. What a lovely occasion! People stood in line for two hours to say kind words to us. Packing then began in full swing and dinners in homes continued every night for a week.

The Christ Church newsletter on May 23, 1993, read as follows:

> *"Dr. Wallace Thomas was appointed by the former Bishop Robert Spain to be Senior Pastor at Christ Church effective June 1, 1989. His orders from the bishop were clear: restore order, bring healing, and give direction to the church so that it would be effective and a strong institution in the 1990s and beyond. Through Dr. Thomas' efforts over the past four years, his mission has been accomplished. We are now a more unified and cooperative church. Our congregation is not only larger but also warmer. Our level of enthusiasm is higher. There is a strong feeling of positive momentum. Most importantly, our church and its people are more spiritual. We are closer to God. His spirit is moving among our membership, enabling us to more effectively do His work.*
>
> *Under Dr. Thomas' tenure, a Strategic Plan has been developed and implemented; Sunday school attendance has increased; job descriptions and evaluations have been written and have been completed for all staff members; 100% of our apportionments are being paid; a pension plan for staff members has been established; key programs in areas such as evangelism, stewardship, and the singles ministry have been fortified. Our church has dramatically improved its missions and outreach effort through the development and growth of the Portland Mission. These are a few of the more formal activities that Dr. Thomas has developed and fostered. One cannot count nor fully appreciate the hours engaged in hospital and home visits,*

marital counseling, and both scheduled and impromptu individual counseling. One thing is for sure: Dr. Thomas was always there for the members of his congregation no matter what hour of the day, no matter what day of the week.

Our congregation will not soon forget the positive spirit and Christian presence that Kay Thomas brought to Christ Church. Her influence and leadership are evident in all aspects of our Church life: counseling and inspiring young mothers, serving as the Membership Chairperson of United Methodist Women, starting four new UMW circles, beginning the Partners in Christ Class for newly married persons. Kay has left her mark on this Church. Her impact will be felt for many years to come.

Each of us has been touched by Wallace and Kay Thomas in some fashion during their stay at Christ Church. During the last days of their stewardship, take time to reflect upon their impact on your life and their personal display of Christian living and discipleship. Take a moment to wish them well.

God bless both of you. Thank you for everything over the last four years.

Signed: The Christ Church Staff-Parish Relations Committee

Our final Sunday was on May 30, 1993, and we packed all day on Monday. The movers loaded the van from 9:00 a.m. until 2:00 pm. We reached the district parsonage in Campbellsville at 8:30 that evening. Food was waiting in our kitchen, and the lawn was freshly mown. Wally and I were excited to be sent to the district of our choice and happy that the last six years of our active ministry would be lived out where our home churches were located. We had now come full circle and had learned over and over again that we can trust Paul's promise "We can do all things through Christ who strengthens us" (Philippians 4:13 NKJV).

Chapter 11

COLUMBIA DISTRICT

In June of 1993, we arrived at what was then the Campbellsville District parsonage. This house was spacious with an office and private entrance in the basement. Like many other parsonages, it needed some renovation. We soon began to look at the needs of the district parsonage which included landscaping in the yard.

There were 55 appointments under Wally's supervision in this district. Among the pastors with whom Wally would be working were 13

Columbia District Pastors' Retreat.

elders, five probationary members, five associate members, seven full-time pastors, 15 part-time pastors, and 10 student pastors.

On June 13, 1993, I joined the First United Methodist Church in Campbellsville, Kentucky. Wally and I went to our district reception in the afternoon at Lindsey Wilson College in Columbia, Kentucky. Each county in the Campbellsville District (later named the Columbia District) brought gifts for us and made us feel welcome to our home district.

The following Sunday we went to my home church, Parrish Chapel United Methodist Church in Cumberland County where Wally and David had preached their first sermons. This was Father's Day and the annual homecoming. That afternoon we went to Albany for another reception which represented Cumberland, Clinton, and Russell Counties. My sisters, Geneva Teal and Jewell Davis, and other members of my family came to this reception.

Invitations to speak in various churches in the district began coming to Wally, and he accepted all he could fit into his schedule. Our district picnic was held two weeks after we moved. Attendance was good at the picnic, as was the spirit among the pastors and spouses.

A week later, we left for Lake Junaluska, North Carolina, for the annual Ministers' Week. We enjoyed the fellowship as the two cabinets from the Louisville and Kentucky Conferences met together for meals and time with Bishop and Mrs. Morgan. We came back by Glasgow to check on Wally's parents.

As we started to leave the nursing home, Mr. Thomas said, "Does he know any?" Wally wondered what he meant, but when we asked Mr. Thomas "Any what?" he didn't answer. Then I asked him if he was referring to Scripture verses, and again he didn't answer. So I shared my favorite verse which is John 14:27 (KJV). "Peace I leave with you, my peace I give unto you: not as the world giveth, give I unto you. Let not your heart be troubled, neither let it be afraid."

Wally shared his favorite verse which is Philippians 4:13 (NKJV), "I can do all things through Christ who strengthens me." I then said, "And

Psalm 23 is good, too." Mr. Thomas nodded approval, so I suggested we say it together. I began the first part of every verse, and he completed each of them. When we got to the last verse, I said, "And I will dwell in the house of the Lord . . . ," and Mr. Thomas immediately formed his version of the last part of the verse as he said, "forever . . . and ever . . . and ever!" I said, "It will be a good house, won't it?" and he replied "Absolutely!" Wally and I later recalled these precious moments many times.

On October 17, 1993, Mr. Thomas went to the house of the Lord. His funeral and burial were in Glasgow, Kentucky. Mr. Thomas was a good, kind, and gentle man, and a devoted husband, father, grandfather, and father-in-law. I will always remember what he said before Wally and I married. He told Wally and Mrs. Thomas that if he ever said anything that he shouldn't around Wally's new wife, he would just take old Thomas (referring to himself) out behind the house and give him a good talkin'. That was never to happen.

Every year the Columbia District held the Acton Camp Meeting at the camp ground near Campbellsville. Wally preached the first camp meeting as was the custom for the new district superintendent. We always enjoyed this experience, and people in the district supported the services. Plenty of lemonade was always available. Katie and Debbie were with us for this first camp meeting. During the week, Katie became very sick and ran a temperature of over 103 degrees. We took her to the local pediatrician and she soon improved. Our family claimed the verse from Isaiah 59:1 (KJV) which says, "Behold, the Lord's hand is not shortened, that it cannot save; neither his ear heavy, that it cannot hear."

Our schedules became busier by the day. Wally visited the pastors and families until it was time to attend the District Superintendent's School at Lake Junaluska. I began to speak in various churches, and we had the annual district potluck meal at the Columbia United Methodist Church.

Mrs. Dorothy Radford, my former elementary school teacher, along with David and me, began making plans for a special youth event in Cumberland County. We called it Heart to Heart, and it was held in the First United Methodist Church in Burkesville where Wally and I were married. We had activities planned for all age groups and had a great turnout. After one of the planning meetings, I heard hymns flowing from an outside speaker at the Christian Church on the square in Burkesville. I parked the car and listened to the old hymn "O They Tell Me of a Home" which was one of my daddy's favorite hymns. It was followed by "How Beautiful Heaven Must Be" which I had heard my mother sing many times. This blessed me so much because I had lost both of them in recent years. Here I was in my hometown hearing the music of my parents' favorite hymns permeating the atmosphere. It felt like they were smiling on our Heart to Heart plans.

Wally completed his first round of charge conferences in November of 1993 and soon it was time for our District Christmas Dinner. Our first District Christmas Dinner in the Lindsey Wilson College dining room was attended by 84 people. I decorated the tables and placed a hand-made favor for the pastors' spouses on each table. It was such a wonderful experience we decided that night to have all the district dinners there. The food was excellent, the personnel were so nice and helpful, and the college is located near the center of the district.

On December 25, our family celebrated our first Christmas in the Columbia District. David came from Cave City and Debbie, Steve, and Katie came from Upton. Katie loved this parsonage. It was roomy and had a nice swing on the back porch. She and I sat out there many times, looking at the lake and singing her favorite songs.

Soon after our Christmas gift exchange, David left for the Urbana Missions Conference. It was at that conference David felt the presence of the Lord in a very special way. Little did he know that attending the same conference was his future wife, Karen Muselman. However, they didn't meet until several months later. I like to think the Lord knew then that David would meet Karen in the future.

In January of 1994, I had all the pastors' wives to the district parsonage for a soup, sandwich, and dessert luncheon. Each person brought their favorite soup, and I made a big kettle of chili using home-canned tomatoes. The following day Wally led the District LITE Day (Leadership, Inspiration, and Training Experience) and returned home just as a major snow storm began. Snows always excited Wally and me. He loved homemade snow cream and always expected me to make popcorn balls with black walnuts to enjoy during the snow event.

Well, I didn't get to do these things during that snow. Instead I ended up in the emergency room of Taylor County Hospital. In the night I began to hemorrhage profusely and needed to go to the emergency room, but we couldn't get either of our vehicles out of our garage and up the steep hill behind the house. Finally, we remembered that our neighbor and pastor at that time, Gene Weddle, had a four-wheel-drive vehicle and he graciously let us borrow it.

After the tests and a colonoscopy, the doctor concluded I had diverticulitis, and he questioned what I had eaten the day before. I told him about my chili made with home-grown tomatoes, and that disclosure pretty well confirmed that the tomato seeds were the culprits.

I soon regained my strength and helped David start a new unit of United Methodist Women for the Cave City-Highland Charge. A week later, I spoke on God's Healing Touch at the Campbellsville First UMC. I had just experienced God's healing touch and could share of my personal experience of healing.

It wasn't long before David received a call from Bishop Robert Morgan saying he needed David at Hodgenville. David felt he was just beginning to get things moving at the Cave City and Highland churches, and he shared that with Bishop Morgan. Bishop Morgan was sure about his need for David to go to Hodgenville. David had promised to go where he was sent, so he agreed. This was the annual conference when David was ordained Elder in full connection, the final step in the ordination process. It was also the year he was asked to speak to the annual conference regarding the possibility for renewal in our annual conference. His message was entitled A Passage of Pain.

David's entire lifetime in the United Methodist Church has been a generation of denominational decline, a trend he and everyone desperately longed to see reversed. David became convinced the work of renewal was more than what human effort and ideas alone could generate. He shared with Bishop Morgan, in a paper entitled A Passage of Pain, that we could not program ourselves into vitality. Only God can renew the church. And He can do this when we get into the grips of heartfelt honesty, allowing the burden of reality to bend our knees in prayer.

Bishop Morgan asked David to share his thoughts with the Uniting Commission that had been appointed to explore the merger of the former Kentucky and Louisville Annual Conferences. This group endorsed David's delivering the same message at the sessions of each annual conference in the spring of 1994, a tremendous honor for David and the key step that led to the gathering of a statewide Concert of Prayer in Frankfort in early 1995.

Two weeks after David arrived in Hodgenville, the youth director there, Clark Hewitt, mentioned to David that he knew the exact girl David should meet. He told David he had studied him ever since he was appointed to Hodgenville UMC two weeks earlier, and he felt he and Karen Muselman, Clark's classmate at Asbury Seminary, would be a great match. David's reply was "Give me her phone number!" David and Karen met in Louisville soon after this, and it is very evident that God was in that match-making!

David and Karen continued to see each other regularly. Karen visited us in Campbellsville in November, and we loved her immediately. We also appreciated the gifts she brought us from her hometown of Berne, Indiana: chocolates, Amish popcorn, and other items.

David brought Karen to our District Christmas Dinner that year. Afterwards, my friend, Brenda Loy, who met Karen at the dinner, called to say how much she liked her. I entered in my journal a verse of

Scripture Karen shared with Wally and me. It was I Corinthians 15:58 (KJV) "Therefore, my beloved brethren, be ye steadfast, unmovable, always abounding in the work of the Lord, forasmuch as ye know that your labor is not in vain in the Lord." That was good advice for us in our first year on the district.

In January, Wally and I left for St. Simons Island in Georgia for the jurisdictional District Superintendents' Conference. We worshiped at Brentwood UMC in Nashville, Tennessee, en route to St. Simon's Island. Cal Turner, Jr., who was a member of Brentwood, had heard of our conference's plans to have a Concert of Prayer and donated $5,000 to assist with it. The Concert of Prayer was held the following month, and this donation was greatly appreciated. David had heard of the Concert of Prayer idea and felt strongly that it could be a blessing for our area. It was held in Frankfort and some 3,500 people attended from both annual conferences in Kentucky. The sight of our bishop and conference leaders on their knees praying will be forever etched in my memory.

After the District Superintendents' Conference, Wally and I spent one night in Hilton Head to celebrate our 39th wedding anniversary. We went from there to Glasgow to see Wally's parents. The following week we attended the pastors' school at Asbury Seminary. Karen was a student at Asbury at that time, and we, David, and Karen attended some classes together.

When we returned from these trips, a faithful prayer warrior, Mrs. Dorothy Radford, called to encourage us in our work in the district. I had Mrs. Dorothy as my elementary school teacher for seven years. She was an encourager then, too. She encouraged me to enter the county spelling bee three different times. Even though I never won, it meant a lot to me to have a teacher encourage me and believe in me. She is 86 at the time of this writing and is still a faithful prayer warrior to this day. She continues to call and encourage us and prays for our family and a host of other people every day. Oh, how our pastors and families need persons who will commit to prayer and encouragement.

On March 16, 1994, David invited me to go with him to Madisonville to get the engagement ring he had ordered for Karen. It was a special and exciting day. I remember that after he picked up the ring, we went to the prayer chapel at First United Methodist Church and committed their future to the Lord.

The following Sunday, Wally and I went to Lawson Bottom UMC to visit that struggling congregation. There were only five or six persons present. We left with sad hearts because it looked inevitable that the church would soon be closing. Church closings were always announced at annual conference, and this was a time we dreaded each year. Communities change and people leave farms to find employment elsewhere. Members who are left grow old and cannot carry on in keeping a church going, but it is still sad to see many of our rural churches declining and dying. However, we were so thankful and pleased that during our years in the Columbia District we also saw many churches revived and renewed.

We believed emphasis on the Sunday school helped in the growth in many of the churches. But the experience that probably helped the most to renew enthusiasm and commitment to work harder to help churches grow was the workshop led by Dr. Rose Sims. Dr. Rose, as she liked to be called, was a pastor in Florida who agreed to be appointed to the Trilby United Methodist Church, a dying congregation. With the Lord's help, this church was restored and became a vibrant congregation. She told our people, "If Trilby can do it, any church can do it!" Dr. Rose and her husband, Jim, led the workshop at Lindsey Wilson College, and Wally and I often recalled the good attendance and renewed enthusiasm among our pastors that day. Many bought the book by Dr. Rose about the rebirth of Trilby Church. Wally and I kept in touch with Dr. Rose over the years, and she has been a faithful prayer warrior for Katie.

On March 21, 1994, David proposed to Karen. Two weeks later Karen and her parents came for dinner with David and us in Campbellsville. The following day we all went to Louisville to make plans for the wedding at Christ Church, for the reception at the Seelbach Hotel, for lodging for the family at the Holiday Inn, and also met with the florist. Wally and I left the following day for Montgomery, Alabama, to visit Bishop and Mrs. Duffey. We took turns driving all the way because both of us were totally exhausted.

On April 27, 1994, Debbie and Steve took Katie to Elizabethtown for evaluation by the Child Evaluation Center associated with the University of Louisville. I heard the concern in Debbie's voice when she called to give us the report. They were told Katie might be mildly autistic and that she could be tested further later. They also speculated Katie might have a thyroid problem. The person who did the testing said Katie seemed like a bright child and seemed to absorb everything, but she was given the label of PDD. Tests later disproved the thyroid problem.

After Debbie's call, I went immediately to the local library in Campbellsville. I pored through all the books related to autism, which were not many at that time. Katie's pediatrician agreed with Katie's parents for her to wait another year for further testing, and she said she had suspected autism since Katie was 6 months old. I will never understand why a doctor would delay talking to parents if this possibility existed. Starting therapies early is so crucial in order to help children with autism.

Later on, Katie was tested at the Weisskopf Child Evaluation Center at the University of Louisville. She saw a speech-language pathologist, a developmental pediatrician, a psychologist, and an autism consultant. The team concluded Katie should have the label of autism even though they were reluctant to give it. In order for her to receive the services she would need, however, they had to give the diagnosis. We will always hold on to the threads of hope expressed to the family that day.

One book that inspired me the most during these days was *Let Me Hear Your Voice* by Catherine Maurice. Catherine had two children with autism, and both are normal today. Catherine shared her desperation for help, and her mother told her that they needed to storm heaven with prayer. They organized a prayer chain, and this inspired me to do the same for Katie.

I wrote 50 letters to persons who believe in prayer. I asked them if they would be willing to take one day each week and pray for Katie. Every single one of them said yes. A few members of the prayer team have already gone to Heaven, but nearly all of them are still praying today after these 16 years have passed. I entered in my journal at this time these words from Matthew 8:17b (RSV), "He took our infirmities and bore our diseases." I know God is working in Katie's life, and that keeps my hope alive.

Katie has been and is a joy to our family. One day she took Wally by the hand and set him down in front of the curio cabinet which contained many figurines of the birth, life, crucifixion, and resurrection of Jesus. As they sat there studying the contents of the curio cabinet, she began singing "Jesus Loves Me." These were precious moments with Grandpa.

On May 6, 1994, we finished dividing up the furnishings in Wally's parents' home so Wally's nephew and his wife could move into the house. We had a wonderful visit with Mrs. Thomas in the nursing home afterward. It was her birthday. I wrote in my journal after that visit:

> *We had a sweet visit with Mrs. Thomas today. I thanked her for the things Wally would inherit. She told me how much she loved me and what a good daughter-in-law she felt I have been. She said, "Kay, we never have had a short word, and we always worked so good together, didn't we?" I assured her this was true. Then we recalled memories of many good times together.*

Now, back to David and Karen's wedding. On September 1, 1995, Karen's bridesmaids' luncheon was held at Jean Flowers' home in Hardin County. That night we went to the Louisville Boat Club for the rehearsal dinner. We were able to have it there due to the kindness of our friends, Jim and Sue Syers, who were members of the Boat Club.

This was a beautiful evening. The food was excellent, and the sharing was even better. Many testimonies were given, some of which were funny and some serious. Wally and I remember the eloquent words of Karen's dad when he said, "Marriage is an experience of taking one through the hallowed halls of the highest human happiness."

The wedding day is a beautiful memory. The busy morning was filled with the ladies' hair appointments and getting pictures taken. Bishop Morgan described the wedding ceremony as being one of "the most energized services I have ever attended." David sang "Arise My Love" as Karen listened and waited before entering the sanctuary at Christ Church. Between 850 and 900 people attended the wedding from 22 states and Costa Rica.

Angels were watching over things that day, too. When the wedding party reached the Seelbach Hotel in downtown Louisville where the reception was held, it was suddenly evident that Sarah, Karen's little 3-year-old niece, was not with the group. It was one of those times when each person thought Sarah was with someone else. Fortunately, Sheila Gilbert, a member at

Wedding day for David and Karen.

Christ Church found Sarah and took care of her until her parents could return to the church.

Soon after the wedding, Wally became busy again with New Life Gatherings (charge conferences) all over the district. On November 4, we had all the retired pastors and wives to the parsonage for a Thanksgiving meal, and we continued to do this during our six years in the district.

My brother, Allen Radford, had open heart surgery on June 30, 1995. About six weeks later, he had surgery for a hernia. Allen had been told to do anything he felt like doing, but on October 4 he had a heart attack while walking in the city park. A cousin of mine died the same day and both bodies were in the funeral home at the same time. Wally officiated at Allen's funeral on October 8, in Burkesville, Kentucky, with burial in the city cemetery.

In January of 1996 we returned to St. Simons for another Jurisdictional District Superintendents' Conference. We stopped in Glasgow en route to check on Mrs. Thomas. Coming home, we spent one night in Charleston, South Carolina, for our 40th anniversary. Wally and I exchanged anniversary cards, and they turned out to be identical. We had even underlined the same words! When we returned home, David and Karen and Debbie and Steve gave us a nice 40th anniversary dinner at the Hodgenville UMC. The roads were iced over, but we still had a wonderful turnout of family and friends.

The following week, Wally had a Growing the Sunday School Workshop in Burkesville for the entire district. This was a very helpful experience. I later led a Sunday school workshop for the United Methodist Churches in Cumberland County.

Dr. Ron Crandall led a workshop in our district on Inviting People to Church. Slowly but surely, growth was taking place in our churches. Wally spent a lot of his time working with struggling and discouraged churches. The lay people of the district seemed to continue to hear in their hearts what Dr. Rose Sims had said earlier, "If it can happen at Trilby Church, it can happen anywhere!"

Wally always believed there is hope for renewal in many of our churches. I hold on to that hope as well. One church in our district decided to close for lack of attendance. After some time passed, it happened that a few couples came to the church one Saturday afternoon. No one knew that anyone else was coming. They all were grieving over the closing of their church, and they spent time at the altar in prayer. After an extended prayer time, they agreed to re-open their church. They also agreed they must develop a ministry to the children in the area if they hoped to reach the young adult parents.

So this small group began to meet regularly for worship and prayer. They bought nice playground equipment, had a Vacation Bible School, and started other programs for children and youth. Soon the church came alive and is going strong today. The truth in Dr. Rose Sims' words resounded in their hearts.

Wally was so proud of the 13 churches which had grown enough to be called Turnaround Churches. He also had 36 churches in the Columbia District that were designated as Vital Congregations by the annual conference. Wally insisted every pastor in the Columbia District make sure there was a directional sign to each of their churches. He was always so pleased to come up on one of these many signs throughout the district, and he was pleased with all the churches who responded to suggestions for growth and improvement.

A great blessing came to the Columbia District through Wally's helping establish a Methodist Opportunity Store in Burkesville. There was a need in this area for an extension of the Methodist Mountain Mission Store in eastern Kentucky. When Wally first mentioned this idea to me, I wondered if it would ever become a reality. So often with Wally, when he was convinced of a need among people and when he also saw a possibility to meet that need, he set out to bring it to pass. Today, the Methodist Opportunity Store in Burkesville has blessed untold numbers of people. Many people come from neighboring towns to shop in this mission store.

Recently, a single father raising a teenage daughter had lost his mobile home in a fire. Everything was destroyed, but thankfully, no one was hurt. My sister, Jewell Davis, called the Methodist Opportunity

Store and explained this family's desperate need. Her son, Daryl, met the father and daughter at the store and helped them load their needed items. The store manager told them to pick out anything they needed, and it would be free. Jesus said, "Inasmuch as ye have done it unto one of the least of these my brethren, ye have done it unto me" (Matthew 25:40b KJV).

Wally and I were continuously trying to help meet Katie's needs. We began attending workshops on autism whenever possible. Our first one was on How to Prepare an IEP (Individual Education Program). Debbie and Steve joined us for this one. The whole idea of an IEP was Greek to us, but we were committed to seeking information on autism any way we could. I continued to read and research autism. When I couldn't find a certain book in the local library, I borrowed it through the inter-library loan program.

David and Karen gave wonderful support in behalf of Katie. On March 28, 1996, Debbie and Steve and we met with David and Karen at their parsonage in Hodgenville. David recounted the positive things he had learned at an autism conference. We viewed a video from Dr. Bernard Rimland who was an authority on autism in California. Dr. Rimland had researched the benefits of vitamin therapy using concentrated doses of vitamin B6 and magnesium. The urgency to do everything possible for Katie as soon as we could was heavy on our hearts. Katie's parents used this therapy for a while. However, most authorities on autism agree it is a combination of therapies that brings the best results.

Every passing day was crucial. We were committed to do everything in our power to help Katie, as well as rely on God's guidance and wisdom. A year had already passed since Katie's original diagnosis of PDD. At the end of our session together in Hodgenville, Karen offered to prepare a scrapbook-type binder for Katie about all the things in Katie's life. She did this, and it was a beautiful work of art which Katie enjoyed and still has today.

Soon it was time for another revival at Camp Acton. This time Dr. Howard Olds was the preacher. We enjoyed Howard and his wife Sandy so much. Howard was a great preacher, and people responded to his messages. He decided to offer a prize to the person with the best attendance. On the last evening, Howard asked for a show of hands for those who had attended every service, but no hands went up. He had clued Wally and me that there likely would be no person in attendance on the last night who had come to every service. He said if this happened, he wanted us to have something to give to the neighborhood dog as he made his nightly stroll in front of the podium.

So I made a big "grand champion" blue ribbon with tape on the back that would stick to the dog long enough for him to walk proudly in front of the congregation. Sure enough, about the time Howard asked if anyone had attended every service of the revival and no hands went up, here came the dog walking happily as usual in front of the congregation. Wally slapped the blue ribbon on the dog. He acted like he was expecting the award and just kept going right on. The crowd broke up with laughter.

Perfect Attendance Award, Acton Camp Meeting.

In August of 1996, we went to the uniting service for the Louisville and Kentucky Conferences. Dan Stokes from Christ Church directed the choir which numbered several hundred people. It was estimated there were 13,500 people in attendance for this historic event. Not long after this occasion, the 14 previous districts were re-aligned to make 12 districts. This is when the Campbellsville District was re-named the Columbia District. The district parsonage was later located in Columbia.

In September of 1996, we had our first Ministers' Wives Retreat since the conferences united. We were blessed to have Dr. Evelyn Laycock as our keynote speaker. We drew prayer partners at the opening session. Our name tags were made from colored paper in the shape of the state of Kentucky. The state had been cut in half, and each person had to find her matching half. I thought I would never find my prayer partner and realized Dr. Laycock was still searching for her matching half, too. You guessed it! Our halves of the state matched, and we are still prayer partners today. What a blessing Dr. Laycock has been to Wally and me over the years. Wally came to know her when they sat on the Hymnal Revision Committee at the 1992 General Conference. We have shared many experiences at Lake Junaluska together as well.

That year the ministers' spouses put together a cookbook with recipes from all the districts. Each district was assigned a specific category of food. The recipes were sent to me for editing and for finding a printer who would copy and bind the books. What a task! Several wives in our district helped complete the project, and we packed the boxes of recipe books in the trunk of my car. When I arrived at the retreat site, I injured my back as I lifted boxes of books out of the car. I was miserable for several days.

I wanted so much to attend a Christian Writers' Conference in Nashville a few days later on October 4-5, 1996. I felt a call on my life to write, and I had published a few articles at that time. My friend, Joyce Joines, who lived in Madisonville and was interested in writing as well, offered to go with me and to help me walk. We had attended a writers' conference at Taylor University in Upland, Indiana, earlier, and it blessed both of us. (We later learned that David's future wife, Karen Muselman, was attending Taylor at the time we attended that writers' conference.)

So off to Nashville we went. I could barely put one foot in front of the other, and I leaned heavily on Joyce's shoulder. I remember waking up in the night to go to the bathroom and being determined I wouldn't wake up Joyce. So I crawled toward the bathroom. As I turned the corner of my bed, I broke down in tears from the pain and I cried out to God in a whisper, "OK, Lord, if I am to be crippled for the rest of my life, I'm yours. Use me!"

The next day I sat alone in the large meeting room at the motel. Even though I wanted so much to attend the workshops, walking was just too painful. I decided to wait while others attended workshops, and I felt grateful that at least I could hear the keynote speaker in the large meeting room.

Donna Goodrich from Mesa, Arizona, who was a part of the staff at the writers' conference, happened to have some free time and sat down by me. I shared with Donna how I longed to see a Kentucky Christian Writers Conference established near the center of our state. She quickly replied, "Well, why don't you start one?" I told her I didn't know how to start a writers' conference. She confidently said, "I will help you." That is how the Kentucky Christian Writers Conference began. We had our 15th conference in 2011, and Donna Goodrich flew in from Mesa, Arizona, to be with us.

Later in 1995 during the month of October, David preached a revival in my home church, Parrish Chapel UMC in Cumberland County. Wally and I attended one service. Five people joined the church as a result of that revival, and three were baptized. Two of these were older men. I believe the Holy Spirit, along with the visits with prospects by David and Mrs. Dorothy Radford, helped bring about the responses from these five persons. I entered these words in my journal after this revival: *"Thank you, Lord, for still saving souls!"*

A highlight of Christmas that year was David and Karen presenting a program of music for our District Christmas Dinner at Lindsey Wilson College. Another highlight was for David, Karen, Steve, and Debbie to join us at the Executive Inn in Louisville for dinner during the Christmas season. During our eight years at Shively a part of our Christmas experience was going to the Executive Inn for a meal and hearing the beautiful violinists play. David played the violin in the Louisville Youth Orchestra for six years, and this was an extra special experience for him. Our friend, Tony Fontane, gave us the money for our first experience at the Executive Inn (about $20 took care of the four meals back then!). Wally and I saved enough money to do this each year until we moved to Madisonville.

On March 2, 1997, Wally called me from the cabinet meeting to say that Bishop Morgan had asked him to leave the cabinet meeting for one hour that day. When Wally returned, Bishop Morgan told him that he was sending David to Centenary. Wally immediately asked him which Centenary, and Bishop Morgan replied, "Lexington."

Wally's immediate response was, "You can't do that, Bishop." The bishop reminded Wally that he was the bishop, and he *could* do this. He said, "This was not a cabinet decision; it was God's decision." Then he explained he had thought of other persons to go to Centenary but always found himself coming back to David.

Wally asked the bishop to take a walk with him. He reasoned with Bishop Morgan that things were going well at Hodgenville, that there would be peer jealousy if David went to Centenary, and that it would be difficult to raise a family while serving as pastor of a large church like Centenary. However, Bishop Morgan's decision was made. He said he had never felt the presence of the Holy Spirit in a meeting as strong as it was when he told the cabinet (while Wally was outside) how he felt in his heart about sending David to Centenary UMC in Lexington.

David and Karen did not know about Bishop Morgan's plans before he asked them to come to the episcopal residence the night after the cabinet meeting was over. It was during dinner that Bishop Morgan shared his thoughts. Later, Martha recalled Bishop Morgan's telling David where he was being sent. She said David had eaten only one bite of food at that time and didn't take another bite during the entire meal.

Wally and I appreciated the trust Bishop Morgan had in David and Karen, and we also appreciated those who sincerely believed in David enough to think he could have a successful pastorate at Centenary UMC. They were a rare group of colleagues in ministry. Sadly, several ugly remarks were made to David regarding this appointment. I have never prayed so hard in my life as I did over this appointment. David finally said to me, "Mom, don't you trust me?" I assured him I certainly did trust him, but that I trusted God most of all.

On April 7, 1997, the Discipleship Team of the newly united Kentucky Annual Conference gathered the clergy together for a Day of Renewal at Centenary United Methodist Church in Lexington. As chair of the Discipleship Team, David led in the planning of this day devoted to worship, repentance, and heartfelt petition for renewal across Kentucky United Methodism. At this stage, many ministers were still becoming acquainted with one another, and this was the best way for doing that: in prayer and faith for new beginnings and the outpouring of the Holy Spirit in our churches. Comments indicated later that some degree of renewal did take place.

Five days later, Wally went with pastors from our district to Camp Loucon. (This name is derived from our former **Lou**isville **Con**ference.) He realized many of the pastors had never been to our wonderful camp near Leitchfield, Kentucky. While he was doing this, I met with the committee to plan the Clergy Partners Conference for the upcoming Monday of General Conference in Louisville.

On April 27 Wally and David spent a day together to talk about David's new challenge as pastor at Centenary. I have saved for 15 years the list of suggestions Wally gave David. Here are some of them:

1. Slow down your delivery of sermons. Listen to tapes of your sermons.
2. Add humor when appropriate.
3. Schedule your responsibilities carefully: study time, administration, staff appointments, lay leadership, pastoral duties, counseling, hospital visits, family crises, deaths and funerals, and weddings.
4. Try to take a day off every week if possible—have family time.
5. Become familiar with how staff relates to various committees: trustees, education, council on ministries, etc.
6. Have a master calendar for staff meetings.
7. Orientation: study budget, policies, facility, weddings, etc.
8. Study.
9. Secure a copy of the Sunday schedule.
10. Avoid doing church work at home.
11. Analyze the budget.
12. Prepare a stewardship profile.
13. Ask for job descriptions for staff. Have these in front of you before you talk to each staff member.
14. Do a lot of listening. Take notes with each appointment.
15. Keep a daily diary log.
16. Stay as relaxed as possible.
17. Keep your focus on vision, nurture, and preaching.
18. Rely on the Lord at all times.

This was a time of high stress in our lives. We were concerned about the challenge in front of David and Karen. Also, our hearts were heavy as we longed to see more therapies used to help Katie. As Wally often did, he wrote me a letter of encouragement. He reminded me the Lord loves us and cares for our concerns. He said that in God's timing He would come to us with supernatural power and give us strength and grace to get through these difficult times. I reminded myself, too, that God is sovereign, and with Him all things are possible!

Following the 1997 Kentucky Annual Conference, Wally and I left for Hyden, Kentucky, to help with the Hammering in the Hills Habitat for Humanity house. The entire conference cabinet and several spouses were assigned one house to build in a week's time. We accomplished our assignment! One highlight of the week was when former President Jimmy Carter visited our house. He had on his blue jeans and was ready to help wherever needed.

We came back from Hyden and attended David and Karen's Covenant Service at Centenary. From there we drove to Athens, Georgia, for the funeral of Eugene Dunn, our friend and Wally's colleague in ministry during seminary days. Eugene was the senior pastor of the Zebulon-Fincher Charge we mentioned earlier. From the funeral we came to Kentucky just in time for me to attend our first Kentucky Christian Writers Conference. I will always be grateful to Joyce Joines and Brenda Loy for their wonderful support and help in getting this first Conference off the ground. They continued to help on the planning committee the second year along with Karen Hart and Maxine Powell.

I enjoyed my relationship with our pastors' wives. We were divided up in prayer pals and also had a Grandmothers' Prayer Group. On August 7, 1997, six other grandmothers and I met at Trinity United Methodist Church in Columbia to start a prayer group for our grandchildren with special needs. I could hardly believe the wide range of needs mentioned at our first prayer time: attention deficit disorder, obsessive compulsive disorder, Treacher Collins syndrome, autism, diabetes, osteogenesis imperfecta, profound deafness, and unexplained weight loss and weakness. We prayed often for our grandchildren with special needs and have seen great improvements in them over the years.

Wally always enjoyed being in the pastor role as a district superintendent. He was so good to spend time with his pastors. Wally had a manner that seemed to encourage pastors to come to him with their concerns as well as their joys. He was never too busy to sit down with them for good heart-to-heart discussions. I remember his visiting one pastor's son who was in jail.

Many of our pastors were facing discouragements, and some even wanted to quit the ministry. As far as I know, no one quit during Wally's total of the 12 years on two districts. Many of the pastors stayed for long pastorates where Wally appointed them. Some are still serving in those churches where he appointed them 12 or more years ago. I believe that if a pastor is doing his job and the congregation is doing theirs, long pastorates are best.

Wally left on October 15, 1997, for the Purpose-Driven Church Conference led by Pastor Rick Warren at Saddleback Church in Los Angeles. This was an exciting and inspiring experience for all who attended this meeting. Some of Rick Warren's methods of evangelism gave a new impetus to our pastors to go home and try new ideas. Some churches in the district turned around, and are still growing and trying new ministries. Other churches in our conference (and elsewhere) have planted new congregations in recent years after the Saddleback experience.

During these years Katie's challenges with autism and a public school that didn't meet her needs occupied much of our thought and time. Her first IEP meeting as she began first grade produced no goals or objectives for Katie. This meant she would have no plan for her learning experience. No one offered an explanation, nor did anyone seem concerned about it. This was somewhat of an omen of what lay ahead. Efforts to get a program planned for Katie seemed impossible. We made several suggestions to try to help with the situation, but to no avail.

On November 3, 1997, our whole family met with the school principal and Katie's teacher. Nancy Dalrymple, an autism specialist, came prepared to train the teachers on how to teach a child with autism. Nancy had previously videotaped Katie in the school in order to gather suggestions for helping plan a workable program. Unfortunately, neither the faculty nor the principal had anything positive to say about Katie. We pled with them for something to be done. No response. It turned out they already had a meeting set to transfer Katie to Lincoln Trail

Elementary School in Elizabethtown, which would mean an hour on the bus for Katie every day.

Going to Debbie and Steve's for lunch that day, Nancy Dalrymple said Katie could not survive in that environment. On December 11, there was a meeting at Katie's school to move her to Lincoln Trail School. The Lincoln Trail principal was not pleased to have a new student with autism. However, after Katie had been in the new school for a little over a month, her parents received a note from the Lincoln Trail teacher saying Katie was a joy to teach.

Stormy times were happening in the weather, too. On February 17, 1998, a tornado came through Barren County and did a lot of damage in the area where Wally's parents had lived. Their house was not damaged as much as some, but one barn, the garage, and a storage building were shifted several inches on their foundations. The yard was in total disarray, but we were thankful no one in the family was hurt. However, three persons in the area were killed.

We were just a little over a year from retirement, so Wally and I began to get serious about where we would then live. Wally felt strongly we should live in a condo in Louisville to be close to medical facilities. We had built a small get-away house in Doe Valley near Brandenburg, Kentucky, 13 years earlier, and it about broke my heart to think we would never permanently live in our own home. We were always grateful for our parsonage homes, but unless one has lived in a parsonage for 42 years, it would be difficult to understand my feelings.

I didn't say much about selling the house and moving to Louisville, but my heart ached. I decided to prepare a nice colorful "For Sale" flyer and I put it out in front by the street. I guess this was my way of surrendering my heart's desire to whatever God willed.

In no time at all, a couple came to our door and just happened to find us there. They were very interested in our house, and the man said he was ready to write the check that day. Since we had never lived in the house full-time, we decided to check out what the capital gains tax would amount to. When we did, we were shocked at the amount we would have to pay! That clinched Wally's decision to retire in Brandenburg, and I praised the Lord! We began the work of adding a garage in the back of our house and some rooms over the garage.

In August of 1998, Bishop Morgan came to preach our revival at Camp Acton for the second time. Everyone enjoyed him and Martha, and the Morgans enjoyed coming to Campbellsville. Bishop Morgan especially enjoyed the butterscotch pie at OK Country Restaurant in Columbia as well as our country ham. On the last night of the revival, our people in the district gave Bishop and Mrs. Morgan a cherry wash stand, bowl and pitcher, and two towels.

On September 23 of that year, Wally's heart went into atrial fibrillation. We called Dr. Charlie Smith in Louisville who had treated Wally once before for the same thing. Dr. Smith suggested Wally see Dr. David Montgomery in Campbellsville. Dr. Montgomery said he had no choice but to put Wally in the Taylor County Hospital where he underwent several tests, was put on a monitor, and began taking the drug digoxin. At 1:00 the next morning, Wally's heart stabilized. We were so thankful. In November the doctor said his EKG was good, but that Wally had some heart enlargement. He found some weakness in the heart muscle but no blockage. He also said stress may have caused the flare-up, and this was a believable possibility.

I remember how Wally seemed to have a new lease on life after this incident and enjoyed all of the New Life Gatherings that fall. The entry in my journal said of the Adair County New Life Gathering, *A great one! Church packed! Children's choir! Net gain in membership in the county's churches and a great spirit! Thank you, Lord.*

Wally's time serving as district superintendent on the Columbia District was near the end. One of the great surprises of our lives was when David and Karen, along with the help of some family and friends plus our old car and a little help from us, presented us with a new Buick. What a wonderful blessing and retirement gift! Our old car had ridden the circuit long enough, but we never dreamed of a surprise like this.

On May 16, 1999, our Columbia District gave us a wonderful retirement reception at Lindsey Wilson College. It was always a joy to work with Lindsey Wilson under the excellent leadership of Dr. John Begley and Dr. Bill Luckey, his successor. One of our treasured possessions from the reception is a video of that event. We have always been grateful to Rev. Bill Davenport and all who assisted with the reception—all the pastors and spouses, the lay people in the Columbia District, and our families and friends—who made this day such a treasured memory.

On June 3, the movers came early as so often happens. They began grabbing boxes before I could get them taped up. Wally was busy in his office giving books away to pastors who had dropped by. I was told to wrap our large grandfather clock, which was a challenge to say the least. As I ever so gently wrapped the pendulum, I thought of just how quickly time passes. Wally had completed 42 years of active ministry, and it seemed only yesterday that he received his first appointment.

I also remember how excited we were to begin to live as permanent residents in our own home near Brandenburg! We left our home district to retire to our first house we could call our own. Our hearts were grateful for the way God has always blessed us, and we looked forward to many more good and fruitful years in retirement.

Our retirement home.

190

Chapter 12

RETIREMENT YEARS

One of our retirement gifts was a clock that had a brass plaque on the front saying, "Now your time is your own. Enjoy!" Yet Wally's time was never completely his own. God owned him, and his heart always longed to introduce people to Christ. Joan Wilson, Chair of Evangelism at Brandenburg United Methodist Church, said of Wally, "Wally always had a heart for lost people." He and Joan led an Exploring Membership Class four to six times each year in the Brandenburg UMC. Wally always looked forward to these sessions when he and Joan discussed four topics

Brandenburg United
Methodist Church.

related to the Brandenburg UMC with prospective members: What We Believe, What We Offer, Who We Are, and What We Expect.

Wally's retirement service at the Kentucky Annual Conference was on June 11, 1999, at 10:00 a.m. Wally's sister, Helen, and her husband, Doug Whitlow, came to the service along with our children and their families. Wally was asked to give the response statement for the entire group of pastors who were retiring that year. Some of Wally's remarks on behalf of all the retirees that year were: "There are no words that are adequate to express the gratitude in our hearts today. So, I want to gather all our thanks for every kindness into a bundle and give it to the Lord. He is the one who really deserves the tribute. He is the One who gave us our call. Through the cabinet, He gave us our appointment. He has given us ideas for our sermons. He has been our strength all along the way as well as our source of joy. He has given us our story through His life, death and resurrection, and the presence of the Holy Spirit in our lives. In the words from the book of Joshua, 'Have I not commanded you? Be strong and of good courage; be not frightened, neither be dismayed; for the Lord your God is with you wherever you go'" (Joshua 1:9 RSV).

Bishop Robert Morgan was not feeling well during this conference. His voice sounded weak, and Bishop Lindsey Davis assisted in presiding. On the last day of conference Bishop Morgan was taken to the hospital by ambulance, and Bishop Davis continued to preside through the final part of the program which was the reading of pastors' appointments for the coming year. Bishop Morgan recovered and is living a full and rewarding life now in retirement.

On the following Monday morning when we were back in our retirement home, I entered these words in my journal, *"Wally felt lost today. He didn't know what to do with himself. We are in a sea of boxes and don't know where to begin."* We were exhausted. Our active ministry was over. Where would we go from here?

I remember Wally walking aimlessly through the house. He passed by me once and said, "Kay, what is the matter with that phone? It hasn't rung one time all day!" I reminded him that we were retired now, and the phone probably would never ring as much again. It was somewhat of a gloomy day for us, but with my first ever Social Security check coming in the mail that afternoon, things began to look brighter. A few days later, our children and families visited us, which made us feel more at home. We soon celebrated Karen's birthday and Father's Day together.

In November of 1999, my nephew, Doug Davis, had to have his leg amputated due to complications from diabetes. Doug was one of the most courageous persons I have ever known. He was Sunday school superintendent at his church for many years. He died on December 12, 1999. My sister, Jewell, Doug's mother, was by his bedside when he went to heaven. I shared at my extended family's Christmas dinner that year that Doug was a person who embodied all the gifts of the Spirit: love, joy, peace, patience, kindness, goodness, faithfulness, gentleness and self-control.

Also in November of that year more sadness came to our family. Wally's mother died on November 25, and her funeral was held on November 27. David sang with Karen accompanying him. Wally's cousin, Gayle Steenbergen, also sang. I loved Wally's parents, and we always had a good relationship. I was only 18 when Wally and I married. I learned a lot about cooking from Wally's mother as well as my own mother. Wally's eulogy was a beautiful tribute to his mother.

My nephew's wife, Sharon Davis, lost her father during that same fall, and another nephew's wife, Brenda Teal, lost her mother. Through it all, God was faithful and met our every need.

On Wally's birthday, January 13, 2000, he led a men's retreat at St. Meinrad, Indiana. Years earlier, Dr. Bill Croft, a good friend of ours, invited Wally to be a part of his group of Christian men from Indiana. They met for support and accountability. Most of this group came into a closer relationship with God through the Emmaus Walk experience. Dr. Croft and his wife, Mae, visited us often at Doe Valley, and they always enjoyed my fried Vidalia onion rings. The cooks at St. Meinrad baked a special cake for Wally, and the whole group sang "Happy Birthday" to him. This was a very special weekend for Wally.

Along about this time, David and Karen shared with us they were going to be parents! I well remember how it thrilled our hearts. David said when he announced the news at the three services at Centenary UMC where he was serving, the people clapped in each service. He said after the services, a total of six older women told him they felt like they were going to be a grandma!

The people at Brandenburg United Methodist Church were in the planning stages of a new Family Life Center. Wally and I agreed to be a part of the prayer committee for this effort. This was a good experience and a good way for us to get acquainted with several people in the church. The congregation was eager to undergird the building project with prayer. We had never seen a building process run any more smoothly. People were willing to sacrifice in order to support this effort. We organized a 24-hour prayer chain, and it was easy to get people to commit to a block of minutes to pray.

One little 4-year-old boy, Tate Wilson, printed his name neatly in one of the blocks on the prayer chart. I was still new in the church and didn't know Tate. But his printing, though well done, showed he was a child. I asked our pastor's wife at that time, Marlene East, if we should try to have an adult to be praying also in Tate's block of time. Marlene quickly answered, "Are you kidding? If Tate signed the prayer chart, you can be sure he will be praying during that time." If I had previously known Tate I wouldn't have had any doubt either.

At this time our 8-year-old granddaughter Katie seemed to be making progress in several areas. Her eye contact was better; she was more verbal now and her eye-hand coordination was improving. During one of Katie's and Debbie's visits an interesting thing happened. Our stereo suddenly came on during the night. Wally and I went to the den and heard the song "I Believe" playing. To this day we don't know what made the stereo come on! We were praying so hard for Katie's recovery from autism, and we are still praying and believing God hears every prayer. Healing will come for Katie—if not in this life, then in the life to come when she is with our Lord.

In April of 2000, David and Karen made a trip to England and Scotland. David wanted to take Karen to the very spot on the Isle of Skye where he committed his life to the ministry. Karen's parents, Art and Gloria Muselman, visited us during this time. All four of us surprised David and Karen at the airport in Louisville as they returned from their trip. All four parents welcomed the news a little later that we would be grandparents of a baby boy!

Around this same time David was honored when he was invited to be a candidate for the position of Executive Director of the World Methodist Council. He prayed long and hard about this decision. We were visiting Bishop and Mrs. Duffey in Montgomery, Alabama, at the time the offer came to David. David was spending some quiet time at our home in Brandenburg. He sought Bishop Duffey's advice in this decision, and as always, Bishop Duffey spoke words of wisdom.

At one point while he was at our house he went downstairs to play the piano awhile. The music to "Because He Lives" was on the piano. As he played this song, he glanced at a little shadow box that contained a thimble he had given me. He purchased the thimble on the Isle of Skye in Scotland where he surrendered his life to ministry. David had never noticed before the symbol on the front of the wooden thimble. It was identical to the symbol of the Trinity used in various ways at Centenary UMC where he was pastor. He had written on the thimble the date when it was purchased. It was the same date he was assigned to Centenary.

This somehow seemed like a sign to him that Centenary was where he belonged, but he still struggled with the decision. As always, he weighed the pros and cons and prayed hard for God's guidance. Finally, he decided Centenary is where he should serve. David felt it is in the local church that he would have more opportunities for soul-winning. The little symbol on the thimble seemed to be a sign from God to continue his ministry in Lexington, and he served there for nearly 12 years.

Time moved on, and on May 27, 2000, Wally's home place was auctioned off. There were several tables and wagons of household items. We were afraid the weather was going to be bad because tornado warnings were coming over the weather channel. But not a drop of rain fell during the four and half hours of the auction.

A couple of months, later Wally and I attended the national meeting of the Autism Society of America (ASA) in Atlanta. The workshops began at 7:30 each morning. I attended seven workshops the first day and wanted to soak in all the information that might be helpful for Katie. This was one of the most exhilarating experiences of my life. Wally wasn't quite as enthusiastic, but he supported me wholeheartedly. I shared every new thing I learned with him, and we attended many workshops together.

A special blessing was meeting Dr. Ruth Sullivan who started the ASA. Dr. Sullivan encouraged me in writing my book *Grand-parenting A Child with Autism—A Search for Help and Hope*. I was so touched by the commitment of parents and grandparents of children with autism who were in attendance at this conference. In one workshop Wally and I sat by a young mother from China. She was there on behalf of her son with autism, wanting to learn all she could. Her husband stayed home to take care of others in the family while she was in America for an indefinite time.

I became acquainted with a grandmother who brought her grandson with autism with her to the conference. She told me she would not get to stay for the whole week because her funds were running out. She gave up her room and hid her luggage away somewhere. I offered to keep her luggage in our room and regretted that we didn't have a spare bed to offer her. She took me up on the offer to leave the luggage in our room. Early the next morning, she came for it. I asked her if they found a couch or somewhere to sleep. She answered, "No, my grandson and

I slept under some tables down in the display room. No one found us there." That seems like real commitment to me.

A few days after Wally and I returned from the ASA Conference in Atlanta, we attended a Grandparents' Conference at Eastern Kentucky University in Richmond. This conference focused on the role of grandparents in the lives of children with autism. Rita Brockmeyer, chair of the conference, offered to add a chapter to my grand-parenting book and I gladly accepted the offer. Three professors at EKU contributed to this chapter as well. We attended several more of these conferences in the following years.

On August 17, 2000, our first grandson, Luke Christian Thomas, was born. David proudly carried Luke from the delivery room and explained his name. He said, "Luke means Bearer of Light and Christian is Karen's Grandpa Muselman's name." Friends from Centenary gathered around the nursery window, and we had a prayer of thanksgiving. What a special experience! As we left the hospital these words came to me, "On the grayest of days, Luke Christian will be a beam of light for his family." He is just that.

The weekend following Luke's birth is a special memory. On Saturday before our annual family reunion, there was a reunion for past students of the little one-room elementary school I attended for eight years. This reunion was held at the site of the school. The small building had been vacant for many years, and being there brought back so many good memories. My friends at this little school gave me a handkerchief shower when I left in 1950 to attend the county high school. I treasured these handkerchiefs until they were stolen in a burglary several years later at our parsonage in Shively. I included this story in my devotional book *New Every Morning*, and to this day I continue to receive handkerchiefs from people throughout the area.

In April of 2001, David visited Kwang Lim Methodist Church in Seoul, Korea. This was a life-changing experience for him. He joined the thousands of prayer warriors on Prayer Mountain for long periods of prayer and was so touched by the commitment of these dear Christians.

Their lives center each day around the practice of prayer, and the growth of this largest church in Methodism is living proof of the power of prayer.

In May of 2001, I had a wonderful experience with Katie I will always treasure. We were at church, and Katie was sitting between Wally and me as she usually did when she came for visits. The congregation was enjoying singing "O How He Loves You and Me," and Katie kept lifting her hand and turning my face toward her. I whispered for her to sing, and I continued singing myself. Each time she pulled my face toward her, she seemed more urgent. Finally I reached down to see what she wanted to say. She whispered in my ear, "*I love Jesus.*" I have often thought: *What if I had missed hearing her say those words?* When a child with autism wants to talk, their words should be cherished because many of these children are not verbal. Katie's three words that day will always ring in my heart.

Another precious experience was with Luke when he was around 10 months old. Wally and I and David, Karen, and Luke were attending our denomination's Kentucky Annual Conference. Billy Graham was leading one of his crusades in Louisville at the same time. One night when there was no program at our conference, I suggested that I keep Luke, and everyone else go to the crusade.

During that evening I gave Luke a stroller ride in the hotel where our annual conference met. As it neared Luke's bedtime, I decided to take him to our room. On the way I passed by our conference prayer room, and found myself pushing Luke's stroller inside. I parked the stroller by a small table "waterfalls." I felt a need to have a time of prayer and thought the waterfalls would interest Luke for a little while.

I prayed out loud, and soon tears were running down my cheeks. When I looked up to check on Luke, his eyes were riveted on mine. He had big tears in his own eyes. I believe Luke understood my heart that night, at least enough to share my emotions. I believe he, in his sweet, sensitive heart, empathized with my repenting heart.

Here is why I was repenting. That afternoon I went to a nearby department store to pick up a wedding gift. As I waited for the gift to be wrapped, a disheveled woman in a tattered dress and worn out shoes stood beside me.

"I missed the bus to the Billy Graham Crusade last night," she confessed sadly. It's the only time the bus will come by Dosker Manor this week." I remembered that Dosker Manor was a low-rent housing complex in Louisville.

"Billy Graham is a wonderful man," I replied, weakly pursuing the conversation as the stench from her body wafted by my nostrils.

"She is attending a conference here in town," the sales clerk interjected as she apologized for taking so long to wrap my gift.

The lady turned to me, with her sad, whiskered face in full view now. She then lifted a foot and showed me the see-through holes in the soles of her worn-out tennis shoes.

"Guess it wasn't meant for me to go tonight," she continued. "I would have probably got my feet wet. But I sure love that closing song."

"That's 'Just As I Am,'" I said. "It's a great old hymn. It always touches me."

"I love that song," she kept repeating as she slowly walked away.

As I walked back to the hotel that afternoon, I remembered that the opening message of the conference was on God's love. Yes, I needed to stop in the prayer room to pray for God's forgiveness for not recognizing Him. I needed to repent for not sharing God's love by offering to try to get a cab for this precious lady. I had Luke with me to take care of, but I could have helped this dear soul find a way to go a few blocks to hear "Just As I Am" and a moving gospel message.

A story about Luke on a lighter note occurred at Kurtz's Restaurant in Bardstown. Wally and I and our family met there to celebrate David's and Steve's birthdays. On this special day, David and Karen announced Luke was going to be a brother. Luke was 13 months old then. I am not sure he understood what his daddy announced, but something made him smile and giggle continuously that night. While we ate, Luke spent the entire time catching the eyes of people at nearby tables. He would first smile real big, and then if he got a response (which he did every time), he would start to giggle. I know this sounds like a Grandma tale, but at one point every person in the room was laughing! It was an experience I have never had before or since.

In July of 2001, Debbie shared a sweet experience she had on their farm. She has always been connected in a special way with nature and God's wonderful creation. She often advised Wally and me to stop and listen to the bird songs. One day she was walking around in her yard and spotted a beautiful Monarch butterfly. It kept floating by Debbie, back and forth. Debbie extended her arm and pointed her finger toward the butterfly, saying, "Come here, pretty butterfly. I won't hurt you. I love you." In that very moment, the butterfly touched down on Debbie's finger and rested there for several minutes.

From the beauty of that scene I move to the dark day on September 11, 2001. We all remember what a scary day it was when terrorists destroyed the Twin Towers in New York City, but something else scary was going on in my life that day. I was hesitant to mention to Wally that I was having chest pains, and they were not improving as time passed. I also had pain in my right arm. I felt I was headed for the hospital so I began packing. Finally I shared with Wally what was happening, and after a few phone calls, we headed to a doctor in Louisville.

The exam in the doctor's office confirmed I had a heart problem, and I was sent to Jewish Hospital. For the following two days, I went through one test after another. On the third day, I had double by-pass surgery. Wally was with me the entire nine days in the hospital, sleeping on a cot. We were so ready to get out of the hospital, and I will never forget that delicious Wendy's hamburger en route home! My sister, Jewell Davis, stayed a week caring for me, and she and Wally made quite a team with the housework.

My book *New Every Morning—a Daily Touch of God's Faithfulness* was published a few months later, and I was given several invitations for book signings. Wally made nearly every trip with me. He enjoyed visiting with the people who came to the signings. We were anticipating the birth of our second grandson, John Paul. Luke was growing so fast. At 18 months, he was identifying alphabet letters from newspaper headlines and counting French fries when we were at a restaurant.

On February 21, 2002, I entered in my journal,

> *Sweet John Paul was born at 8:05 this morning at Central Baptist Hospital in Lexington. Both sets of grandparents were present plus a special friend, Keene Howard. John Paul weighed eight pounds and 14 ounces and measured 20 inches long. As with Luke, David explained the meaning of John Paul's name. "John" was after John the Baptizer and the special friend of Jesus, and "Paul" after the man who made Jesus known all over the world. John means "grace" and "Paul" means "little," signifying dependence on God. As we left the room to come home that day, David was sitting in a recliner in Karen's room with his little new baby boy asleep across his chest.*

Time moved on. I continued having more book signings and being asked to speak now and then as well. Wally was involved in many aspects of the church we attended in Brandenburg. He was minister of visitation for our church and kept a card with prospects on it in his shirt pocket most all the time. He was gifted in evangelism; he always enjoyed preaching revivals and had more invitations than he could fill. He and I had the blessing of helping organize two new Sunday school classes at Brandenburg.

Wally and I started a ministry for pastors and spouses in our home soon after we retired. We called it "A Time Apart." We invited our guests to come on a weekend—Friday through Saturday or Sunday, whichever their schedule would allow. We enjoyed providing this time of rest and renewal which pastors need so much.

Around this time I received a letter from a friend in Nashville, Betty Stroud. Her husband, Steve, suggested she send with the letter an article about a new social skills camp for children with autism which was associated with Vanderbilt University in Nashville. I called the university and finally tracked down the director of that camp. I asked for permission for Wally and me to come and observe one whole day at their camp. The director graciously agreed and said we could also video and interview all day.

We went to Nashville the night before so we could get to the camp before it began at 8:30 the following morning. What a thrill this was to see the progress being made with these children! I began to dream of such a social skills camp in our area and shared this dream with Debbie and Steve. Debbie got on board immediately and made an appointment with the Director of Special Education in Hardin County who, at that time, was John Roberts. John didn't hesitate to express his interest in such a camp. He viewed our video with us, and Wally and I shared some of the materials we brought back from Nashville. Excitement grew as we formed a committee and met every month for a year.

I met with Linda Polley at Severns Valley Baptist Church in Elizabethtown to see if they would host such a camp. This was later approved by the appropriate committee of the church. Camp TESSA (**T**eaching **E**ffective **S**ocial **S**kills to children with **A**utism) began. Severns Valley has hosted these camps for the past nine years. We will be forever grateful to this wonderful church. This year we had four different camps running simultaneously, blessing children and youth who are at many different places on the autism spectrum. We have a waiting list of children hoping to attend each year.

David was experiencing some answered prayers and what seemed like some miracles at Centenary along about this time. These came about through a broad visioning process which was rooted in prayer and waiting on the Lord. In order for Centenary to continue into future generations, they would need more land. The Ministry Support Study Team identified one desirable parcel of significant acreage available in

Fayette County, but the owner of the land did not want to sell. However, this is not the end of the story. The day after it was reported the last parcel of land of any size in Fayette County was not for sale, a call came to the chair of the committee saying that as a family, the owners had had a change of heart. They felt God directed them to let Centenary UMC buy it.

On October 20, 2002, a congregational vote was taken regarding the purchase of the land. Seventy percent of the people voted in favor of the purchase that night, which was a bit disappointing for David. He had been hoping for a broader consensus. However, the leaders were resolved to keep advancing with the majority. The staff was positive about the move. Phone calls were all supportive. People said things like, "This was a great mandate to move forward." As it turned out, several families joined together and purchased the land to keep it for three years and lease it to the church for a dollar a year. This would give the church time to give careful thought to the whole matter and to raise the needed funds.

The following Sunday David shared from the pulpit what seemed like six miracles that had occurred over the past months:

1. The only possibility of land that could be purchased became available as a family felt inspired by God to sell the land, even though they had refused earlier.
2. A spirit of respect pervaded the church during the months leading up to the vote. (There was no rudeness or personal attacks.)
3. Parking was presenting a challenge, and the idea of shuttling people to park near the University of Kentucky football stadium came as a group of people prayed many hours together one evening. It was implemented and successful.
4. A Festival on The Land was planned. The night before the festival, a huge rainstorm came in that area. Fields were muddy and soaked all around, but not a drop fell anywhere on Centenary's new 100 acres.

5. The square footage projected as needed for expansion came out to be the exact square footage of projected need for expansion that was in the original building plan.
6. God stopped the plans early on until the committee stopped to seek His Presence and power, and they agreed to dig deeper into His Word, and to pray and fast.

Around this time a program called Alpha was started at Centenary. Many people experienced Jesus and grew in their faith as a result of this program. Alpha is a hospitality-based model for introducing people to the foundations of Christian faith. Through friendships formed around a weekly meal together, people grow to feel safe in asking their heart-felt questions in response to talks given about a variety of topics related to Christianity. David now serves on the national board for Alpha.

In January of 2004, we celebrated Wally's 70th birthday. I believe it was one of his happiest birthdays. All of our family and Wally's sister, Helen, and her family came to our home. I was able to surprise Wally by asking people to send his cards to Debbie's home instead of ours. An amazing total of 70 cards were mailed to her address! I gave Wally a beautiful suit he had wanted for several months. We both felt it was too expensive, but I slipped and bought it when it was 60% off. Our children and families gave us a nice grill which Wally enjoyed so much for the next five years.

Wally's 70th birthday.

I continued being involved with the annual Kentucky Christian Writers Conference, leading retreats, speaking occasionally, going to book signings, and writing as I could find the time. Wally and I attended several grand-parenting conferences at Eastern Kentucky University during these years. Wally continued to work in our Brandenburg UMC and picked up the hobby of woodworking in his spare time. One year he made 80 wooden nativity sets for our friends and family as well as for David and Karen to give as gifts to the Centenary staff.

A few months later David and Karen called to tell us that they were expecting a little girl. I squealed so loudly Wally ran upstairs from the basement to see what was wrong with me! David wanted me to let him tell Debbie and Steve, because Debbie was hoping so much that David and Karen would have a little girl. Now Wally and I would have two granddaughters and two grandsons. What a blessing! Someone has said having grandchildren is the only thing in life that is not overrated.

On July 15, 2004, Mary Esther Elaine Thomas was born. She weighed seven pounds and 11 ounces and was 19 ½ inches long. David and Karen chose Mary as a part of her name because the word means "most blessed' as it refers to Mary, the mother of Jesus. Esther, the queen, is remembered in the Bible for her leadership and courage. Elaine is a part of Karen's name, her mother's name, and her niece's name.

Within hours of Mary Esther's birth, David and Karen were told the baby had a heart murmur. A cardiologist was called in and tests were run. This doctor was a devoted Christian, and he assured David and Karen the baby's ventricular septal defect would likely correct itself. Dr. Wilkes, their trusted pediatrician, felt the same. In time the healing happened for which we give God thanks and praise. Our four grandchildren have brought so much joy to our lives.

L to R: Katie Caswell, Luke, John Paul, and Mary Esther Thomas.

The grandchildren loved their times with Grandpa.

Another of Wally's and my favorite memories was our trip to The Greenbrier in White Sulphur Springs, West Virginia, in November of 2004. The three days there were a bit of a splurge for us, but we were grateful to Christ Church for their very generous going-away gift many years earlier of which we used a part for this special experience.

Later in November, we realized our efforts to get a social-skills development program started for Katie. The lack of appropriate social skills is one of the three main deficits in children with autism. We will always be grateful to the assistant principal at West Hardin High School, Patty Wren, who stepped up to the task of helping us start a Lunch Bunch for Katie. For the past seven years, Katie has been blessed by this experience of meeting with regular peers for experiences in social skill development. Later at Central Hardin High School, the school occupational therapist, Angela Lily, has been a blessing for Katie and others through implementing a Friends Group. One student, Kasey Smallwood, has been a part of both of these groups. Katie and others have benefited greatly from these experiences.

One experience that verified the positive effect of these social-skills experiences occurred en route to Louisville one day. I happened to be a little low in spirit that day. Katie was sitting in the back seat with me, and she seemed to sense my feelings. She looked over at me and said, "I love you . . . so much!" Then she followed that sentence by saying, "I am so proud of you." These two sentences of encouragement were followed by her singing "For He's a Wonderful Savior." I personally believe that some persons with autism, like Katie, may be advanced in terms of spiritual perception.

Then Hurricane Katrina happened! When David and Karen returned from a short trip, they found Centenary preparing to house 250 refugees from New Orleans. The Red Cross was providing 24-hour on-site police, medical care, and a building manager. David was so proud of his church and the spirit in which they ministered to the refugees for nearly six weeks.

In September of 2005, Wally became pastor of Munfordville First United Methodist Church . . . for the second time! The invitation came to Wally as a result of the church's pastor taking a medical disability leave due to cancer. We moved back into the parsonage that was built during our first tenure there from 1964-69. Parishioners gathered together the bare necessities of furniture. During these nine months, we were there on weekends and sometimes during the week. Several needed improvements were made on the parsonage while we were there.

Wally and I enjoyed this interim time in Munfordville. The church he served in Munfordville during the 1960's had burned a few years earlier, and the congregation had been meeting in the local Presbyterian Church facility since that time. However, the United Methodist congregation elected to build the family life center before their sanctuary, and this first phase was almost finished when we arrived.

While many of our friends had passed away since we left in 1969—and then some died during these nine months—we enjoyed renewing old friendships and making new ones. Wally often said that he could go right to work leading this congregation because he didn't have to establish trust this time. He worked hard during this time to get the church "up and going," and I feel he did do that with God's help.

During our first few months in Munfordville, we continued to have Sunday school and worship in the Presbyterian Church. Everyone was so excited for that first Sunday in the first phase of the new building. It is amazing how quickly a family life center can become a sanctuary for worship.

Just before we were to have the first service, a tornado hit Munfordville! David had arranged to be away from Centenary in order to attend this service. He and his family came and stay with us on the Saturday night before the special service. During the night Karen awakened, and then awakened all of us as she heard the "train sound" of the tornado. We barely reached the basement before we felt the EF 2 tornado's fierce attack on the parsonage. Trees and power lines were brought down in the front yard. A porch post went through the window of David and Karen's van. Much damage occurred all over town. People were in the streets trying to check on neighbors, especially the elderly. Our new church facility immediately became a center for feeding and caring for workers and needy people.

One of the first things we did when we got to Munfordville was have a TIP-OFF which was an all-day "**T**raining, **I**nspiration, and **P**lanning" event for the entire church. The day was well-attended, and a delicious potluck meal was served. People left the meeting motivated to move forward. Attendance picked up. Wally and I helped start a new Sunday school class that brought new life to the church.

Wally helped organize a stewardship campaign, a Time and Talent committee, and developed a plan for inviting and welcoming people. Door hangers inviting people to visit our church were placed on the doors of the houses in the surrounding community. Greeters were in place each Sunday. A delicious meal was prepared in the church kitchen every Wednesday night and was open to the whole community at a very reasonable price.

During our time at Munfordville, Wally and I celebrated our Golden Wedding Anniversary on January 26, 2006, at the Brandenburg United Methodist Church. I was so excited that day, I awakened at 4:20 a.m. I went to the den and sat in my chair, thanking God for our 50 wonderful years together, for our family, and for the multitude of blessings God has bestowed on us over the years.

Many folks from Munfordville and family and friends from other places joined us for the reception. I had mixed feelings about what we should do for this anniversary. I didn't see how I could pull it all together by myself with all the travel to and from Munfordville. Then someone suggested a wonderful lady, Jackie LaTondress, who lives near Brandenburg, would likely be able to cater the reception. What a blessing this was, and what a beautiful job she and her family did with the reception! But the highlight for Wally and me was when Luke and John Paul sang a cute little song about us David taught them and when Katie sang the Lord's Prayer at the close of this happy event. There was hardly a dry eye in the room by the time she sang the Amen.

Wally and Kate's 50th anniversary.

Family Group . . . 50th Anniversary

Wally had suffered for years with hip pain, and now he was facing hip surgery. Many days during those months at Munfordville he could hardly walk because of the pain. Wally seldom, if ever, slowed down. God blessed his ministry during those nine months he served the Munfordville First UMC and Mt. Beulah UMC by bringing 29 people into the Munfordville church either by profession of faith or transfer of letter.

On January 6, 2011, members and friends processed into the new facility as the choir sang joyfully. The instrumental prelude featured a procession of the elements of worship with the cross, worship candles, and offering plates being brought in by members of the church with the acolytes following. The bell choir played the offertory. The nearly-filled sanctuary was spirit-filled, and a congregation of people rejoiced, remembering how God brought them from despair—when their former church building was destroyed by fire—to this happy occasion.

In May of 2011 their beautiful new sanctuary was dedicated.

Munfordville First United Methodist Church's new facility.

David and Karen moved from their present house to a safer neighborhood. A few days later in February of 2006 Bishop James King called David to come to the bishop's office. Bishop King told

David he wanted him to come into the cabinet and serve as a district superintendent. David felt he still had critical work to finish at Centenary. He received a second call to the Bishop's office. Bishop King told David he was bringing him into the cabinet and named the district. They talked for quite a while, and David started to leave. He again told the Bishop he felt strongly that it was not a good time to leave Centenary, but being a United Methodist pastor, he would go where he was sent.

On Friday, February 24, 2006, David was told the bishop would meet with Centenary's Staff-Parish Relations (SPR) Committee that night to announce the move. Karen led a women's retreat in Arizona that weekend, and Wally and I were in Lexington helping with their children. All of us were praying our hearts out for God's will to be done. A pall seemed to settle over their home, and I felt like I was shut up in a tomb. I asked God for a sign that He was working in all of this.

On the day the bishop would go to Centenary, I felt a nudge to look out on the back deck. At first I ignored the nudge, thinking I was too busy and also thinking it didn't make any sense to look out on the deck. After all, wouldn't it be just like it was the last time I saw it? Again the nudge returned. I went reluctantly to the door leading out to the deck. There on the rail in front of my eyes was a beautiful dove. Just one. Waiting, and looking toward the door I opened. I wonder how long it had sat there waiting for me to obey God. I knew in that moment the dove was a sign of hope from God and His Holy Spirit with was us, but I still didn't know what was ahead.

Karen made it back from the retreat in time for the meeting with the Bishop. She and David were struggling to surrender to the Bishop's new appointment for David. Unknown to us at the time, Karen went into every room of the house they had just moved into and prayed a prayer of humble surrender of each space to God. She had worked so hard to get the house cleaned and prepared for their recent move.

Becki Curry, who at that time was the administrative assistant to the bishop, called David and said the bishop would meet David and Karen first in David's office and then meet with the SPR Committee afterward. Wally and I were still praying at their home for God's will to be done.

Bishop King opened the meeting with David and Karen by reiterating how he had felt David should go on a district. But, he said, while he was taking his shower that morning, God spoke clearly to him saying, "It's not right to move David right now." He went on to say he got out of the shower right then and wrote down the words he was sure God had spoken to him, and he had total peace about the decision.

David and Karen rejoiced during the time the bishop was with the SPR Committee. They called to tell us about the answered prayer. After Bishop King and Rev. Paige Williams, district superintendent of the Lexington District at that time, left, David, Karen, and the SPR Committee went into the chapel to pray and sing songs of praise.

I believe God spoke to Bishop King and he heard and obeyed God. I will always believe, too, that a part of the reason God intervened was that David and Karen fully surrendered to God's will, even though their hearts were sad. The entry I wrote in my journal that day is this, *"Thank you, Lord, for intervening. This has strengthened my faith."*

On June 30, 2006, Wally had hip replacement surgery at Baptist East Hospital in Louisville. He did well and I was able to stay with him for the four days in the hospital. The physical therapist released Wally a month later, saying the doctor would be very pleased with Wally's progress. The orthopedic surgeon *was* very pleased, and after walking behind Wally several steps, he teasingly said, "OK, Show Out!" In one more month, Wally was playing golf again.

The year 2007 was another busy year for our family. David was awarded the Harry Denman Fellowship from the Foundation for Evangelism for his Ph.D. studies. We attended meetings to transition Katie into high school. Wally and I went to Madisonville in June for Wally to preach at their homecoming celebration.

Sadly, in June of that year, we lost our brother-in-law, Adron Teal, who was my oldest sister, Geneva's, husband. Adron had been in poor health for many months. He had fought a brave fight to live but gained new life in Heaven. David and Wally participated in the funeral.

The summer of 2007 brought a drought to Steve and Debbie's farm. All of us prayed fervently for rain, but Debbie seemed to have a special line to God. She knelt out in their yard on the steps leading up to Katie's trampoline and poured her heart out to God. It wasn't long before dark clouds boiled up and an 8.8-inch rain fell, salvaging the crops that year.

Then on August 30, a terrible tragedy occurred. Karen's parents, Art and Gloria Muselman, were both killed instantly in a car accident near Karen's hometown of Berne, Indiana. We received the call around 10:15 that evening. The accident occurred about 6:20 Eastern Daylight Time. David and Karen were at the church leading in Alpha meetings, each in a different room. They had their cell phones on vibrate, and neither could answer them as they were in the middle of leading the Alpha groups.

Karen left the church first and immediately checked her messages. When she returned her brother Roger's call, he told her about the collision. Karen immediately turned around, parked her car, and ran into the church screaming and crying.

The person who was directing the Alpha program at that time, Tracey McLarney, ran out into the hall to see what was happening. She saw an unknown woman arm-in-arm with Karen. Tracey held Karen's arm on the other side as they made their way quickly to David's office.

Tracey later shared that as she sat near the door that night, while Karen was speaking in the Alpha group, she noticed this same person appeared three times close up to the window pane in the door. The stranger set her eyes on Karen each time. It appeared that this person was checking on Karen for some unknown reason.

When they arrived at David's office door, the stranger disappeared. Tracy was going to thank her for her comforting presence with Karen, thinking that Karen probably knew the person. However, Karen had never seen the person before. In retrospect, everyone who witnessed this was convinced this had to be an angel from God who was assigned to be with Karen when she received this devastating news. God sent ministering angels to be with Jesus in the Garden of Gethsemane. I believe He still does this today.

A friend of Karen's family sent a small jet to Lexington to get David, Karen, and the children. David and Karen dreaded so much to awaken the children and tell them the sad news that they had to get ready to leave that night. Wally was supposed to preach at a homecoming at my sister Jewell Davis' church on that following Sunday, but we felt we should go to Berne as quickly as we could get there. Thankfully, the Columbia District superintendent, Rev. Darren Brandon, gladly filled in for Wally and was a great blessing to this congregation that day.

Some 900 people attended the funeral for Art and Gloria Muselman. Beautiful tributes were paid to this wonderful couple who had served their Lord faithfully over the years. They were generous-hearted people who had supported so many benevolent programs in their town of Berne and beyond. Heaven becomes nearer and dearer as our loved ones transition from Earth to their homes in Heaven.

On April 2, 2008, which was the first-ever World Autism Day, I was privileged to speak on autism to the Woman's Club of Louisville. I was especially pleased to see around 25 members from our former church, Christ Church United Methodist, in attendance that day.

One month later, a friend of ours, Marsha Wardlaw, passed away after a long battle with cancer. Her husband, Russ, was a member of Wally's Covenant Group at Christ Church. Wally and I prayed so hard for Marsha's healing. Somehow, I felt led to pray for God to restore Marsha's appetite so she would regain her strength. When I received the call that Marsha had passed away, I thought I was going to hear that she was eating better. I remember crying out to God after I hung up the phone, "Lord, I thought you would restore Marsha's appetite as a sign of her miracle," In my heart I heard these words I will never forget: "She is at my banquet table *now*!" After Wally's death I could just envision

Marsha and Wally, along with a host of relatives and friends, around that heavenly banquet table.

More recently another member of the Covenant Group lost his wife to cancer. John "Rocky" Rawlins wife, Sandy, another dear friend, went to heaven in 2011. I can now envision Sandy joining Wally and Marsha around that banquet table! I prayed for Sandy every day for six years. I believe some day we will have answers to all our questions.

In May of 2008, David and leaders of Centenary Church were working hard preparing for Pledge Sunday for The Land, which they began to call the 100 acres. David and other church members began to walk the perimeter of The Land and pray. With each walk they had to climb three fences. On Saturday before Pledge Sunday, they did this seven times following the example in the Bible of Joshua and Jericho. God blessed Centenary with the faith to purchase this property which will be a great resource for Kingdom work for generations to come.

Wally's last summer with us was full of happy activities. We went to family and church reunions, birthday celebrations, and had a wonderful visit to Lake Junaluska, North Carolina. En route there Wally and I spent one night at Pigeon Forge where we enjoyed visiting every year or so. David, Karen and family met us at Lake Junaluska where we shared a house. When they arrived, we heard the children squealing with joy. They know how much their daddy loves Junaluska, and how we as a family loved to go there for a week's stay during many summers of our children's childhood.

We played with them many of the games our children played years ago: Skeeter Cards, Sorry, Jacks, and Pick-up Sticks. We visited places we went to when our children were growing up. We walked the Rose Walk by the lake and visited Waynesville, Ghost Town, and the Cokesbury Book Store. But most precious of all was our visit in the evening to the lighted cross overlooking the lake. It was there that we always had a special time of prayer as a family.

In August of 2008 David shared with his Staff-Parish Relations Committee and the lay leader at Centenary about his feeling that God was directing him to focus full-time on his Ph.D. Soon after, he told his district superintendent, Paige Williams. Then in October of that year David told the entire congregation he would be leaving in January of 2009. He explained that much of what he and Karen had worked for during the past 11-plus years was in place. The staff and leadership were strong. Big financial projects were complete. All facilities were in good order with unlimited potential for expansion. The congregation shared a wonderful spirit of love, unity, and vision. It seemed the ideal time for a new senior pastor to come. Centenary would use pastors already on the staff and others to fill the pulpit until the Kentucky Annual Conference met in June.

On November 15, 2008, we, along with several other couples, were visiting Carl and Judy Austin in their home in Brandenburg. Judy prepared a delicious Thanksgiving feast, and all of us were enjoying a great time of fellowship. In the midst of this scene, Wally's cell phone rang. His sister's daughter, Diane Whitlow, was on the phone to let us know her 51-year-old brother, Tommy Whitlow, had just died. We learned later that Tommy was en route to Glasgow from Smiths Grove when he began to smother. He pulled off the road and flagged down someone who called 911. Tommy died of a heart attack on the way to the hospital. Wally, David, Brian Whitlow, Tommy's son, and Jimmy Melton, participated in the funeral service. Tommy and our Debbie were born 10 days apart, and his untimely death was another stark reminder of the brevity of life.

This last Thanksgiving before Wally died was very special. As a family we named the things for which we were thankful and wrote them down on construction paper. David and the children cut out colorful leaves and later strung them on a string to be hung across the entrance from our living room to the den. Besides the names of family members, many words came from the children: Jesus, food, Kentucky, cars, memories, sports, churches, country, school, nature, friends, animals, freedom, adventure, clothes, books, cross, Holy Spirit, world, and Heaven. Little did we know then that Heaven would soon become so much more real to all of us. These are now a part of my Thanksgiving decorations every year.

In December of 2008, we learned that my oldest brother, Windell Radford, had lung cancer. His wife, Maxine, suggested we let Windell tell us about it, which we did. Windell shared very openly about his condition and the brief projected time he had left. He was never hesitant to talk about Heaven, and he was glad for me to read several pages from *90 Minutes in Heaven* by Don Piper and co-author Cecil Murphy. Windell's daughter, Judy Branham, said her daddy seemed so grace-filled during the last months of his life, and his peace and courage amazed her.

Windell loved to reminisce during those last months of his life. He talked about his time in the Navy and the years he raised seed tobacco. He loved life on his farm and won awards for his fine seed tobacco. At one time he said he hired more people than any person, factory, or business in a 100-mile radius of his home. His family was a great support and all worked with Windell in the seed tobacco for Clay's Seed Company.

On December 21, 2008, David preached his last sermon at Centenary. His sermon was entitled "Being Born Again." He received a standing ovation at each of the three services that morning. As he closed this last service, David knelt at the altar for prayer. Luke and John Paul joined him there (Mary Esther was in the nursery). They said they wanted to thank God for Centenary Church. Then just before the benediction, the choir director suggested David and Karen walk about halfway down the aisle and allow the entire congregation to gather around them for one final prayer. My journal entry that day was, "*Thank you, Lord, for David's commitment to You and Your kingdom on earth. Please continue to guide him in Your way, and teach him your paths.*"

On Wally's 75th birthday, January 13, 2009, seven couples from Brandenburg met us at a local restaurant for a birthday meal. The following day, David and Karen met us at Science Hill Inn in Shelbyville for another birthday celebration. Then on January 18, our family and our extended family and friends met at Glendale for still another celebration. I prepared a digital frame of pictures of Wally's life that ran continuously that evening. Luke, John Paul, and Mary Esther sang a cute little song David had written about Grandpa, and Katie sang "Amazing Grace." We never dreamed this would be the last birthday we would get to celebrate on earth with Wally.

Later in January we had a snow followed by a terrible ice storm. We lost our electrical power for seven days. I came down with strep throat, and all doctor's offices and pharmacies were closed. Finally, we reached our local doctor. Kroger opened their pharmacy by using a generator, and I was able to get some antibiotics. However, the strep throat went into strep synavitis which is a form of crippling arthritis. I could only walk with a walker. We were in a real dilemma. No heat. No lights. No hot water. Little food. Debbie and her family were without electricity longer than we were and were running out of food as well.

Wally kept the fireplace going in the basement day and night which meant he got little sleep. Finally, I felt able for us to go visit David and Karen in Lexington which was a life-saver. We went by Bob Evans and bought dinners for Debbie, Steve and Katie as well as Steve's parents and took them to Upton.

Never has a house looked so good or food tasted as delicious as it did with David, Karen, and family that night. Karen had fresh flowers everywhere. We were a fright to look at as we came into their house. I was stumbling along on my walker. Neither of us had been able to bathe for about three days. We will never forget that, as Wally entered their home and walked through the kitchen, Karen gently said, "Wally, go get in the shower!" I improved every day while we were there, and in a few days we went home.

We returned shortly to Lexington to keep Luke and Mary Esther while David and Karen went to Florida for an Alpha meeting. They took John Paul with them to celebrate his 7th birthday. It was a good visit. I will never forget the laughing contest Wally, Luke, and Mary Esther enjoyed. Each person tried to out-laugh the others. I thought to myself *if laughter is healing as we hear it is, these three are getting a good dose!*

I knew Wally didn't feel very well but did the laughing for the children's sake. A small part of Wally's new hearing aid had come off in his Eustachian tube. The piece that came off in his ear was shaped like a tiny closed umbrella. Even though it was giving Wally a good deal of pain, there was nothing we could do about it until be got back to Brandenburg.

As soon as we got home, Wally went as a walk-in at our Family Medical Center to see Dr. Bryan Honaker. Being a walk-in, he waited around an hour before he saw our doctor. Dr. Honaker called his partner, Dr. Kyle King, in on the situation. They along with two nurses finally removed the little umbrella and found it to now be spread out like an open umbrella. This explained why it was so difficult to remove. The procedure was painful and the ear was bleeding a little. Dr. Honaker gave Wally a prescription for an antibiotic, and he came back home.

When Wally entered the house, he held his hand over that ear and said, "This hurts!" I encouraged him to rest a little while before going to the church, but he went straight to the shower, instead, to get ready for the activities at our church that night. Rick Bard, pastor of Broadway United Methodist Church in Bowling Green, was beginning our revival that night. Rev. Bard planned to meet with some of the church officials at 5:30 before the 7:00 service. Our pastor, Jim Robinson, was sick that night, so Wally was supposed to fill in for him. I arrived later for the service.

Wally presided at the service that night. He had known Rick Bard since Rick was in college, so Wally was ready to tease him a little in his introduction. He talked about their bald heads and told about the removal of the piece from the hearing aid, embellishing it even more than was necessary! The longer he talked, the more the congregation broke up with laughter. Yet, in retrospect, I felt Wally was not quite himself that night. After all the laughter faded away and he came to sit with me, he seemed to wilt. Two ladies in the choir said later that Wally's face turned chalky white when he sat down.

We had driven to the church in two cars, so after the service, I offered to go get Wally's prescription. He insisted he would pick it up, but he walked in our house right behind me and wasn't carrying any medicine. Evidently he either didn't feel like going to the drugstore after the service or had not remembered to do so. I later learned Wally had some difficulty in finding his Trailblazer van in the parking lot that night.

At this point in my journal I entered these words: *These will be the most difficult pages I will ever enter in my journals.*

Chapter 13

GOOD-BYE FOR NOW

When Wally came upstairs after parking the car in our basement garage, he was holding the left side of his head where the ear problem was located. His first words were, "My head is really hurting!" I gave him an Aleve, which had been recommended for pain, and suggested he sit down in his recliner and relax. I then took his blood pressure, and it registered 151 over 86. When I showed Wally the numbers I had written down on a piece of paper, he looked at the paper and then back at me. I will never forget the scared look on his face when he said, "Kay, what is happening to me? I can't read those numbers."

My heart was racing as I became more concerned by the minute. I was determined my face would not reveal the fear welling up in me. I said, "Wally, just relax and we will turn on the news." I handed him the television remote control, but he just stared at it, now with a look of desperation in his eyes. "What is wrong with me?" he asked. "I can't see the numbers on this thing!" I helped him punch the channel number, but he said he was ready to go to bed. I noticed he had some difficulty walking to the bedroom, but I was able to get his pajamas on him and helped him lie down.

I immediately ran down the hall to call the doctor. It was around 10:30 by now, and I was so sorry to call our family doctor at that hour, but I felt I had no choice. Dr. Bryan Honaker suggested I take Wally either to Jewish Hospital or Baptist East Hospital Emergency Rooms in Louisville. Remembering how difficult it was to get Wally to the bed, I knew I couldn't get him down the steps to the car in the basement. Nor could I get him down the seven steps outside to get in the car.

So I called 911, and in 10 minutes the ambulance driver and the assistant were at my front door. I hardly had time to think before Wally was on the stretcher and out the door. Two neighbors, Hope Wix and Martin Bosemer, came to our house immediately. As I ran by them to catch the ambulance, I told them to lock the house and I would see them later.

As we rushed out of the driveway the ambulance driver said she had taken patients with Wally's symptoms to hospitals before, and she insisted we go to Hardin Memorial Hospital Emergency Room in Elizabethtown. She knew, as I did, that time was of the essence. The trip to the Elizabethtown hospital that usually takes around 40 to 45 minutes took 24 minutes that night! I prayed all the way—not only for God to spare Wally but also that we would arrive safely. In between prayers I kept calling David's cell and home phones.

When we reached the hospital I jumped out of the ambulance in order to see Wally before they rushed him into ER. Our eyes met just as he was being whisked from the ambulance. I said, "Wally, it's Kay! I am with you." He saw me waving to him and he waved back. I will always treasure the big smile that came over his face. I knew he was in a critical condition, but I *didn't* think I was seeing Wally conscious for the last time.

I was allowed to stay with Wally only a few brief minutes while his pajamas were being cut off his body. Then I was asked to go into a nearby room. I was surprised to find the ambulance driver along with her assistant waiting for me. They said they would not leave me until my neighbor, Hope Wix, arrived. I found out later that Hope reached the hospital almost as soon as we did and had been waiting until she found out where I was. I will always appreciate so much these dear people who were by my side through such a difficult time.

Thankfully, a neurosurgeon was available at the hospital, which was very unusual at this time of night. The neurosurgeon kept telling me to call in the family. I knew Debbie and Steve would need to get Katie off to school early the next morning, so I waited until after Katie was on the bus before calling them. I decided I would need to have someone in David's church help me awaken him. It was around midnight by now. I tried to call a few people, but there were no answers. Then I tried to call Greg Howard, a former police officer and a member of Centenary where David served as pastor. Greg's wife, Keene, was with us during the births of all three of David's and Karen's children.

Greg answered and immediately went to David and Karen's home. He knocked on the door, rang the doorbell, and called to David until he responded. David and Karen had just returned from the Alpha meeting in Florida and were exhausted. David said this was the first time he could ever remember failing to have a phone by his bed. He was so remorseful that I had trouble reaching him and left almost immediately for Elizabethtown. Hope stayed with me until 3:00 a.m. when David arrived.

The person who attended Wally en route to the hospital later came to Wally's room to find me. She hugged me and said, "I just had to find you. There was something special going on in that ambulance!" My first thought was Wally's sweet smile as he waved to me, and I asked if this was what she meant. She said she couldn't see his smile, but she saw him wave good-bye to me. I told her I did remember his waving, but I was concentrating on his face, hoping he would say a word to me. Later she and I had lunch together, and she mentioned that Wally seemed so peaceful. She said she had been with numerous people who were being taken to the hospital and many of these were very distraught and fearful, but Wally seemed totally at peace. I believe this was because the presence of the Lord was right there in the ambulance that night.

I will always believe Wally willed himself to stay conscious long enough to tell me good-bye. Once he was laid flat on the gurney, blood filled one side of his brain and pushed the other side of the brain over three-fourths of an inch. He never regained consciousness. The neurosurgeon said that Wally had a catastrophic brain bleed.

There was hardly any movement in Wally's body the following day except involuntary muscle movements. The neurosurgeon asked our family to meet him in the conference room early the morning after our arrival. He began telling us we would have to deal with the hard reality. He even spoke of organ donations. It had only been nine hours since I saw the first signs that something was happening to Wally. We could hardly take in all that had happened, let alone discuss organ donations.

God is always on time. Immediately after the neurosurgeon left the conference room, we heard a knock on the door. We were so thankful to see the kind and familiar face of Dr. Charlie Smith. Dr. Smith was a friend from Christ Church and also our family doctor for some 25 years. My first words to him were, "Dr. Smith, you are a God-send." His reply was, "Well, I thought you all might have some questions."

Did we ever have questions! Dr. Smith gently and wisely answered all of them and stayed for two hours. He shared these suggestions with us: (1) Get a second opinion, (2) Give God time, and (3) You will know when it is time to let him go. What wonderful advice! We followed it.

A flood of people began to arrive that day. Ministers constantly lined Wally's room. Most of the people prayed for Wally's healing, and many of them said, "I am in the ministry today because of that man." Debbie and Steve came as soon as they could get there. My pastor Jim Robinson noticed how many times he saw David go into the conference room, and he always had his Bible tucked under his arm. Karen came as soon as she could get babysitters lined up to take care of the children. She pitched in immediately and helped keep a record of the visitors, calls, food, and gift donations.

On Wednesday, February 25, 2009, Karen shared with us the research she had done on the Internet regarding Wally's condition. More and more family and friends came. At one point the ICU personnel limited the number of visitors allowed in the room at one time. I will always regret that we failed to see many people who waited a long time for an opportunity to visit Wally's room.

We are so grateful for the many prayers for Wally's recovery. My niece, Judy Branham, called from Tulsa, Oklahoma, to suggest a person she knew in Mt. Washington who believes strongly in the power of prayer. She asked if we would like for him to come to the hospital and pray for Wally. I told Judy we would be glad for him to come, and we especially appreciated his driving that distance. He was there in 45 minutes, and it was now around 8:30 p.m. Bro. Allen Oliver entered Wally's room, and we introduced ourselves. He pulled up a chair and scooted up close to David and me. He explained a little about his ministry of healing. He said he wanted us to feel comfortable with his prayers. We sensed this man's authenticity.

Bro. Oliver started toward Wally's bed to pray and invited David and me to join him. He only made a step or two when he turned to us and said, "This man is fulfilled. He is in Heaven already." As he made a few steps forward and came closer to Wally's bed, he said, "This room is filled with ministering angels. There is a great celebration going on in Heaven right now!" I immediately thought of how angels ministered to Jesus in the Garden of Gethsemane. With the next step or two, he glanced toward the window, gasped a little, and made a step backward. I honestly thought he might be about to faint. After a moment, Bro. Oliver looked at us and said, "I have just looked into the face of Jesus. He is waiting and welcoming. Glory is strong in this room." I could not doubt what he was saying. He left shortly following his prayer, but we will never forget this servant of God.

Soon after Bro. Oliver left, a second doctor friend came. Dr. Bill Croft from New Albany, Indiana, left work and came straight to Hardin Memorial Hospital. Our friendship with Dr. Croft and his wife, Mae, goes back many years. In fact, David helped Dr. Croft come to faith during a Walk to Emmaus when David served on the team. I signed a waiver for Dr. Croft, as I did for Dr. Smith earlier, giving my permission for him to look at all of Wally's records.

After Dr. Croft finished looking over all the records, he said to us, "It will take a miracle of mammoth proportions." He went on to say, "The damage to Wally's brain has resulted from the brain bleed. It has filled one whole side and beyond." (We later looked at the scans ourselves and could see how the blood had totally filled the brain cavity, and was even down in the spinal cord.) Dr. Croft reiterated what we had been hearing, "The spinal cord and brain injuries don't heal."

On Thursday, February 26, our family doctor, Dr. Bryan Honaker, came. He, too, spent around two hours with us. We were especially grateful he gave up some in his day off from work to be with us. I again signed a waiver so Dr. Honaker could look over Wally's records. He agreed with what the two previous doctor friends had said.

With each passing day, the neurosurgeon became more insistent that we give permission for the life support to be removed. We felt we were moving toward the decision as fast as we could. I continued to recall Dr. Smith's words: "Give God time" and "You will know when it is time to let him go."

I finally told the neurosurgeon that he and we come from two different worlds. I said I respect his world, and I knew he was a brilliant doctor. But we were moving in this as fast as we could move. I told him Wally was a reasonably healthy 75-year-old man. He loved life and loved the Lord. His illness came on so suddenly and unexpectedly that making a quick decision to take life support away seemed like an impossibility. I assured him we would be making a decision soon. He was very upset with me, and when he left, I turned to apologize to Max and Naomi Bowen, our friends from Shepherdsville who had driven down to be with me. Tears were running down their faces. They apologized for the pressure I had been under to make a decision so quickly.

Later that night, before David and I tried to get some sleep, I lifted the sheet from Wally's feet as I so often did to see if they were cold and needed more cover. This time David was standing beside me as though he knew this would be a telling moment. Sure enough, both of Wally's feet were turning dark. In the same split second, we turned toward each other and said in unison, "It's time."

The next morning before daybreak, I was sitting by Wally's bed when a young nurse came in and squatted down by my chair. She softly whispered to me, "Do you need to talk?" I answered "Yes." I explained that I was struggling with the feeling that if I gave permission to take away all life support, I would be playing God. Looking me straight in the eyes, she firmly spoke words of wisdom, "This man is already in Heaven. He is not alive in this body. He is being maintained artificially, and you are playing God by keeping him alive this way." These words were blunt, but I knew they were true. I felt peace fill my heart.

The fourth doctor friend came on this day. Our long-time friend from Christ Church, Dr. Rajah Kara, spent two hours with us as each of the other doctor friends had done. He, too, studied Wally's records and agreed totally with what the other doctors had concluded.

Our family met with the neurosurgeon that afternoon. The most difficult thing I have ever had to do in my life was sign the form giving permission to remove the life support. We had a few minutes with the neurosurgeon to share our hearts, and I mentioned the role faith had played in our decision to wait for awhile before taking away the life support. We wanted to give God time if He chose to heal Wally. It was at this point the neurosurgeon said he could not be in this work if he were not a Christian. With tear-filled eyes both he and the CCU nurse hugged each of us as they were leaving the room. Our family, one by one, had some private time with Wally before sharing in a time of prayer as we encircled his bed.

Life support was removed at 6:25 p.m. All signs of life were gone within 10 minutes. Each of us then shared what we could be thankful for about Wally's life. We all felt peace that we had followed Wally's wishes in his living will. Debbie volunteered to say a benediction over her daddy—a passage of Scripture she had heard Wally use over the years as a benediction in our churches. She stretched her hands out over Wally's body as he used to stretch his hands toward the congregation. She began to pray, "Now unto Him that is able to keep you from falling, and to present you faultless before the presence of His glory with exceeding joy, to the only wise God our Savior, be glory and majesty, dominion and authority, both now and forever. Amen." (Jude verse 25 KJV). I was amazed that Debbie could recall perfectly this verse of Scripture at such a difficult time as this.

When Debbie finished praying, she said, "Now, let's applaud Daddy's home-going, because the angels, loved ones, and friends who are already there are applauding him as he reaches heaven." We clapped our hands and then each of us prayed. After this we went back to the conference room. We asked for a few more minutes with Wally as each of us took turns to be with him alone for the last time on earth. I was the last one to go in his room, and I will never forget those moments when I said my good-bye for now.

(I will always have a hole in my heart from losing the love of my life. On our first wedding anniversary I spent without Wally, David gave me a beautiful silver heart necklace with a hole in it shaped like a tear drop. The poem that accompanied it said God will restore that missing piece on the great Reunion Day. I believe this to be true.)

The following day was a blur. We were busy making funeral arrangements and planning the March 4 service at Memorial United Methodist Church in Elizabethtown. Our pastor at Brandenburg, Rev. Jim Robinson, along with two former pastors, Rev. Russell East and Rev. Willard Knipp, former assistant pastor, Rev. Janet Carden, and Rev. John Bruington who is also on the church staff, decided to plan a shorter service at Brandenburg United Methodist Church following the visitation on March 3.

The line of people who came to both services seemed endless. It was estimated there were over 200 at the Brandenburg service, and around 500 at the Memorial UMC in Elizabethtown service. Seventy-five pastors and many spouses came to the Elizabethtown service. Rev. Jim Robinson presided over this service. Sharon Meredith and John Rawlings, friends from former churches, gave beautiful testimonies about what Wally meant to them. Other participants included Bishop Robert Spain and our district superintendent, Rev. Coleman Howlett. David gave a beautiful eulogy and sang "Until Then" by Stuart Hamblen, with whom we visited when Wally helped with the funeral of our friend, Tony Fontane, at Forest Lawn in Los Angeles. Debbie prayed the beautiful Scripture benediction she had prayed over Wally at his death. She held her hands out over the congregation as she prayed like her daddy used to. Many people said the service was like a revival meeting. Trumpets were played as a part of the funeral program, and hearts were touched by the entire experience.

Wally was buried in the Municipal Cemetery in his hometown of Glasgow, Kentucky. Wally's sister and brother-in-law's church provided a wonderful meal for our family following the burial. In the pages that follow I will reflect on many of Wally's qualities that have blessed so many lives during his 75 years. I Thessalonians 1:3 will continue to linger in my mind, "We continually remember before our God and Father *your work* produced by faith, *your labor* prompted by love, and *your endurance* inspired by hope in our Lord Jesus Christ" (NIV). (Emphasis mine.)

Chapter 14

REFLECTIONS

In closing, I want to share some reflections on Wally's life and ministry. Wally was a person of honest humility. He had a transparent and genuine quality that drew people to him and to his Lord. I believe there are hundreds of people who will spend Eternity in Heaven because of Wally's witness.

He had a loving heart and never gave up on people. Wally kept note cards in his pocket every day with names of unsaved people on them. After his death I found a list of 65 prospects in the Brandenburg area alone. He was convinced no one was beyond the reach of the Lord, from the vilest sinner to the hesitant good person. Wally was a person who was real and totally dedicated to God. He had impeccable moral character in all areas of his life.

Wally had a strong work ethic imbedded in him from the long hours of labor on the farm. He began to drive the tractor at the age of nine, even though he had to stand in order to see where he was going. He got up every morning at 3:00 to help milk a herd of cows on his parents' dairy farm.

Wally persevered during discouraging times and drew strength and courage from his life verse, "I can do all things through Christ who strengthens me" (Philippians 4:13 NKJV). He was not hesitant to take a stand for what he felt was right. He served churches and districts in the same manner: with kindness, firmness, understanding, and love. As a pastor, he cared for the people in his churches as well as those in need in the community. As a district superintendent, he cared for the pastors as well as the lay people in the churches. Twenty-one young men entered or re-entered the ministry during the time Wally served as a pastor and district superintendent.

Wally was a loving father, and he was the same person at home as he was in public. He was always ready to go the second mile for his family in whatever way they needed him. The following pages give some thoughts Debbie and David shared in writing about their dad:

FATHER

F is for always finding time for *family* and *friends*.
A is for *always* being there to listen and lend a helping hand.
T is for *taking time* to reach out to those in need and minister to a hurting world.
H is for his *happy* spirit and *holy* walk with God.
E is for his *eagerness* to be reunited with loved ones and friends.
R is for his *reaching* his final destination . . . his eternal home!

Debbie Thomas Caswell
2009

Lessons From A Life Well-Lived
Wallace Edwin Thomas
1934-2009

Love your kids unconditionally. Be their #1 encourager.

Sacrifice for your family.

Love your wife all your life. Support her dreams, as she has yours.

When it is all good at home, you can face anything.

Take your family places. Memories you make are worth the money.

Build traditions.

Honor and care for your parents until the end.

Love your relatives and in-laws. Try to help them.

Listen until it is all talked out. Think before you speak.

If God gives you a burden for somebody, act on it.

Drop in and see people, or give them a call.

Be willing for your heart to break with others.

People need the Church. People should have a good church.

Make the situation better. Help people grow.

Sing with gusto!

Build up the next generation.

Try something new and bold.

Leading people to Christ is the most important thing.

Spend wisely. Go for quality. Splurge a little!

Dress well. Keep your car and home in good condition.

Have a note card handy. Write neatly.

Why not strike up a conversation?

Make it easy for people to open up.

Work hard.

Laugh more.

Give second chances.

Stay humble and gentle.

Be you. But try to improve.

Be the same at home as you are out front.

Grow on past your past.

Always remain teachable.

Being a country boy is a good thing.

It's OK to cry.

Own your mistakes.

Even if no one notices, do the right thing anyway.

Pray daily.

Use common sense.

Keep going even when life hits hard.

All things are possible through Christ.

A wise son heeds his father's instructions.
Proverbs 13:1
David R. Thomas
2009

I found many more words of wisdom among Wally's notes and papers in his office cabinet, desk drawers, and books. Here are some:

If I were beginning my ministry over, I would:

- Give more time to my family.
- Have a more disciplined devotional life.
- Realize I can't do everything.
- Set a more realistic pace and schedule.
- Do more of what I think is right instead of what others think is right.
- Maintain the Sabbath plus a day off.
- Be less institutional.
- Participate in an accountability group.
- Develop a hobby or fun activity earlier in my life.

Our family often set goals for ourselves, especially at the beginning of a new year. On his list of 1999 goals (the year we retired) Wally simply listed:

- Adjust to retirement.
- Get settled in our own home—first time in our marriage.
- Exercise.
- Walk as closely with God as is humanly possible.
- Have a joyful heart.

Wally listed "Have a joyful heart" on several of his goal cards. Sometimes that was a challenge as he often took upon his shoulders the hurts and burdens of his people. He knew he needed to consciously make an effort to do all he could to help others and then give the remainder to the Lord.

Wally had a good sense of humor, although some people may have not seen this in him. I have mentioned earlier that the night before he became unconscious we were keeping Luke and Mary Esther in Lexington. He and the children had a laughing contest. I wish I had a sound track of this event. How could I have imagined that the following night Wally would become unconscious . . . never to regain consciousness again in this life? I have often thought about how difficult it was for the grandchildren to have the laughter resounding in their ears one night, and the next night, to hear of the seriousness of their grandpa's critical condition.

Wally loved Christmas. There is no time in his life he enjoyed more (besides leading people to Christ) than having our family together at Christmas. Wally was like a kid again when Christmas arrived. He started looking for our children and their families long before they were scheduled to arrive. He loved getting candid shots of all of us. Every year he filmed me in the kitchen. The video was almost the same every year, but that didn't stop him from getting an up-to-date account of my menu. His parents gave us a nice 35-millimeter camera for our wedding gift, and we have enjoyed photography ever since.

David expressed so well his remembrances of Christmases with his dad in a letter he read to the family the first Christmas after Wally died:

Christmas 2009
Dear Dad,

I can't remember when it became a part of our family tradition to exchange messages in Christmas cards to one another. But as we are doing that today, I wanted to write a few things to you. Perhaps you somehow hear me. Even if you don't, maybe these are words I need to hear. Maybe all of us do.

This is in many ways the Christmas we have always dreaded: the first one in which our family circle has been broken by the absence of one we love so much. We are really, really missing you, Dad. It all still seems so hard to believe, to accept as real that you are physically, permanently away from us on earth. I still feel like it shouldn't be so, that you are not actually gone—especially at Christmastime. Few people I have known loved Christmas any more than you. It was a load of work for you and Mom, and as the years went by, that load became a heavier one to carry. But when we got to this moment every year, no man was ever happier to have his home transformed into a Christmas wonderland, his wife beside him, and his family all gathered in, than you were. Christmas was a deep treasure to you. That is why you programmed your garage automatic door opener in a way to remember Christmas. That is why you and Mom went to all the trouble to make every part of Christmas so holy and beautiful. And that's why we're hurting today: your absence this first Christmas is so sharp.

All of us are missing you, Dad, but certainly Mom most of all. Did you see her tears as she made the Wally's Cheese Ball? Did you know the ache in her heart as she wrote in all our cards by herself? We have tried to fill in some gaps in the decorating and in the mailing list (I thought of you as we put up the same things you and I took down just 11 months ago). But Mom has carried your load and hers in all the preparations. All the runs to Kroger, all the trips up and down the stairs, all the vacuuming, all the cards to friends, all the gifts for family and friends. It has been so hard for Mom not to go to Christmas Eve Communion with you, not to put a gift for you under the tree, and not to have one there from you. It has been so tough for her to go about the traditions we cherish in such a quiet house. Thank God she has not been alone. The Christmas promise of "Emmanuel" has been even more real for Mom and all of us this year: God is with us. But it's the love He gave us for one another that makes our absence from one another so painful. You would be so proud of the way Mom has persevered throughout this year and especially this last month.

We are missing you keeping watch from the side porch of the house for our minivan to pull up. I miss your help with our luggage and hearing your excitement over all the presents we add to the ones already under the tree. I miss meeting up in the back porch over the snack table and building a fire in the fireplace with you—we both loved that. We miss your prayers at mealtime, you sitting at your spot at the table and in your twin chair beside Mom as we come together now. We miss you having that handy pocket knife for cutting tape and ribbons and getting into the packages. The kids will miss seeing you in a Santa cap and having their cuddle time in your lap on these mornings. I will miss you frying up the country ham tomorrow morning and searching me down with a little piece for an advance taste. We will miss you raving about the food at all the meals and snacks, saying again how Mom "never stops," but that she is never happier than when she is cooking for her family. We'll miss taking a walk with you on Piping Rock Road to "make room" for more of those goodies. We have some chocolate-covered peanuts here today as a little reminder of all the delights you enjoyed on Christmas that are dimmed for us today without you.

But it's not all these little bits and pieces, Dad. It's just you. We just miss you. We would give up any and all of the trimmings of Christmas just to have you here with us today. That's because you never failed to keep Christmas centered for us and your churches. You loved all of Christmas, but you loved the Christ of Christmas best of all. I remember you saying so many times how much you loved preaching at Christmas, how good it was to tell others about Christ at such a holy time. I would usually roll into this day really tired from Christmas Eve services, and you always spoke a word of unique understanding to me knowing that Gospel proclamation is really the most important part of all. Your heart for the Lord was the best gift you ever gave us or anyone, Dad, and we are missing that tender Christmas love you had for God in our circle today.

But we thank God that all you preached about Christmas is true, and all you gave us to make our celebration so special each year was not wasted. We are here, continuing the traditions and renewing our love for Jesus and for one another. We are comforting one another in the love that came down at Christmas. That comfort will be enough today as it has always been and will be every Christmas and every day until we finally make it Home where you are. What a celebration you must be enjoying in the presence of the One we adore. Being happy for you about that and looking forward to joining you there one day has been our greatest source of strength this Christmas.

So thanks again, Dad, for always giving us Christmas experiences that were so abundant, always more than what you had growing up, always so full of sacrifice and joy. You have given us the gifts that are still giving. We miss you and love you, and we will see you soon. Merry Christmas, Dad.

Your son,
Dave

Wally was very serious about the call of God on his life. He was convinced that God's hand was on him. Once he was on his dad's tractor, and he felt that God nudged him to stop. Wally sat down under a tree and felt God speak clearly to him, "Go on . . . I will be with you." So many times I have heard him say he never felt he was "caught up" in his work as a minister. There was always something else he wished he could do or have done. He was always troubled that so many people take so lightly their vows of church membership and the call of God upon their lives.

Wally had a heart for helping people. You saw an example of that with the Patera family story in the Munfordville chapter. He cared for those addicted to alcohol and established an AA group everywhere we served if there was need for a group. Wally was great in counseling with people, regardless of the problem involved.

Wally was an encourager. If a minister complimented Wally's tie, he would usually take it off and give it to the person. He encouraged his pastors with practical suggestions for ministry. I recall one young minister in particular who was hesitant about going to seminary. This person knew he needed to continue his education but lacked the confidence to start. After a long conversation and a prayer time, this pastor left Wally's office, drove to Asbury Seminary, enrolled that day, and he never stopped until he completed his requirements. When pastors became discouraged and dropped out of ministry, Wally seemed to have a way of getting them back on track. He always had a keen eye for members of the churches he pastored who missed more than one Sunday and would follow-up with a visit and a word of encouragement.

Wally loved to sing and often led the singing when he served smaller churches. I came across a list of songs he picked out for the Munfordville UMC during the recent nine-month pastorate there. Some of his favorites were: "Victory in Jesus," "When We All Get to Heaven," "How Great Thou Art," "My Jesus, I Love Thee" (his all-time favorite), "Until Then," "Take Time to Be Holy," "He Touched Me," "Trust and Obey," "Blessed Assurance," and "Because He Lives."

Wally loved the church. I found an article he wrote entitled "Let Me Tell You How Much the Church Means to Me." It read, "The church is a place of affirmation, acceptance, vision and nurture. It is the place where I met Jesus and gave my life to God. It is where Kay and I married, our children were baptized, and later were married. The church is the place where love is a venture that keeps spreading in ever-widening circles." Wally closed this article with these words, "What a gospel! What a Lord! What a faith home is our church! What a hope for all seasons of life!"

I found numerous note cards and pages with quotable quotes. My apologies to the authors of any of these statements which might not be originally Wally's words:

- God doesn't want a church full of people as much as He wants a people full of God.
- We need to take our atmosphere with us. We don't have to be changed or destroyed by a hostile and alien environment.
- Hope in the future takes the sting out of the present.
- If you know God's hand is in everything, you can leave everything in God's hand.
- People don't care how much you know until they know how much you care.
- Our programs are worthless without the Lord's anointing.
- The business of the Church is discipleship development, and the product of the church is changed lives.

- If we always do what we have always done, we will always be where we have always been.
- Whatever God calls us to do, we can be sure He will equip us to do.
- The pessimist complains about the wind. The optimist expects it to change. The leader adjusts the sails.
- Encouragement is oxygen to the soul.
- To have a worthwhile, meaningful life, a person must be a part of something greater than himself.
- Pray unceasingly.

Wally strongly believed in the power of prayer, and he prayed every day. I loved to hear Wally pray. We prayed together at every meal, in times of need, and each night before we went to sleep. In my mind's eye, I can see our family as we formed a circle of prayer when we learned of a death, accident, sickness, or struggle of any kind. I am so glad to find many prayers Wally has written and prayed during his years in ministry. I want to include one of these here:

"Heavenly Father, as I enter this new day, I commit everything to Your care: my soul, body, and all my activities. I pray that You will watch over me and my family. Cause my heart to follow Your ways. Transform me into Your image . . . just like a potter forms the clay.

"Help me to live by Your Spirit, completely covered by the armor of God, and shining a light that cannot be put out.

"Help me to be able to live in this sinful world and remain unstained by wickedness. Direct all my words today according to Your wisdom and according to what will bring good. Help me to speak each word as if it were my last word and walk each step as if it were my last step. If life should come to an end today, let it be my best day. Through Christ our Lord. Amen."

What a blessing it is to have the privilege of praying and also to be blessed by someone's prayer. I appreciate so much a prayer a friend from Munfordville, Jane Dobson, sent to me on February 28, 2009, the day after Wally died:

"Father God, there are many broken hearts from the loss of Wally Thomas from our lives. His soulmate, Kay, is on my heart. There is an emptiness now as she contemplates life without her Wally to share it. Lord, cover her with Your Holy Spirit's presence. Be with her to sort out her feelings through the fog and uncertainty of the days to come. Then hold her through the rawness of grief and the unexpected times of realization of death: planning meals, baking Wally's favorite pie, or eating country ham and cornbread—all of the things a loving wife does to please her husband. Especially be with her when she is alone and friends and loved ones have gone home; at night when the busyness of the day and distractions have ceased; when she faces head on the loneliness that comes in long stretches. Help her to know these are the times when You are there as always. We can all revel in knowing that Wally is with You and that healing will come. We will grieve as Your children, but already rejoice in having known Your servant Wally Thomas, and that You greeted him in Heaven saying, 'Well done good and faithful servant.' Amen."

As I mentioned earlier, one of Wally's favorite spots to do ministry was around the kitchen table. I will never forget the times he came home from visiting prospects and shared with me how he and the couple or individual sat around the kitchen table. Often one or more persons accepted Christ into their hearts during these visits. Many people who wrote notes to our family following Wally's funeral mentioned his "kitchen table ministry." I can almost envision Wally fellowshipping now with a group around the banquet table in heaven.

Since Wally's death, we have listened to the first sermon he preached following his four-month recuperation from the wreck in 1973. In that sermon, he said, "Sometimes in God's providence, He spares us. And, sometimes in His providence, He calls us home." He closed that service by singing his favorite hymn, "My Jesus, I Love Thee."

It is difficult to bring this book to a close. There is so much more I would like to share. I would like to mention every family member and friend by name. So many of you have made an indelible imprint on our lives.

I believe God ordained Wally's and my life to cross. It was no coincidence that, at the Freshman Reception at Western Kentucky University in 1954, both of us knew there was something special between us. That feeling never changed during the 55 years I knew him.

I gave Wally a little card a couple of years ago entitled "My Wonderful Husband." He kept it in his sight on his desk all the time. It reads like this:

> "You're my joy,
> and my strength,
> the source of my comfort,
> the person in whom I confide—
> The friend of my heart,
> who knows me completely
> and fills me with such love and pride."

Our hearts were one. A favorite story of mine is about the little daughter of a couple, Syd and Donna Tate, in my Love One Another Sunday School Class in Madisonville. I remember so well the evening when they told Wally and me they were expecting their first child. Little Monica was a joy. She loved to learn, and Donna taught her the alphabet at an early age. Donna would ask Monica what each letter of the alphabet says, and she always answered correctly. When Donna asked Monica what the letter "K" says, without hesitation, Monica would always reply, "K says Wally!" Monica was right.

I don't know what lies before me, but Jeremiah says to "Ask where the good way is; and walk in it, and find rest for your souls" (Jeremiah 6:16b RSV). I am trying to do this every day. I can go forward unafraid because I know who holds my tomorrows. I claim the words of St. Augustine: "Trust the past to God's mercy, the present to His love, and the future to His providence."

Following Wally's funeral, a member of the Brandenburg United Methodist Church, Beverly Furnival, wrote and gave me this poem in memory of Wally:

"This Child of God"

This child of God,
Who unwrapped every day like a gift,
Delighted in fairways and chocolate,
Scattered laughter and comfort
Like a trail of bread crumbs.

This child of God,
Whose heart spilled over with love for his Creator,
Running in rivulets,
Through every corner of creation.

This child of God,
who humbly poured from the Cup of Peace,
A soothing balm
Over many a sin-sick soul.

This child, the angels missed so much
They approached God and said,
"It's been too long!" And God replied,
"Go, and fetch him home, then."

Wally is in his Heavenly home now. One day all of us who love the Lord and have given our hearts to Him will be at home with Him, too . . . together forever. Thanks be to God!

Chapter 15

A Celebration Of The Life And Ministry Of Wallace E. Thomas

Words of Tribute and Truth
March 4, 2009
by
David R. Thomas

On behalf of our entire family, we want to thank all of you for the amazing ways you have blessed us and supported us with your love and your prayers these last nine days. We especially appreciate the generous hospitality of Memorial United Methodist Church in hosting us today.

As you can imagine, they have been, beyond comparison, the most heart-wrenching days we have ever experienced.

But they have not been days that were ever lacking in love. They have not been days of fear. And this and all the days to come will never want for hope.

We do not grieve as those without hope. That is the Christian victory we're anchored in today, and the invitation and opportunity my dad gave to so many people all his life.

You're here because you knew my dad, and you loved him. You've heard some stories about him already.

A refrain in your comments to us over the past week has been something like, "Wally was one in a million. He was just about the most gentle, sincerely Christian guy I've ever met."

And that really is no exaggeration. To hundreds of people in every newcomer retreat at Centenary, my story began by saying my parents remain two of the most authentic Christians I have ever known. They made the Christian life seem so winsome, so appealing, that it really would have seemed ridiculous to rebel into something else.

Dad was always the same man at home all week that Debbie I saw up front on Sundays.

Mom reminded me of my saying to Christ Church once when Dad allowed me to preach there during seminary that if you cut Wally Thomas anywhere, he bleeds love.

Wally Thomas was so genuine, so humble, really so full of grace. Dad was not judgmental. He felt safe to people. He was understanding and accepting of people, while all the while summoning up the better person he could see inside of us.

There was something about Dad saying, "It'll be OK," that made you believe it would be.

He was loyal. He went to bat for people. He worked hard to dispel rumors. When he heard about a pastor getting hurt in the crossfire, I've heard him say, "That wouldn't have happened if I had been the district superintendent."

Dad was very hard-working, an early riser from his upbringing on a dairy farm.

He was creative, enjoying penmanship and photography and his woodworking shop in retirement.

Dad was expressive. He was a man who could talk it out, say what he felt, put his love into words. He had this disarming honesty and compassion toward people that kind of melted them. People at all stations in life—rich or poor, urban or rural, sophisticated or simple—people tended to trust Dad quickly, easily, and then always. He was so kind and approachable, a good man through and through.

But he wasn't afraid to speak the word that needed to be said—sometimes the tough word. Dad was very gentle. But he was no pushover. I have seen him take gutsy stands that required great courage.

I think Dad was born with a kind of a high relational IQ, an unusually strong inner compass, and a future of blessing and lifting the lives of people in Jesus' name: what he has done for us all as **pastor, friend, father, husband,** and **man of God.**

Jim Robinson mentioned last night at the service in Brandenburg that there was an innocence about Dad, and there was—always. You can see that in his face from boyhood photographs. He met Jesus as a little boy and never strayed.

He would get up from the dinner table, put his arm around his dad's neck, and ask him to pray out loud with the family for their meal. Eventually Grandpa Thomas did, and his prayers became a family treasure. Dad's way of calling people to experience more of God began very young.

When Grandpa got sick during Dad's college years, Dad came home from Western to run the farm. It was during that time he sensed God calling him out of agriculture into church leadership, which he resisted, feeling so inadequate.

One night, when he threw himself across the bed to say "Yes" to God's call upon his life, Dad prayed for a word of encouragement from the Bible. And when he opened it up, his eyes fell on Philippians 4:13 (NKJV), which became Dad's life verse: "I can do all things through Christ who strengthens me." His ministry proved that promise true.

Dad has been a pastor's **pastor,** influencing a generation of young leaders in our conference as a mentor and model.

All the churches Dad shepherded flourished. He was very bold as a pastor, inviting Tony Fontane to Munfordville and Shively, having Miss America give her testimony in Madisonville, introducing

Kentucky to Lay Witness Missions and the Walk to Emmaus, helping people grow closer to God.

He was always reading about ministry, always staying current. If I got interested in a book, he would get it to read along.

He had a gift for healing in churches, helping congregations in that way as a pastor and district superintendent, many times invited back to churches he had served before to bring some encouragement and restoration and fresh vision.

God used Dad to heal people. He was always involved with men and women in recovery. Alcoholics loved Dad. In their humility and transparency and desperate love for Jesus, I think Dad felt at home with them.

Most of all as a pastor, Dad is one of the few people I know who truly did have the spiritual gift of evangelism. He had an unusual—really supernatural—ability to introduce people to Jesus. Evangelism was his passion and the centerpiece of his work.

Many times, I remember him saying, "Oh just give me some corner in a church somewhere, and let me lead people to Christ there." I think that's one of the reasons these Brandenburg years of retirement have been so fulfilling for Mom and Dad: years of ministry that were just about people. Not the buildings and the operations, just the people.

Dad would get a burden for people.

Last night after the visitation in Brandenburg, a man told me about talking to Dad about his son. "I've not met that son, have I?" "No." "Is he a Christian?" Dad asked him right off the bat. "Well, I think so." "Has he made a profession of faith?" "I don't know for sure."

"I'd really like to meet him." So this guy calls his son. "Son, my friend, Wally Thomas, would like to meet you." "OK, Dad. We'll do that." "Well, what are you doing right now?" "Nothing really."

Dad went over. He sat down at the kitchen table, his favorite place for doing work in the soul. This father went on to say, "David, they sat down and talked for an hour. And Wally led my son to Christ right then. He made a profession of faith. No one had ever explained how he could give his life to God. Wally did."

I always remember Dad getting a burden for people, kind of a prompting in his spirit.

He wouldn't let go until he had done all he could about it. And God bore great fruit through it. Both in programming and personal witness, Dad had a supernatural giftedness in evangelism.

In the last minutes of Dad's life, my wife, Karen, said she could just imagine the standing ovation for him in Heaven from those who were there because of how God had reached them through Dad.

He was an evangelist, a pastor's pastor.

And he was a great **friend**. Men loved Dad, in every place, laymen and pastors.

I have never seen so many weeping men as I did at the foot of his bed at Hardin Memorial Hospital last week. Someone said last night, "I only met Wally a short time ago, but I feel like I've known him for a lifetime."

Deep, personal relationships with men were a real power center in his ministry. He had an eye for talent in people. He could see ways they could serve and grow and lead and influence and change before they could see those things, which is a high-level mark of leadership. Dad did that: he grew men.

A lot of that happened on the golf course, where Dad could be just a blast to be with.

Doe Valley golfers talk about "Wally's Gimme." If the ball got within six feet of the hole, Dad would pick it up and say, "Oh, that's a gimme." Dad once hit the ball into the woods and a friend asked, "Wally, you want me to kick it out?" "No, I don't. You wouldn't kick it far enough!"

He'd crack a joke, and then get back into the cart and say, "So now tell me, how are things at home?"

Many people in this room are better people—better men and women—because of your friendship with Wally Thomas. That's certainly the case for me.

Pastor, friend, and **father**: Dad has been such a great dad. He loved our home life together as a family. He said, "Son, if things are good in here, you can face just about anything out there." He set that tone of priority and joy and love in our household.

When I would check voicemails while we were in the hospital last week, more than one of them were from guys I knew growing up who said something like, "David, Wally was the dad I always wished to have."

Debbie and I have always been so proud to claim him as our dad. The best part, for me, of going to annual conference each year was just getting to sit with Dad in meetings, having rooms next door in the hotel, eating snacks at night that Mom brought from home.

Dad sacrificed for Debbie and me to give us opportunities he never had and to shield us from hardships he had faced.

To us as kids, Dad gave us the gift of unconditional love. He gave us freedom. He never once put expectations on us because we were preacher's kids.

I was the only one in my confirmation class who held back on coming on into the church, and Dad never pushed me. I did it on my own a couple of months later, from a much deeper place of faith.

When I was looking at seminaries, he went with me to his *alma mater* at Emory, but then left to let me finish out the visit on my own. "It's your decision," he said, tucking a $20 bill in my hand as he left. "Get yourself a good meal here in Atlanta."

As I became an adult and could look back on my growing-up years, I was able to talk that out with Dad, even the disappointing parts, with forgiveness and understanding and no shame.

He was always so eager to listen to Debbie and me, to try to help. Most every drive home after every night's meeting at Centenary these past 12 years was spent on the phone with Mom and Dad. And there was often an email the next day to the effect of, "Been thinking about you today and what we were talking about last night. And have you thought about this? Just know we're praying for you, Son, and we're so proud of you."

Dad has been my main mentor. He's been Debbie's big ally in supporting our precious Katie in meeting the special challenges she faces. Camp TESSA was the obvious choice for memorials honoring Dad because of the way he championed that or any way for his granddaughter's life to be enriched.

And the same goes for all his grandkids. What a Grandpa: "Poppy"! All four—Katie, Luke, John Paul, and Mary Esther—have loved to snuggle in Grandpa's lap. As babies, when nothing else could get them to sleep, Dad could do it.

That calming effect, that love that's always celebrated with his kids in good times and hurt with us in bad, that wisdom and prayer cover and playfulness with our children: we were not in any way ready to give that up.

But we never would have been, even after 53 years of marriage like Mom had enjoyed: pastor, friend, father, **husband**.

Mom and Dad kind of grew up together. Dad had been nervous to tell Kay he believed he was going to be a preacher. Mom was unsure about marrying Wally, wondering if agribusiness would allow her to fulfill her commitment to serve Christ with all of her life.

So when they discovered this calling to ministry God had given each of them separately, that sealed a love-bond that has been really exceptional and so used by God. Mom and Dad have been a team in every way.

She typed his papers in seminary. He typed her manuscript for her book in his retirement. Mom enhanced his leadership so much in the churches. In retirement, Dad would often run the vacuum cleaner or fold a load of clothes without being asked. Mom writes notes to people at night. Every morning she woke up to the notes in the mailbox, the paper brought in, the coffee ready, two bowls of cereal poured. Dad just loved his "Kay." Always bragged on how pretty she was, how good she was.

And their love for one another stretched out into our extended family. Nieces and nephews on both sides received so much love and advice and encouragement. Dad was the family pastor, really making the whole clan better, and being instrumental in many of our relatives coming into a relationship with Jesus.

Someone said last night that "Wally and Kay" has always just sounded like one word.

They have been each other's greatest cheerleaders. Dad has modeled for me a servant strength toward his wife and his family.

I've told Mom and Dad many times that perhaps the greatest thing they ever gave to Debbie and me was their marriage.

A week ago Monday night, Dad came home from church and was not himself. By the time Mom called 911, he wasn't able to answer questions or say more than a few words.

The ambulance made it to the hospital in record time, Mom praying along the way from Isaiah 59:1: "Surely the arm of the Lord is not too short to save, nor his ear too dull to hear" (NIV). She got out as they took Dad in. "I'm here, Wally." And Dad smiled and waved. By the time Mom got in the emergency room, Dad was in a coma.

It was as though Dad had willed to last long enough to see his Kay one more time and wave goodbye.

The ambulance drivers came to the hospital and the visitation last night to see Mom, so touched by just that hour of their marriage.

Pastor, friend, father, husband, **man of God**.

I can stand before you this afternoon as the son of Wally Thomas and say without question that when it comes to the heart of a man, I have never known one better than my Dad.

I am so thankful I didn't wait until now to say these things. Dad heard them from me a lot through the years, that when it comes to the character of a man who loves God and loves people, he sets the bar.

What I said 20 years ago has remained true: when you cut Wally Thomas anywhere, he bleeds love. And who does that sound like, other than the one who shed His blood out of love for us all?

Jesus Christ was deeply and firmly formed into the life of Wally Thomas, and we're all the better for it.

I really believe he was too humble to have ever known the depth of his impact, the far stretch of his legacy in all our lives.

And that legacy was of the very best kind: building the Kingdom of God; introducing people to Jesus Christ; helping people grow and heal and change; empowering the local church to reach its potential; having friends who love you and a family that respects you and a wife who adores you. What could be better than that?

Dad would say, "As good as it has been, Son, where I am now *is* better than that."

Dad spent his life helping people become prepared to go to the place where he is now, to the place where Jesus prepared for Dad, and for us, as we heard Jesus say in the words Coleman read just a minute ago: "'Do not let your hearts be troubled. Trust in God; trust also in me. In my Father's house are many rooms; if it were not so, I would have told you. I am going to prepare a place for you'" (John 14:1-2 NIV).

There is a real place being prepared for us, a place of reunion. I know many of you are reliving your own losses as we experience ours today. And you can be sure Jesus is preparing a place of reunion for you and those you love who have put their trust in Him.

This will be a place of relief where we'll be set free from the sickness and mental illness and disability and broken families and addictions and wounds that have at times made us wonder if life will ever get better.

In that place, our lowly bodies will be transformed to be like his glorious body, Paul wrote the Philippians.

Jesus has gone ahead to prepare a place of reward for us. "'Blessed are you when people insult you, persecute you and falsely say all kinds of evil against you because of me. Rejoice and be glad, because great is your reward in heaven'" (Matthew 5:11-12b NIV).

So we can be bold in this life. You can lay it on the line for the Lord—at your work, with your time, with your money, with your investment into the lives of people, knowing that whatever hardship your courage produces, God will reward you in Heaven.

Because of what's waiting for us in heaven, these remaining days on Earth *can* be ones that never lack in love, days that *are* free from fear, days now and always that *will* never want for hope.

And if Dad were here, he would say, "Believe me, it's true!" That's why Paul could write to the Colossians, "Since, then, you have been raised with Christ, set your hearts on things above, where Christ is seated at the right hand of God. Set your minds on things above, not on earthly things" (Colossians 3:1-2 NIV).

It couldn't be a service celebrating the life and ministry of Wally Thomas if we didn't say that of all these things we know about heaven, we are sure of this most of all: Jesus wants you there.

If you will open your life to God and invite Him to come in, not holding anything back, but giving Him your simple and total trust, there will be a day when you and all of us will get to Heaven, and we'll all be able to say what I kind of think Dad said when the standing ovation of his welcome finally subsided: "Wow! Thank You, Jesus. Thank You for preparing all of this for me, and thank You for making the way for me to get here!"

All Things Through Christ

Postal orders: Kate Thomas
      586 Piping Rock Rd.
      Brandenburg, KY 40108

Telephone and fax orders: 270-422-4897

Price: Softcover – $19.99, hardcover – $35.99

Shipping: $ 3.00 for first book and $ 1.00 for each additional book to cover shipping and handling within the US, Canada, and Mexico. For international orders, add $ 6.00 for the first book, and $ 2.00 for each additional book.

Please send *All Things Through Christ* to:

Name _____

Address _____

City _____

Zip Code _____

Telephone: (_____) _____

_____ **book(s) @ $19.99 each**   _____

_____ **book(s) @ $35.99 each**   _____

Kentucky sales tax (.06 per dollar)   _____

Shipping/handling ($3.00 per book)   _____

$1.00 for each additional book   _____

TOTAL: _____

(Contact http://bookstore.westbowpress.com/, www.amazon.com, www.barnesandnoble.com or your local bookstore.)

CPSIA information can be obtained at www.ICGtesting.com
Printed in the USA
LVOW112227180512

282384LV00002B/6/P